DICTIONARY
of the
Bible

By D M McFarlan

GEDDES &
GROSSET

Abbreviations used in this book:

O.T   Old Testament
N.T.   New Testament
A.V.   Authorized Version
R.S.V   Revised Standard Version
N.E.B. New English Bible

Published 2005 by Geddes & Grosset,
David Dale House, New Lanark, ML11 9DJ, Scotland
First published 2003, reprinted 2005

Text written by D M McFarlan

ISBN 1 84205 312 4

Printed and bound in Poland

POLSKABOOK

Preface

The purpose of this book is to set down as plainly as possible the essential facts about people and places of the Bible from Aaron to Zion. Some other topics are also included, e.g. articles on Parables, Miracles, the Sermon on the Mount, so that scattered references to these themes may be brought together for study. Book, chapter, and verse references are to the Revised Standard Version of the Bible. Little-known individuals and obscure places have been omitted, and there are no articles on theological or philosophical terms. Although this volume is primarily a reference book of names and such topics as will assist students in senior schools and colleges who are making a study of the literature of the Bible for examinations or essays or general discussion, the contents of this handbook will also be of interest to the general reader.

A

Aaron The elder brother of Moses and his constant companion when he faced Pharaoh and led the children of Israel out of Egypt and through the desert. Sometimes Aaron acted as spokesman for Moses because he could speak well. When the people complained that Moses had gone away from them at Mt. Sinai, Aaron made a gold calf for them to worship as a god.

Aaron also appears in the Bible as the first high priest and head of the Levites. Later on it came to be believed that all priests must be descended from Aaron, who was himself said to be a great-grandson of Levi the son of Jacob. As the priesthood became more important the O.T. writers added to the story of Aaron and his family, e.g. their anointing and priestly clothing and duties.

Aaron's blessing, as it is called, is still used as a prayer in Jewish and Christian custom:

'The Lord bless you and keep you:
The Lord make his face to shine upon you, and be gracious to you:
The Lord lift up his countenance upon you, and give you peace.'

[*Refs.* Exodus 6: 20; 7: 1-2; 32, 39. Numbers 6: 23-6. 1 Chronicles 6: 49.] *See also* LEVITES; PRIESTS

Abba The Aramaic word for 'father', used by Jesus when he prayed in Gethsemane. It was the family word used by children to their father at home. Paul mentions it in that sense when referring to prayers containing the words 'Abba, Father'. Probably the earliest form of the Lord's Prayer began with this word. [*Refs.* Mark 14: 36. Romans 8: 15. Galatians 4: 6.]

Abednego One of the three Jewish youths who were Daniel's companions in Babylon.When they refused to bow down before the golden image which Nebuchadrezzar set up they were cast into the fiery furnace, but were delivered unharmed. [*Refs.* Daniel 1: 7; 3: 12-30.] *See also* DANIEL

Abel The second son of Adam and Eve in the Genesis story, and brother of Cain. Abel was a keeper of sheep, and Cain a tiller of the ground. When they brought their offerings to the Lord, Abel's offering was accepted but Cain's was not. In anger Cain killed his brother and was cursed by God.

In this story we see an age-old rivalry between the shepherd people and the farming people in ancient Israel. The shepherd is the ideal figure in a great deal of Jewish thought and writing. In the N.T. Abel is a symbol of the suffering of the innocent. [*Refs.* Genesis 4: 1-12. Matthew 23: 34-5.]

Abiathar A priest who escaped the attack of Saul and fled to join David in his outlaw days and throughout his reign as king. He was rewarded by being made priest in Jerusalem along with Zadok, both guardians of the Ark of the Covenant. When David was on the point of death, Abiathar and Joab, the commander of the army, sided with Adonijah, David's eldest son, who proclaimed himself king. When Solomon seized the throne he banished Abiathar, but did not put him to death 'because you bore the Ark of the Lord God before David my father, and because you shared in all the afflictions of my father'. According to the Gospel of Mark, Jesus referred to Abiathar as high priest in the time of David. [*Refs.* 1 Samuel 22: 20*f*; 23: 6*f*. 2 Samuel 8: 17; 15: 24*f*; 17: 15; 19: 2*f*. 1 Kings 1: 7, 19, 25; 2: 22, 26-7. Mark 2: 25-6.]

Abilene *See* LYSANIAS

Abimelech A king of Gerar on the southern coast of Palestine who made a covenant with Abraham at Beersheba. The same story is told later of Abimelech and Isaac. [*Refs.* Genesis 21: 22-33; 26: 26-33.]

Abner Commander of the army of Saul, and also his cousin and right-hand man. After the death of Saul, Abner followed the fortunes of the king's son, Ishbosheth. Then he plotted to join David the popular leader and future king. Joab, who was David's right-hand man, feared Abner's influence and hated his treachery. He feigned conversation with Abner and struck him down suddenly with his dagger. David called for national mourning for Abner and lamented him thus: 'Do you not know that a prince and a great man has fallen this day in Israel?' [*Refs.* 1 Samuel 14: 50; 17: 55-7; 26: 13-16. 2 Samuel 2: 8 to 3: 39.]

Abomination Something that causes disgust or loathing. In the Bible the word is widely used for some kinds of animals for food, certain people or tribes, some kinds of work, horrible disease, sexual offences, dishonesty, idols and idol-worship. [*Refs.* Genesis 46: 34. Leviticus 11: 10, 13, 20. Psalm 88: 8. Revelation 21: 27.]

'The abomination that makes desolate' refers to the heathen altar to Zeus which Antiochus Epiphanes set up in the Temple in 168 B.C. when he tried to wipe out the Jewish faith. This impious act was one of the things that led to the Maccabean Revolt. *See also*: DANIEL, THE BOOK OF

A similar 'abomination' mentioned in the N.T. may refer to the Emperor Caligula's plan to set up his statue in the Temple at Jerusalem. He died before his order was carried out. [*Refs.* 1 Maccabees 1: 54. Daniel 11: 31; 12: 11. Matthew 24: 15. Mark 13: 14.]

Abraham Abraham is held in honour by the Jews as the father of their race and also as the friend of God. Genesis 11-25 contain a series of stories from different sources which tell of his leaving Ur and Haran in Mesopotamia to become a nomadic tent-dweller in the land of Canaan. We may picture Abraham and his clan as a small part of the Semitic migrations which passed through the Fertile Crescent during several centuries. The stories point to Mesopotamia as the original home of the Hebrew people, the link is maintained by marriage in the days of Isaac and Jacob.

Later the Jews were proud to remember their shepherd ancestor and call themselves sons and daughters of Abraham.

Throughout the Bible, however, Abraham is more significant as the man of faith than as a figure of history. Genesis 12 speaks of Abraham as a man who was called by God, who responded in trust, who was given a promise. The Bible writers teach their people to identify themselves with faithful Abraham and enter into the three-fold promise: that they will possess a land of their own, that they will become a great nation, that through them all the families of the earth will be blessed. They are to be 'the people of the God of Abraham'.

The N.T. continues these ideas. Matthew traces the family tree of Jesus back to Abraham to show his true descent, and the patriarch is frequently mentioned by the N.T. writers as the 'father' of their people. Paul follows the theme of God's call and promise when he says that the true children of Abraham are all who put their trust in Christ. [*Refs.* Genesis 11: 27 to 12: 9. Psalm 105: 9-11. Isaiah 41: 8. Matthew 1:1. Luke 1: 55. Galatians 3: 6-9, 28-9. Hebrews 2: 8-10.]

Absalom The third son of David, a favourite with his father, handsome, vain and spoiled. Absalom 'stole the hearts of the men of Israel' and led a rebellion against his royal father. David had to flee from Jerusalem, but his commander-in-chief, Joab, defeated the rebel army. Absalom fled on a mule but was caught by his long hair in the branches of an oak tree. Joab killed him as he hung there. David's lament over his loved son is memorable: 'O my son Absalom, my son, my son Absalom! Would I had died instead of you, O Absalom, my son, my son!' [*Refs.* 2 Samuel 14: 25; 15: 1-6, 13*f.*; 18: 6-15, 33.]

Ashaia The ancient name for the part of Greece which included Corinth. In N.T. times it was a Roman province. Paul was there several times and was brought before Gallio the governor for causing unrest among the Jews. The believers in Achaia sent an offering for the poor Christians in Jerusalem. [*Refs.* Acts 18: 12-17, 27. Romans 15: 26. 2 Corinthians 1: 1. 1 Thessalonians 1: 8.]

Achan A man of the tribe of Judah who broke faith when Jericho was destroyed. In spite of the fact that everything in the captured city was 'devoted' to destruction, Achan secretly took some of the spoils and hid them. When the men of Israel were subsequently defeated at Ai, they looked for a culprit. A search was made and Achan had to confess his sin—he had stolen 'a beautiful mantle from Shinar' and some silver and gold which he had hidden in the earth beneath his tent. Achan and all his family and beasts were taken to the valley of Achor, stoned to death, and burned. [*Ref.* Joshua 7.]

Acts of the Apostles This book is volume two of a single work by the author of the Gospel of Luke and is dedicated to the same person, Theophilus. It may be called the first history book of the Christian Church. The book of the Acts takes up the story of 'all that Jesus began to do and teach' (i.e. the Gospel of Luke) and continues it in the life and work of Christ's followers, from Jersalem, the capital city of the Jews, to Rome, capital of the Empire.

It is usually accepted that the whole work was by Luke, the friend and companion of Paul and 'beloved physician' as the latter calls him. (*See* LUKE, THE GOSPEL OF for fuller N.T. references). The 'we' sections [Acts 16: 10-17; 20: 5 to 21: 18; 27: 1 to 28: 16] suggest he was with Paul on his second and third missionary journeys.

It is plain that Luke selects and arranges his material in this part of his work just as he does in his Gospel. For example, Peter is prominent as a leader of the Church in the early chapters, but he disappears from the story at 12: 19 and, apart from one brief reference, is not heard of again. For the rest of the book Paul is the dominant figure. In fact, the very title of the work is misleading, for apart from some instances of Peter at work and a lengthy account of Paul's missionary journeys, we hear practically nothing of the 'acts of the apostles' in the early days of the Church. Perhaps a better title for the book would be: 'the acts of the Holy Spirit'. Acts 1: 8 states the plan and span of the contents: 'You shall receive power when the Holy Spirit has come upon you; and you shall be my witness in Jerusalem and in all Judea and Samaria and to the end of the earth.' It is the Spirit who guides their way, from the Pentecost onwards. The speeches of Peter, Stephen, Paul, were not taken down word for word but are to be read as containing the thinking and teaching of these leaders of the Church. Luke is not at all concerned with History step by step. Even his faithful account of Paul's work is not always accurate in its dating. That is not Luke's prime concern. Rather, he relates how Paul in particular led the early Church out of the legalistic confines of Judaism into the Gentile world. The account of Pentecost, the words and work of Stephen, the gospel in Samaria, Philip and the Ethiopian, Peter's visit to Cornelius, and the missionary journey of Paul and Barnabas all point in this direction. The key phrase which brings the issue into the open is at Acts 13: 46—'behold we turn to the Gentiles.' The Council of Jerusalem described in Acts 15 makes the matter authoritative. The gospel of Jesus Christ is for the whole world.

A brief outline of the contents of the book is:

(a) *A picture of the early Church*

Acts 1: The Ascension of Jesus and the company of the upper room in Jerusalem. Acts 2: Pentecost and the preaching of Peter. Acts 3 to 5: The growing Church in Jerusalem.

Acts 6: 1 to 8: 3: Stephen, the first martyr, and the persecution of theChurch. Acts 8: 4 to 12: 25: From Jerusalem to Judea and Samaria.

(b) *The work of Paul*

Acts 13: 1 to 14: 28: The first missionary journey.

Acts 15: 1-35: The Council of Jerusalem.

Acts 15: 36 to 18: 22: The second missionary journey.

Acts 18: 23 to 21: 14: The third missionary journey.

Acts 21: 15 to 23: 22: Paul in prison in Jerusalem.

Acts 23: 23 to 26: 32: Paul in prison at Caesarea.

Acts 27: 1 to 28: 15: The voyage to Rome—storm and shipwreck. Acts 28: 16-31. Paul in Rome.

The dating of the Acts is very difficult, and the nearest we can come to it is the second half of the first century A.D.

Adam The name of the first man in one of the Creation stories of the book of Genesis. The word Adam also stands in the Bible for mankind in general. [*Refs*. Genesis 2: 7, 15*f*.; 3. 1 Corinthians 15: 22, 45-50.]

Adonijah The fourth son of David, Adonijah plotted to declare himself king just before his aged father died and he won Joab, David's general, on to his side. Nathan the prophet, however, urged Bathsheba to speak to David to proclaim her son Solomon the true heir. David did so and Solomon was anointed by the priest and hailed by the people. Later Solomon had Adonijah put to death. [*Refs*. 1 Kings 1 to 2: 25.]

Adullam A cave in the hills where David hid when he was a fugitive from Saul and where he gathered a company of outlaws and rebels. David became their leader and some of them became his 'mighty men' and personal bodyguards in later years.

Agabus A prophet from Jerusalem who foretold to the Church at Antioch that there would be a great famine 'over all the world'. This brought about a relief collection to aid the Christians in Judaea. Agabus later warned Paul at Caesarea that he would be imprisoned in Jerusalem. [*Refs*. Acts 11: 28-30; 21: 10-11.]

Agag A king of the Amalekites whom Saul spared when he destroyed his people. Samuel rebuked Saul and himself hewed Agag in pieces. [*Ref*. 1 Samuel 15: 7*f*.]

Agrippa *See* HEROD

Ahab Son of Omri and king of Israel 869-850 B.C. He married Jezebel, a Phoenician princess, who brought idolatry and persecution of the prophets to Israel. Jezebel's Phoenician priests spread the cult of Melkart (called Baal in the O.T.) and of Asherah, a heathen goddess, thus reviving ancient fertility rites which had threatened the true faith of Israel ever since the chosen people settled in Canaan. The queen's action called forth fierce protest from Elijah who challenged Ahab to bring the prophets of Baal and all the people to a test of true worship at Mount Carmel. There, says the dramatic tale, 'the fire of the Lord fell', and Elijah was able to check Jezebel's pagan cult. In the affair of Naboth's vineyard, which Ahab coveted for himself, Elijah again confronted the king, this time with a moral demand. Ahab had killed and taken possession, and God's justice would bring disaster on him and his whole house.

After Ahab's death, in battle against Syria, Elisha, the disciple and successor of Elijah, instigated an army revolt against the family of Ahab. Jezebel and the sons of Ahab were wiped out, together with all their friends and supporters in Israel.

The O.T. is mainly concerned with the menace of Ahab's marriage to the worship and moral claims of the Lord. Archaeology reveals that Ahab was an able warrior who took part in the coalition of kings of Syria and Palestine against the growing threat of Assyria. In the famous battle of Qarqar, Ahab led 2,000 chariots and 10,000 soldiers.

Athaliah, daughter of Ahab and Jezebel, married Joram, king of Judah, and brought Baal worship and political trouble to the southern kingdom. [*Refs*. 1 Kings 16: 29-33; 18: 1 to 19: 3; 21; 22: 29-40.] *See also*: ATHALIAH; BAAL; ELIJAH; JEZEBEL

Ahaz King of Judah, c. 735-715 B.C. When Syria and Israel joined forces to besiege Jerusalem, trying to compel Judah to join them against Assyria, Isaiah warned Ahaz to have nothing to do with 'these two smouldering stumps of firebrands'. Ahaz appealed to Tiglath-Pileser for help and paid him tribute from the gold and silver of the Temple. The Assyrians destroyed Syria and Israel, and Judah became a vassal state. Ahaz is condemned by the Bible writers for sacrificing his son to the fire-god Molech and for indulging in Canaanite fertility rites. We have a picture of the situation in Judah at this time in the early chapters of Isaiah, and also in Micah and Hosea. [*Refs*. 2 Kings: 16. Isaiah 1: 1; 7: 1-9. Hosea 1: 1. Micah 1: 1.]

Ahaziah (1) Son of Ahab and king of Israel c. 850-849 B.C. He is mentioned as a worshipper of Baal, and therefore an evil king in the Bible view. Succeeded by his brother Jehoram. [*Refs*. 1 Kings 22: 51-3. 2 Kings 1: 2-4, 17.] (2) Grandson of Ahab of Israel, son of Jehoram of Judah and king of Judah c. 842 B.C. On a visit to his uncle Jehoram (king of Israel) Ahaziah was shot in his chariot by Jehu the rebel general and died at Megiddo. [*Refs.* 2 Kings 9: 14-28.] *See also*: AHAB; JEHU

Ahithophel A highly esteemed counsellor of David who sided with Absalom during his conspiracy and rebellion. The latter, however, rejected his tactical advice. Ahithophel foresaw disaster, went home to his own city, set his house in order and hanged himself [*Refs.* 2 Samuel 15: 12, 31; 16: 15*f*; 17: 1-23.] *See also* ABSALOM

Ai A town in the hill country of Canaan, not far from Bethel, which was completely destroyed by Joshua and reduced to a heap of stones. [*Ref.* Joshua 8: 1-29.]

Alms Money or other gifts given to the poor in the name of God. Jesus taught that alms should be given, not boastfully, but in secret. [*Refs.* Matthew 6: 1-4. Acts 3: 2-5; 10: 2.]

Alpha The first letter in the Greek alphabet. It is used along with Omega (the last letter) to express the greatness of God. Also as a title of Christ, 'the first and the last, the beginning and the end'. [*Refs.* Revelation 1: 8; 22: 13.] *See also* OMEGA

Altar A table of earth, stone, wood, precious metal, on which sacrifices were offered to God, usually by burning them and allowing the smoke and smell to rise heavenwards. There are hundreds of references to altars in the Bible, mostly in the O.T. In early times a simple altar of earth or a heap of stones with a flat rock on top marked the place which men felt to be sacred. The favourite site for an altar was the top of a hill, and 'high places' of heathen worship were often condemned by the prophets.

The altar of burnt offering was one of the most important features of the Temple in Jerusalem. It was there that animals were slaughtered by the priests and burned in sacrifice to God, to beg forgiveness and blessing for the worshipper. Several chapters of Leviticus are taken up with the proper use of the altar, the priests who serve at it, and the sacrifices to be made there. [*Refs.* Genesis 8: 20-1; 12: 7. Exodus 20: 24-6. Leviticus 1-7. Deuteronomy 12: 2-3.] *See also*: PRIEST; SACRIFICE; TEMPLE

Amalekites A nomadic tribe which raided and plundered the Israelites during the desert wanderings of the Exodus, and later in the settled land of Canaan. [*Refs.* Exodus 17: 8-16. Deuteronomy 25: 17, 19. Judges 6: 3-4. 1 Samuel 15: 1-9; 32-3.]

Amen One of the few Hebrew words to come into the English language. It was originally an adverb meaning 'firmly', or, as we might say, 'surely'. Used as a religious response, *Amen* means 'So be it' or 'Let it be so'. Amen was spoken at the end of prayers, blessings, wishes, even curses.

In the N.T. Jesus uses the word to introduce a solemn statement where it is sometimes translated 'verily, verily' or 'truly'. In Revelation, Christ is called 'the Amen, the faithful and true witness'. [*Refs.* Psalm 41: 13; 106: 48. Deuteronomy 27: 14-26. Nehemiah 8: 6. Matthew 8: 10. John 3: 3. Galatians 6: 18. Revelation 3: 14; 22: 20.]

Ammonites A Semitic people, said to be descendents of Lot and thus related to the Israelities. They lived east of the Jordan and the Dead Sea and throughout O.T. times there was bitter warfare between the Ammonites and the tribes of Israel. The Ammonites were notorious for cruelty. [*Refs.* Genesis 19: 38. Judges 11. 1 Samuel 11: 1-11. 2 Samuel 12: 26-31. Nehemiah 4: 7-8.] *See also* JABESH-GILEAD

Amon Son of Manasseh and king of Judah c. 642-640 B.C., Amon was assassinated by his own servants. [*Ref.* 2 Kings 21: 1-26.]

Amorites A Semitic group of tribes who invaded the Fertile Crescent from the desert about 2000 B.C. The name means 'people of the West' and the Hebrews were part of the Amorites. They are often mentioned in the early books of the O.T. as enemies whom the Israelites had to overcome in order to conquer Canaan. [*Refs.* Exodus 3: 17. Deuteronomy 1: 19-20. Judges 11: 22. Ezekiel 16: 3.]

Amos, The Book of Amos is the first of the teaching prophets and his book is one of the 'Latter Prophets' of the Hebrew Scriptures and one of the twelve minor prophets of our O.T. Amos was 'a herdsman and a dresser of sycamore trees' who belonged to Tekoa in the southern kingdom of Judah. His oracles, however, deal with Israel, the northern kingdom, about the middle of the eighth century B.C., in the reign of King Jeroboam II. An autobiographical fragment at 7: 10-17 tells of his utterance against the royal house at the king's sanctuary at Bethel, and the furious reaction of Amaziah the priest.

The book of Amos may be divided into three parts:

(a) Amos 1-2: These chapters contain seven short oracles about surrounding nations introduced by the warning words 'Thus says the Lord'. They deal in turn with Damascus, the Philistine cities, Tyre, Edom, Ammon, Moab. Each oracle speaks of judgment and destruction. An additional passage concerning Judah was probably written by a different hand. Finally there is an oracle against Israel, warning her of forthcoming punishment because of the social injustice to be found throughout the kingdom: 'they sell the righteous for silver, and the needy for a pair of shoes'. The Israelites will by no means escape judgment just because they are God's chosen people.

(b) Amos 3-6: These chapters are largely taken up with denunciations of the social abuses Amos saw in the land of Israel, especially in Samaria, the capital city. We have a grim picture of a sick society—the luxury of the rich, their sumptuous winter houses and summer houses filled with ivory furnishings and soft couches, the pampered, well-fed women with their oils and perfumes, the trickery and dishonesty of merchants in the market-place, bribery in the law-courts, hypocrisy at the shrines. Meanwhile the poor of the land languish in the dust, stricken and oppressed by their fellow-men. In the name of a righteous God Amos declares the inevitability of doom: 'You only have I known of all the families of the earth; therefore I will punish you for all your iniquities.' God takes no delight in religious festivals which are but a hypocritical show, nor in burnt-offerings and sacred songs. His demand is moral: 'let justice roll down like waters, and righteousness like an everflowing stream'.

(c) Amos 7-9: Here one vision of doom succeeds another—locusts, fire, the plumb-line, a basket of summer fruit. The repeated refrain is death, exile, the end of Israel. The note of hope which comes oddly in the concluding verses of the final chapter is almost certainly by a later writer.

The whole Book of Amos might be entitled 'a cry for justice'. He is pre-eminently the prophet of passionate anger against 'man's inhumanity to man', constantly reminding the rich, callous citizens of Israel that they are of one family with the poor of the land and that a rightous God will require them to look to their brothers' welfare. In the eyes of Amos, righteousness is written into the very fabric of the universe. If cause is on the side of right, effect will be moral, too. Those who think and live otherwise will inevitably bring doom upon themselves.

Anakim The Anakim or 'sons of Anak' were a legendary race of giants mentioned a number of times in the stories of the conquest of Canaan by the Israelites. [*Refs.* Numbers 13: 28, 33. Deuteronomy 1: 28; 9: 2.]

Ananias (1) A member of the Church in Jerusalem in the days when the believers had all things in common. He sold a piece of property, secretly kept some of the money, and brought only a part of it to the apostles. When Peter rebuked him, Ananias fell down and died. (2) A disciple in Damascus who, inspired by a vision, sought out Saul and helped to restore his sight. [*Ref.* Acts 9: 10-19.] (3) The high priest in Jerusalem before whom Paul was brought as a prisoner for examination to find out if he had broken the Jewish law. [*Ref.* Acts 23: 1-5.]

Anathoth The home town of Jeremiah the prophet, not far from Jerusalem. At the time of the siege of Jerusalem by Nebuchadrezzar, Jeremiah was in prison in the royal palace because his advice did not please the king. In spite of impending disaster the prophet bought a field in Anathoth as a sign of hope for the future: 'For thus says the Lord of hosts, the God of Israel: 'Houses and fields and vineyards shall again be bought in this land'.' [*Refs.* Jeremiah 1: 1; 11: 21; 32: 1, 6-15.]

Andrew One of the twelve apostles. Andrew was a fisherman of

Galilee who, along with his brother Simon, was called by Jesus to follow him. John's Gospel tells how Andrew was first a disciple of John the Baptist and that he belonged to Bethsaida. [*Refs.* Mark 1: 16-18. John 1: 35-41, 44.]

Angels The Greek word *angelos* means 'messenger' or 'bringer of news', but in the Bible an angel is usually taken to mean a messenger from God, and especially a superhuman being. Since the name of God was held in reverence by the Jews and was not directly spoken, it was quite common for 'the angel of God' to be used as a roundabout way of telling of God's dealings with men or to signify that God was appearing in human form. Thus 'the angel of the Lord' called to Abraham from heaven to prevent him slaying his son Isaac, 'the angel of the Lord' appeared to Moses in a flame of fire out of the midst of a bush, 'the angel of the Lord' came to Gideon and to the mother of Samson—where he is also called 'the man'. These beings speak and walk and look like mortals and yet appear and disappear at will. It is an angel-man who wrestles with Jacob at Peniel on the river Jabbok. Perhaps the idea of angels began in primitive animism with spirits of the groves, trees, fountains and the sky. Certainly we find Persian influence here. It may be that the bright stars of the Eastern sky suggested fiery and celestial beings. A great deal of imagery developed round the idea of divine messengers in Hebrew thought. Angels ascended and descended the ladder set up at Bethel in Jacob's dream; they are called 'heavenly beings' in the poetry of the Psalms, as well as helpful ministers of God. The book of Job sees them as 'the sons of God'. In the N.T. it is 'an angel of the Lord' who appears to Joseph in a dream to announce that his wife Mary will bear a son, legions of them are mentioned in the same Gospel of Matthew, and in Luke 'the heavenly host' appears to the shepherds in the fields near Bethlehem. Again in Matthew angels minister to Jesus in the wilderness, and Luke tells that 'an angel from heaven' appeared to Jesus in the agony on the Mount of Olives before his arrest and death. Angels are mentioned here and there in the teaching of Jesus, including an unusual reference to 'guardian angels'. 'An angel of the Lord' directed Philip the evangelist to meet the Ethiopian on the Gaza road, and another came in shining light to deliver Peter from Herod's prison.

The letter to the Hebrews and especially the book of The Revelation have a good deal to say about these divine ministers. In the latter writing angels busy themselves greatly in the final holocaust, sealing the faithful on their foreheads, swinging their sickles, pouring out bowls of wrath, and sounding their trumpets to proclaim the judgment of God. It should be noted that bad angels as well as good appear in the O.T. and the New, thus providing John Milton with his *dramatis personae* for *Paradise Lost*.

Once poetry and the visual arts take over, angels are elaborated. They are clothed in gleaming white or brilliant colours, with widespread wings and sheathed in a radiance not of this world. They preside over the mysteries of birth and of death. Popular mythology has added its own imagery all through the ages. Though angels belong entirely to the world of man's imagination, they have powerfully affected religious art and symbolism and have provided many a comforting link with the supernatural. In that sense angels are indeed ministers of the grace of God. [*Refs.* Genesis 22: 11-12; 24: 7, 40; 28: 12; 32: 24. Exodus 3: 2. Judges 6: 11-22; 13: 3, 6, 11. 1 Kings 19: 5. Job 1: 6. Psalm 103: 20. Matthew 1: 20; 4: 11; 18: 10. Luke 2: 8-14; 15: 10; 22: 43. Acts 8: 26; 12: 7. Hebrews 1: 4, 7. Revelation 1: 20; 8: 2; 15: 7.]

Anna A prophetess, a very old widow, who visited the Temple daily and who saw the dedication of the infant Jesus. [*Ref.* Luke 2: 36-8]

Annas Former high priest of the Temple, father-in-law of Caiaphas. According to John's Gospel, Jesus was taken before Annas as soon as he was arrested. Annas later took part in the trial of Peter and John. [*Refs.* John 18: 13. Acts 4: 6.] *See also*: TRIAL OF JESUS

Anoint To pour oil on the head or body, usually in a sacred ceremony. In Bible times sweet-smelling oil was used to welcome a guest, and oil or ointment was used to heal the sick. Religious anointing was for three kinds of people: prophet, priest, or king. It was, as it were, an outward sign of God's choice and approval. Thus Samuel anointed Saul and later David to the sacred task of being God's chosen king over Israel. The Hebrew word Messiah and the Greek equivalent Christos mean 'anointed' and the N.T. writers spoke of Jesus in this sense of being God's chosen one. Sacred objects and furnishings are also mentioned as being 'anointed'. [*Refs.* Genesis 28: 18. Exodus 30: 22-32. 1 Samuel 10: 1; 16: 13. Isaiah 61: 3. Mark 6: 13. Luke 10: 34. Acts 10: 38]

Antioch (1) Antioch in Syria on the river Orontes, about fifteen miles from the Mediterranean, was the capital city of the Roman province of Syria. It was the third city of the Roman Empire and had a large Jewish population. Many Jewish-Christian refugees fled to Antioch after the martyrdom of Stephen, and the followers of Jesus were for the first time called Christians in Antioch. The Church in Antioch sent out Barnabas and Paul on their first missionary journey, and to Antioch they returned to report the success of their mission to the Gentiles. Antioch was one of the most important centres of the Christian Church during the first three centuries. [*Refs.* Acts 11: 1-26; 13: 1-3; 14: 26-8.] (2) Pisidian Antioch, a town in the highlands of Asia Minor, in the Roman province of Galatia, visited by Paul and Barnabas on their first missionary journey. The Jews of the synagogue there strongly opposed their message, and it was in this Antioch that Paul declared he would turn to the Gentiles. [*Refs.* Acts 13: 14-50.]

Antipas *See* HEROD

Apocrypha The word literally means 'hidden', and it is normally applied to certain Jewish writings which have not been included in the accepted canon of sacred Scripture. A dictionary defines the Apocrypha as 'those books included in the Septuagint (the Greek version of Jewish Scriptures) and the Vulgate (the Latin version of the Bible approved by the Roman Catholic Church) which were not originally written in Hebrew and which, after the Reformation, were excluded from the canon of Scripture by Protestants'. The canon of sacred Hebrew Scriptures was fixed by the time of the Council of Jamnia in A.D. 90. The Hebrew canon included the Law and the Prophets and certain Writings, forming, in fact, the O.T. as we usually know it in the thirty-nine books of our English translations. There were also, however, Jewish writings composed at various times from about 300 B.C. to A.D. 100, during the era of Greek and Roman rule. They include the fourteen books which form the Apocrypha:

1 Esdras
2 Esdras
Tobit
Judith
The rest of Esther
The Wisdom of Solomon
Ecclesiasticus
Baruch, with the Epistle of Jeremiah
The Song of the Three Holy Children
The History of Susanna
Bel and the Dragon
The Prayer of Manasses
1 Maccabees
2 Maccabees

For one reason or another the Jews excluded these books from the Hebrew canon of sacred Scripture. The early Christian Church which used the Septuagint was not so rigid and was prepared to regard some of these writings as sacred. The Latin Vulgate did include the Apocrypha and so also did the original Authorized Version of the Bible in English of A.D. 1611. But the Protestant reformers in Britain were doubtful about the validity of these books. The Thirty-nine Articles of Religion of the Church of England (1563), for example, declares: 'In the name of the holy Scripture we do understand those canonical Books of the Old and New Testament, of whose authority was never any doubt in the Church' (i.e. the thirty-nine books of our O.T.). 'And the other Books the Church doth read for example of life and instruction of manners; but yet doth it not apply them to establish any doctrine' (i.e. the fourteen books of the Apocrypha). The Westminster Confession of Faith (1647) explicitly states: 'The Books commonly called Apocrypha, not being of divine inspiration, are no part of the canon of the scripture, and therefore are of no authority in the Church of God, nor to be any otherwise approved, or made use of, than other human writings. 'The Bible Societies of a later age tended not to include the Apocrypha in versions of Scripture circulated in the British Isles.

Apollos An eloquent Jew of Alexandria who came to the city of Ephesus to speak of repentance and baptism in the manner of John the Baptist. Priscilla and Aquila heard him teach in the Synagogue and took him and instructed him in the meaning of the life and teaching of Jesus. Thereafter Apollos proclaimed the Christian Gospel. He was apparently a speaker of great power. In Corinth a group of his followers declared that Apollos was greater than Paul, and this led to some party rivalry among Christian believers. It was on this account that Paul wrote to the Church in Corinth about Christian unity and their one Lord, Jesus Christ. [*Refs.* Acts 18: 22-8. 1 Corinthians 1: 10-13; 3: 4-6; 16: 12.]

Apostle The Greek word *apostolos* means 'one who is sent as a messenger'. The name is used mainly of the twelve men chosen by Jesus from among his followers to be witnesses of his life and work. Each Gospel has its own list of the twelve. After the Resurrection the word apostle was also used of others, such as Matthias, Paul and James. [*Refs.* Matthew 10: 2-4. Mark 3: 14-19. Luke 6: 13-16. Acts 1: 26; 14: 14; 15: 22. Romans 1: 1. 1 Corinthians 15: 7-9.]

Apphia A Christian woman of Colossae, probably the wife of Philemon. [*Ref.* Philemon: 2.]

Aquila A Jew who belonged to Pontus, on the Black Sea coast of Asia Minor. When Paul met him in Corinth he and his wife Priscilla were fugitives from Rome, expelled along with other Jews by the emperor Claudius. Aquila and Priscilla were tent makers and Paul stayed with them in Corinth because he was of the same trade. They went with Paul to Ephesus and became well-known Christian teachers in the early Church.

Wherever they went their home was a centre of worship. One of their most noted pupils was Apollos. [*Refs.* Acts 18: 1-3, 18-19, 24-6. Romans 16: 3-5. 1 Corinthians 16: 19. 2 Timothy 4: 19.]

Arabia The largely desert peninsula which lies between Egypt and Mesopotamia and is bounded by the Red Sea, the Indian Ocean and the Persian Gulf. From Arabia in earliest Bible times came the Semitic migrant tribes which populated the Fertile Crescent from Mesopotamia to Canaan. In o.t. narrative Arabia is mentioned as the desert home of nomad traders. In the N.T. Arabian visitors to Jerusalem are mentioned as being present on the day of Pentecost. Paul claimed to have spent some time in Arabia, no doubt in meditation. [*Refs.* 1 Kings 10: 15. 2 Chronicles 9: 14. Isaiah 13: 20. Ezekiel 27: 21. Acts 2: 11. Galatians 1: 17.]

Ararat This is best known as the range of mountains where Noah's ark came to rest when the waters of the Flood went down. [*Ref.* Genesis 8: 4.]

Archelaus *See* HEROD

Areopagus The 'hill of Ares (Mars)' in Athens where Paul stood up in the council of Greek philosophers and preached the God of heaven and earth to them. [*Ref.* Acts 17: 22.]

Arimathea A town in the hill country of Judaea, north-west of Jerusalem. It was the home of Joseph, a rich man and member of the Jewish council, who took the body of Jesus and gave it burial in his own tomb. Arimathea is the same place as Ramah, the town of Samuel, in the o.t. [*Refs.* Matthew 27: 57. John 19: 38.] *See also*: JOSEPH

Aristarchus A Macedonian from Thessalonica and a faithful companion of Paul. He was seized in the riot at Ephesus when the silver craftsmen cried out that their trade was being ruined by Paul's preaching. Later Aristarchus sailed with Paul on his fateful voyage to Rome. The Letter to the Colossians mentions him as a 'fellow-prisoner', presumably in Rome. [*Refs.* Acts 19: 29; 27: 2. Colossians 4: 10. Philemon: 24.]

Ark The word means a 'box' or 'chest'. In the Bible it refers to

the large, floating covered boat in which Noah and his family
and pairs of every living creature were kept safe during the
Flood which covered the earth. [*Refs.* Genesis 6: 14*f.* Hebrews
11: 7.] *See also*: FLOOD, NOAH

Ark of the Covenant The box made of acacia wood which was
believed to contain the two stone tablets given by God to Moses
on which the Ten Commandments were inscribed. According
to Jewish tradition the Ark of the Covenant (or Ark of the
Testimony) accompanied the Hebrews through all their desert
wanderings until they came into the promised land. The account in Exodus 25: 10-22 tells of the making of the box, overlaid with pure gold within and without, with gold rings to
support the carrying poles. Other accounts vary, and it must
be remembered that they all belong to a much later age. The
Ark was kept in the inmost shrine of the Tabernacle and later
of the Temple in Jerusalem. Many traditions are recorded
regarding this most ancient symbol of the faith of Israel. It
was carried on the shoulders of Levitical priests when the Israelites crossed the dry bed of the river Jordan; it was borne
round the walls of Jericho, later captured from the shrine at
Shiloh by the Philistines, brought to Jerusalem by David, and
at last enshrined in the Temple by Solomon. After that no
more is heard of it, nor can anyone tell what happened to the
sacred Ark. Perhaps it was looted by one conqueror or another, or even removed by the iniquitous King Manasseh.
Certainly it was lost long before the building of the second
Temple. A later legend tells that Jeremiah hid it in a cave in
the hills.

The synagogues of Judaism after the Exile and to the present
day have contained a box called the Ark which holds the
scrolls of sacred scriptures used in the Jewish services. The
Ark is separated from the main room of the synagogue and
screened by a curtain except when the scrolls are taken out,
carried round the congregation, and unrolled to be read from
the reading-desk. [*Refs.* Exodus 25: 10-22. Numbers 10: 33-
6. Deuteronomy 10: 15; 31: 9. Joshua 3: 17. 1 Samuel 4: 1 to

7: 1. 2 Samuel 6: 1-19. 1 Kings 8: 1-9.] *See also*: SYNAGOGUE;
TABERNACLE; GATH; UZZAH

Armageddon *See* MEGIDDO

Artaxerxes I King of Persia, 464-424 B.C. He gave his cupbearer
Nehemiah permission to go to Jerusalem to rebuild the walls.
[*Ref.* Nehemiah: 2: 1.]

Ascension The ascent of Jesus to heaven on the fortieth day
after his Resurrection is referred to in the book of Acts and
celebrated in the Christian Church on the Thursday ten days
before Whit Sunday. The idea of the ascent of Jesus to 'the
right hand of God' is often referred to in the preaching of the
early Church. [*Refs.* John 20: 17. Acts 1: 2, 9-11; 2: 33; 5: 31.
Ephesians 4: 8-10. 1 Timothy 3: 16.]

Asenath *See* EPHRAIM

Ashtaroth, Ashtoreth, Asherah Names for the female counterpart in Canaanite fertility cults to Baal, the male 'lord' or 'master'. In the O.T. Asherah usually refers to the symbolic wooden
pillar or sacred tree carved in female form, misleadingly translated 'grove' in the Authorized Version. The names *Asherah,
Ashtaroth, Anath*, the Babylonian *Ishtar* and the Greek goddess
Astarte are all linked in pagan worship. We can trace the same
goddess in Greek mythology as Aphrodite and in Roman as
Venus. The Hebrew prophets were emphatic in their condemnation of all Canaanite fertility worship. [*Refs.* Judges 2: 13;
10: 6. 1 Samuel 7: 4; 12: 10. 1 Kings 11: 5; 16: 32-3. Jeremiah
7: 16-20; 44: 15-30.]

Assyria The great empire which lay along the river Tigris in
Mesopotamia, its capital being first at Ashur and later at
Nineveh. Assyria is mentioned many times in O.T. history as a
dark threat for many a century to the kingdoms of Israel and
Judah. In the days of Menahem, king of Israel, Tiglath-Pileser
III of Assyria (called Pul in the Bible) marched against Israel
and forced Menahem to pay tribute. Tiglath-Pileser III later
devastated the north of Palestine and carried away many cap-
tives to Assyria. His successor, Shalmanezer V, laid siege to
Samaria, the capital of the northern kingdom, for three years,

and after him Sargon II at last destroyed the city and carried the Israelites away to exile in Assyria. Thus the kingdom of Israel disappeared from world history.

The southern kingdom of Judah was left defenceless, and Sermacherib of Assyria came against all the fortified towns of Judah and took them. At first Hezekiah of Judah paid tribute, stripping the Temple of its gold and silver to do so. Later, encouraged by the prophet Isaiah, he refused to give in, and the Bible graphically describes how the Assyrian army besieged Jerusalem but failed to take it because plague broke out in their camp. The immediate threat was removed, but Judah was a vassal to Assyria during the reign of the next two kings. In 612 B.C., however, the Assyrian capital city of Nineveh was itself overrun by the Medes and Chaldeans of Babylon, and the Assyrian empire was at an end. [*Refs.* 2 Kings 15: 17-20, 29; 17: 3-6; 18: 9 to 19: 37. Isaiah 8: 7; 10: 5-6; 36: 1 to 37: 38. Nahum 1: 1; 2: 1-12; 3: 1-7, 18-19.]

Athaliah Daughter of King Ahab of Israel and Jezebel his Tyrian queen, and wife to King Jehoram of Judah. She followed her mother's example in encouraging the worship of Baal and tried to wipe out the royal line of David. After her son Ahaziah had been killed in Jehu's rebellion, Athaliah seized the throne and put to death, as she thought, all the royal family of Judah. But she overlooked Joash, the infant son of Ahaziah, who was hidden away from his aunt for six years. At length the Temple priests and the army proclaimed the boy Joash king and they destroyed Athaliah. [*Ref.* 2 Kings 2: 1-20.]

Athens A city state of Greece in N.T. times, and famous centre of learning and pagan worship. On his second missionary journey Paul preached in Athens, in the synagogue, the marketplace, and on the Areopagus. [*Ref.* Acts 17: 15-34.]

Atonement, Day of *See* HIGH PRIEST

Augustus Augustus Caesar was the official title of Octavian, the first Roman emperor who ruled 27 B.C. to A.D. 14. [*Ref.* Luke 2: 1.]

Azariah *See* UZZIAH

B

Baal The word means 'lord' or 'master' and it is applied as a general term in the O.T. to the Canaanite gods encountered by the Israelites in their settlement and possession of the promised land. The Baals (in Hebrew, *Baalim*) were male fertility gods to which sacrifice was made to produce bountiful crops in the fields and vineyards, fecund flocks and herds, as well as family blessing in sons and daughters. The female counterpart to Baal was Ashtaroth. The worship of Baal belonged to high places, mountain tops and cultic poles where, year by year, offerings were made in anticipation of the bounty of harvest or in thanksgiving for it. Sexual rites were mixed up with the cult of Baal.

Time and again the O.T. prophets and writers cried out against the spiritual and moral danger of bribing and placating the gods of field and farmyard. The Hebrew God of the desert tradition was austere, holy, not to be worshipped in idol form or any image, and always righteous, beyond the reach of bribery. He is thus described as a 'jealous' God, who recognizes no other gods. But frequent reference to the struggle with the Baals, as well as many place-names and personal names in the O.T., shows how deep the apostasy went.

The moral stuggle is best illustrated in the encounter between the prophet Elijah and Jezebel the Phoenician queen of Ahab, king of Israel. Other kings and queens were sternly denounced by the prophets through at least three centuries.

Manasseh, for example, is portrayed as the most wicked king in the whole story of the Jews because he filled Jerusalem and the Temple with Baal images, tapestries, priests and cult prostitutes. Josiah, on the other hand, is extravagantly praised because he rooted out all the heathen ornaments and burned them with reforming zeal. Only with the Exile, however, did the Jewish people at last shake off the influence of fertility gods of hills and valleys and return contrite to the worship of a God whose true sacrifice was not in gifts of grain or oil, wine, or even human sacrifice, but in spirit and in truth. The supreme lesson of the Exile was that there was but one God. It might be argued, however, that Baal worship came back in subtle fashion not in fertility cults but in the religious fanaticism which marred post-exilic Judaism, when the Temple in Jerusalem and its elaborate system of sacrifice became a fetish rather than a symbol of faith. [*Refs.* Judges 2: 11-14; 10: 6. 1 Samuel 7: 3-4. 1 Kings 16: 32; 18: 18*f*. 2 Kings 21: 3-7; 23: 4*f*. Jeremiah 2: 28. Hosea 2: 13.] *See also*: ASHTAROTH, ASHTORETH, ASHERAH

Babel The Hebrew name for Babylon. The Tower of Babel was a seven-storey temple-tower built up on terraces, each stage smaller than the one below. It was known as 'the house of the terrace-platform of heaven and earth'. The writer of Genesis 11 uses it as a symbol of the overweening pride of the city-dwellers who sought to build a tower to the heavens and rebel against God. The story tells that God scattered the people of Babel and confused their language so that they no longer understood one another. Thus the many languages of mankind are accounted for. [*Ref.* Genesis 11: 1-9.]

Babylon A very ancient city on the Euphrates in Mesopotamia. Apart from Jerusalem, no place had a greater influence on Jewish culture and literature, especially if we remember that Babylon often stands for the country and peoples of Chaldea (Babylonia) in O.T. writings. In that sense Babylon was the original Hebrew homeland; its gods and beliefs appear in their religion, its writings lie behind many pages of Hebrew scripture, and its land provided home and shelter in the days of exile. Shinar, in the early chapters of Genesis, refers to Babylonia.

The city of Babylon is best known in Bible times as the capital of Nebuchadrezzar, who destroyed Jerusalem and carried off the Jewish people into exile. Excavations have revealed how wonderful it was, with massive double walls, towers, gates covered with coloured tiles, a palace with hanging gardens, as well as temples of the gods. Babylon was later conquered by Cyrus of Persia who allowed the Jews to return to their own land. Just as Jerusalem was the place of their chief joy, so the name Babylon lingers symbolically in Jewish memory as the city of their desolation and utter grief. In N.T. times the name is used to signify Rome, the capital of the new oppressor: 'Babylon the great, mother of harlots and of earth's abominations.' The name has passed into the language as a symbol of a great, luxurious, wicked city. [*Refs.* 2 Kings 24: 11. Ezra 1: 11. Psalm 137: 1, 8. Isaiah 13: 19. 1 Peter: 13. Revelation 14: 8; 17: 5.] *See also*: NIMROD

Balaam A soothsayer summoned by the king of Moab to curse the invading people of Israel. But Balaam had a vision of God forbidding him to curse the blessed and victorious nation. Later, when Balaam saddled his ass to go to Moab, the ass saw the angel of the Lord standing in the way with a drawn sword in his hand. When Balaam beat him, the beast spoke reproachfully to his master. Then Balaam saw the angel, was reproved by him, and in spite of being bribed to say the opposite, he spoke God's blessing of Israel in the hearing of the king of Moab. This very ancient tale illustrates the Israelite belief in their invincibility under God in the face of every foe. [*Ref.* Numbers: 22-4.]

Barabbas A robber or rebel in prison in Jerusalem at the time of the trial of Jesus before Pilate. When Pilate offered to release Jesus, the leaders of the Jews stirred up the crowd to have him release Barabbas instead. Some ancient versions say his full name was Jesus Barabbas. So Pilate's question may have been. 'Whom do you want me to release for you, Jesus

Barabbas or Jesus who is called Christ?' [*Refs*. Matthew 27: 15-21. Mark 15: 7. Luke 23: 18-19. John 18: 40.]

Bar-Jesus *See* ELYMAS

Barnabas A Jewish Christian named Joseph, a Levite and a native of Cyprus, who was given the nickname Barnabas by the disciples in Jerusalem in the early days of the Church. He sold a field which belonged to him and gave the money to help the needy. In the Church at Antioch, Barnabas was called a prophet, teacher and apostle. It was he who sought out Paul and brought him to Antioch as leader of the Church there, just as he had already vouched for him among the disciples in Jerusalem. Barnabas and Paul made their first missionary journey together, taking with them John Mark, nephew of Barnabas. No one is more memorable in the story of the early Church for his encouragement of others. It is not for nothing that the author of Acts calls Barnabas 'a good man'. [*Refs*. Acts 4: 36-7; 9: 26-7; 11: 25-6; 13: 1-3; 14: 12; 15: 12, 35, 39.]

Bartholomew One of the twelve apostles mentioned by Matthew, Mark, Luke. He may be the same man as Nathanael in John's Gospel. [*Refs*. Matthew 10: 3. Mark 3: 18. Luke 6: 14. John 1: 45.]

Bartimaeus The blind beggar by the roadside outside Jericho who hailed Jesus as 'Son of David' and whose sight was restored. [*Ref*. Mark 10: 46.]

Baruch The friend and secretary of Jeremiah who wrote down the prophet's message on a scroll and then read it in the hearing of the people of Jerusalem. The scroll was later taken to the king who was sitting in the winter house with a fire burning in the brazier before him. The king listened to the oracles of Jeremiah, cut up the scroll bit by bit with a penknife, and threw the pieces in the fire until the entire scroll was consumed. When Jeremiah heard of it, he ordered Baruch to write another scroll containing words of doom to the king and the kingdom of Judah. It is likely that Baruch's record contains a part of our Book of Jeremiah. The prophet and his faithful scribe were both eventually carried off to Egypt. [*Refs*. Jeremiah 32: 9-16; 36: 4-32; 43: 6.]

Bashan A district east of the River Jordan which was famous in O.T. times for its rich pasture, fat cattle, great oaks, and many-peaked mountains. It is frequently mentioned in the stories of the attack on Canaan in the time of Moses when the Israelites defeated the giant Og, king of Bashan, and his people. [*Refs.* Deuteronomy 3: 1-11. Psalm 22: 12; 68: 15. Isaiah 2: 13.]

Bathsheba Wife of Uriah the Hittite whom David took when her husband was on the field of battle. David gave orders that Uriah was to be put in the front line of battle, where he was slain. The king then took Bathsheba as his wife, but he was rebuked for his wicked act by Nathan the prophet. Bathsheba's son was Solomon, and when David was very old she begged him to promise that Solomon would reign after him. [*Refs.* 2 Samuel 11; 12: 9, 24. 1 Kings 1: 28-31.]

Beautiful Gate A gate of the Temple in Jerusalem in N.T. times usually identified with the Nicanor gate which led to the inner court. It was made of valuable Corinthian bronze. Peter healed the lame beggar who sat there. [*Ref.* Acts 3: 2, 10.]

Beatitudes *Beatitude* means a special blessing or happiness of the highest kind. In Hebrew poetry it is common to find phrases of this kind, particularly in the Psalms or Proverbs, which declare: 'Blessed is the man who...' or 'Happy is the man who...'. Such beatitudes are also scattered in the Gospels. The name is usually applied, however, to the sayings of Jesus at the beginning of the Sermon on the Mount in Matthew 5: 3-12 and the parallel passage in Luke 6: 20-3.

Matthew's Gospel has eight (or nine) Beatitudes, where Luke has four. No doubt they share a common source of material containing some of the teaching of Jesus. But where Matthew spiritualizes the sayings, for example 'Blessed are the poor in spirit...', Luke sets his in the real, everyday world: 'Blessed are you poor..'. Luke thus more nearly echoes the Messianic promises of Isaiah 61: 1-3.

The Beatitudes portray the blessings and rewards of those who share in the kingdom of God—the poor, the merciful, the pure in heart, the peacemakers, the persecuted and reviled. It may be noted that Matthew 5: 11 forms a statement rather than the usual exclamation. That is one reason why some scholars would limit the Beatitudes in Matthew to eight rather than nine, and suggest that verses 10-11 show a later extension of some original words of Jesus about suffering. Luke's version of his fourth beatitude on the same theme is also extended beyond the one short sentence. It must be remembered that the writing of the Gospels came from days when the disciples of Jesus were indeed being persecuted. Luke also adds four 'woes' as if to balance his four 'blesseds' and these, too, are a reminder of troubled days for the community of the early Church. [*Refs.* Psalm 1: 1; 32: 1, 2; 65: 4. Proverbs 8: 34; 16: 20. Luke 1: 45; 7: 23; 14: 15. Revelation 14: 13; 22: 7.]

Beelzebub The name means 'lord of the flies'. *Beelzebub* or *Beelzebul* is the Greek form of Baalzebub, a heathen god of Ekron, the Philistine town of Canaan. In N.T. times the name came to signify 'prince of the devils' in the teaching of the Pharisees. [*Refs.* 2 Kings 1: 2, 6, 16. Matthew 12: 24-7. Mark 3: 22. Luke 11: 18-19.] *See also:* SATAN.

Beersheba One of the oldest towns in the Bible story, on the edge of the desert in the south of Palestine. Beersheba means 'well of the oath' or 'well of the seven' and its plentiful water supply made it an important oasis for Abraham, Isaac and Jacob with their large flocks and herds. The phrase 'from Dan even to Beersheba' later became a favourite description of the north-south limits of the promised land. [*Refs.* Genesis 21: 25-32; 46: 1. 1 Kings 4: 25.]

Belshazzar The book of Daniel wrongly describes Belshazzar as the son of Nebuchadrezzar and the last Chaldean king of Babylon. Belshazzar gave a feast for a thousand of his lords, during which they drank wine from the sacred vessels which had been taken from the Temple in Jerusalem. During the feast 'the fingers of a man's hand appeared and wrote on the plaster of the wall of the king's palace'. When none of the wise men of Babylon could explain the words, Daniel was brought to read the writing. He made known its meaning, predicting the downfall of Belshazzar's kingdom. [*Ref.* Daniel: 5.] *See also*: DANIEL

Benjamin The twelfth and much-loved youngest son of Jacob, by his wife Rachel who died at Benjamin's birth. His name appears in the stories of Joseph, his full brother. His descendants are mentioned as the tribe of Benjamin, said to be brave warriors. Two famous members of the tribe were Saul, the first king of Israel, and Paul the apostle. [*Refs.* Genesis 35: 16-18. 1 Samuel 9: 1-2. Romans 11; 1.]

Bethany A village (literally 'the house of dates') on the eastern slope of the Mount of Olives about two miles from Jerusalem. Jesus' friends Lazarus, Martha and Mary lived there, and also Simon the leper. Jesus visited their homes. Luke says the Ascension took place near Bethany. [*Refs.* Mark 11: 1, 11; 14: 3. Luke 24: 50. John 11: 1, 18; 12: 1.]

Bethel The name means 'house of God'. Bethel was a well-known holy place in O.T. times. The town stood high in the central range of Palestine hills and was important because of its ancient connection with Abraham and Jacob. It was at Bethel that Abraham first pitched his tent and built an altar and worshipped God. Jacob's dream of a ladder reaching from earth to heaven took place there. In the days of the Judges the Ark was kept at Bethel for a time. After the division of the kingdoms Bethel fell within Israel. Jeroboam I erected a shrine at Bethel and set up a golden calf and appointed his own priests. The place became a royal shrine. In the eighth century Amos prophesied at Bethel against the royal house. Later King Josiah of Judah pulled down the altar and heathen symbols of Bethel and destroyed the shrine. [*Refs.* Genesis 12: 8; 28: 10-22. Judges 20: 18. 1 Kings 12: 29, 32-3. Amos 7: 10-11. 2 Kings 23:15.]

Bethesda The name means 'house of mercy'. Bethesda was a place outside one of the gates of Jerusalem where there was a pool of water with porches round it. Sick people lay there waiting to step down into the waters when they saw them 'disturbed'. Jesus healed a man who bad been waiting there for thirty-eight years. [*Ref.* John 5: 2-9.]

Bethlehem The name means 'house of bread'. The town of Bethlehem lies in the hills about five miles south of Jerusalem and is famous as the birthplace of David and of Jesus. The town is mentioned also in the O.T. story of Ruth, traditionally an ancestor of both David and Jesus. Although Jesus' birth at Bethlehem is mentioned only by Matthew and Luke, a great wealth of legend, song and story has grown up about this hallowed place. [*Refs.* Ruth 1: 1, 19, 22. 1 Samuel 16: 1-4. Micah 5: 2. Matthew 2: 1, 5, 6. Luke 2: 4, 15. John 7: 42.]

Bethphage The name means 'house of figs'. Bethphage was a village on the slope of the Mount of Olives, near Bethany. Jesus sent two of his disciples to Bethphage to fetch an ass for his entry into Jerusalem. [*Refs.* Matthew 21: 1. Mark 11: 1. Luke 19: 29.]

Bethsaida The name means 'house of fishers'. Bethsaida was a town on the north shore of the Sea of Galilee, near the mouth of the river Jordan. It was the home of Peter, Andrew and Philip. Near there Jesus fed the five thousand and healed a blind man. [*Refs.* John 1: 44. Mark 6: 45; 8: 22.]

Birthright *See* FIRST-BORN

Boanerges The name means 'sons of thunder'. This surname was given by Jesus to the brothers James and John when he appointed them to be his disciples. [*Ref.* Mark 3: 17.]

Boaz The name means 'swiftness'. In the idyllic tale of Ruth, Boaz was a wealthy farmer of Bethlehem who befriended Ruth, the Moabite woman who was the widow of his kinsman. The story ends with Ruth becoming the wife of Boaz. The child born to them was the grandfather of David and ancestor of Jesus. [*Refs.* Ruth 2: 1; 4: 13, 17. Matthew 1: 5. Luke 3: 32.]

Booths A booth is a temporary dwelling made of woven branches. The Jewish Feast of Booths, one of the three great festivals of the religious year, takes place in the autumn and is a reminder of the days when the Israelites wandered through the desert from Egypt to the promised land and lived in tents. The Feast of Booths is also known as the Feast of Tabernacles ('tents') or *Sukkoth* in the Hebrew language. The festival lasts for eight days and was originally held as a joyful harvest thanksgiving. The instructions for it are in Leviticus 23: 33-6, 39-43. After the return from Exile the Jews kept the festival by building booths of 'branches of olive, wild olive, myrtle, palm and other leafy trees' and set them up on the flat roofs of their houses and in their courts. [*Refs*. Deuteronomy 16: 13-17. Nehemiah 8: 13-18. John 7: 2, 8.]

Burnt-Offering An animal sacrifice offered to God by burning. In primitive times it was believed that a god could be influenced or placated by burning such an offering on his altar. The smoke and smell ascended to heaven and the sweet savour pleased the god and brought his favour. Burnt-offerings are frequently mentioned throughout the O.T. at times of personal and public crisis, thanksgiving, festival, and particularly in the elaborate ritual of the Temple in Jerusalem. The laws for the burnt-offering are set down in great detail. They are described as a command of God: 'My offering, my food for my offerings by fire, my pleasing odour, you shall take heed to offer to me in its due season.' The animal for the burnt-offering was to be a male without blemish. It was brought to the priest and killed at the altar. The blood was dashed round about the altar and the animal was cut in pieces and completely burned. The offering of animal sacrifice eventually became part of the daily worship of the Temple, a ritual in which the priesthood had a strong vested interest. Many of the O.T. prophets condemned the sacrificial slaughter of animals as a means of offering atonement. As early as the story of Samuel it is written:

'Behold, to obey is better than sacrifice,
and to hearken than the fat of rams.'

(1 Samuel 15: 22)

The prophets of eighth century B.C., Amos, Hosea, Isaiah and Micah, reiterated the moral claims of God:

'For I desire steadfast love and not sacrifice,
the knowledge of God, rather than burnt-offerings.'

(Hosea 6: 6)

Micah's plea for the true offering of justice and kindness in place of slaughtered animals is the very peak of O.T. religion. Not burnt-offering of calves or thousands of rams, not ten thousands of rivers of oil, not even the sacrifice of his first-born, but:

'He has showed you, O man, what is good;
and what does the Lord require of you
but to do justice, and to love kindness,
and to walk humbly with your God?'

(Micah 6: 8)

The prophetic theme is echoed in the comment of a scribe quoted in Mark's Gospel who declares that to love God 'with all the heart, and with all the understanding, and with all the strength, and to love one's neighbour as oneself, is much more than all whole burnt-offerings and sacrifices'.

Animal sacrifice came to an end with the final destruction of the Temple in Jerusalem in A.D. 70. [*Refs.* Genesis 8: 20-1. Exodus 29: 38*f*. Leviticus 1: 1*f*; 22: 18. Numbers 28*f*. Isaiah 1: 11. Mark 12: 33.]

C

Caesar The name taken by successors of Julius Caesar as a title for rulers who became Roman emperors. The Caesars mentioned in the N.T. are: Augustus, Tiberius, Claudius and Nero. [*Refs.* Luke 2: 1; 3: 1. Acts 11: 28; 25: 11-12.]

Caesarea A Roman town on the Mediterranean coast of Palestine, built by Herod the Great and named in honour of Augustus Caesar. Caesarea was the military headquarters of Pontius Pilate when he was governor of Judea. It had a well-built harbour, and therefore a lot of shipping. Philip the evangelist lived at Caesarea, Peter visited the home of Cornelius the centurion there, and Paul was imprisoned at Caesarea for two years before being sent to Rome to stand trial before Caesar. [*Refs.* Acts 8: 40; 10: 1, 24, 48; 23: 33.]

Caesarea Philippi A town situated in the hills of northern Palestine near the source of the river Jordan. It was rebuilt by Philip the tetrarch near a shrine of the heathen god Pan and was named by him in honour of Caesar. Caesarea Philippi is of importance in the Gospel record because it was there that Peter confessed Jesus to be the Messiah in the words: 'You are the Christ.' [*Refs.* Matthew 16: 13. Mark 8: 27.]

Caiaphas Joseph Caiaphas was high priest of the Temple in the Gospel account of the trial of Jesus. He was son-in-law of Annas and succeeded him as high priest, ruling from A.D. 18-36. Caiaphas is remembered mainly for the leading part he played in the arrest, trial and Crucifixion of Jesus. [*Refs.*

Matthew 26: 3, 57. Luke 3: 2. John 11: 49; 18: 13-14, 24, 28. Acts 4: 6-7.] *See also*: TRIAL OF JESUS

Cain The elder son of Adam and Eve in the Genesis story. Cain killed his brother Abel, was cursed by God, and became a wanderer on the earth. [*Ref.* Genesis 4: 1, 8.] *See also*: ABEL

Calvary The place outside the walls of Jerusalem where Jesus was crucified. The name, from the Latin *calvaria* ('skull'), is a translation of the Aramaic word *golgotha* which has the same meaning. There is no mention of a hill in the Bible. The church of the Holy Sepulchre stands on the site today. [*Ref.* Luke 23: 33.]

Cana A village in Galilee where Jesus did two miracles. He turned water into wine at a wedding, and he told the Capernaum official that his son was healed. Cana is also mentioned as the home town of Nathaniel, the disciple. [*Refs.* John 2: 1-11; 4: 46-54; 21: 2.]

Canaan The O.T. name for 'the promised land' which is first mentioned in the stories of Abraham, Isaac and Jacob, and to which Moses led the children of Israel from slavery in Egypt. The land of Canaan lay between the Jordan and the Mediterranean coast, east to west, and between Syria and Egypt, north to south. In comparison with the bleak desert, it was pictured as 'a land flowing with milk and honey', fertile and fruitful.

The Canaanites were the inhabitants of the land when the Israelites invaded Canaan. They included Amorites (a Semitic people), Hittites and Hivites. The spies whom Moses sent out described them as being giant in size and as living in walled cities. The land and its peoples are mentioned repeatedly in the accounts of invasion and conquest in the books of Joshua and Judges.

Canaan was later known as Palestine. [*Refs.* Genesis 10: 19; 12: 5; 17: 8. Numbers 13: 17, 27-33. Psalm 105: 11.] *See also*: AMORITES; HITTITES; HIVITES

Capernaum A city on the northern shore of the Sea of Galilee, west of the mouth of the Jordan. Capernaum was a busy and prosperous fishing port with a customs post and a Roman military station. Jesus made his home there with Simon Peter and the other fishermen disciples, and Capernaum was the centre of much of his healing and teaching mission in Galilee—in the synagogue, at Peter's home, and in the surrounding countryside. [*Refs.* Matthew 4: 13. Mark 1: 21, 29; 2: 1. Luke 4: 31. John 2: 12; 6: 24, 59.]

Caphtor *See* CRETE

Carmel The name of a range of hills stretching from Samaria to the headland of Mt. Carmel which stands out on the Mediterranean coast of Palestine. Carmel was proverbially leafy and fertile with flowers, trees, olive groves. Mt. Carmel was the scene of the contest between Elijah and the prophets of Baal. [*Refs.* Song of Solomon 7: 5. Isaiah 35: 2. 1 Kings 18: 19-20.]

Centurion A soldier in charge of a hundred men in the Roman army; not an officer, but in rank like a sergeant-major today. Several centurions are mentioned in the N.T., and all are portrayed in a favourable light. Jesus healed a centurion's servant at Capernaum. A centurion was in charge of the Crucifixion. Cornelius, a centurion of the Italian Cohort, was one of the first Gentile converts baptized in the name of Jesus Christ. [*Refs.* Matthew 8: 5. Mark 15: 39. Luke 7: 2; 23: 47. Acts 10: 1-2; 22: 25; 27: 1.]

Cephas The Aramaic form of the name Peter, meaning 'rock' or 'stone'. It was the name Jesus gave to Simon, his first disciple. [*Refs.* John 1: 42. 1 Corinthians 1: 12; 15: 5.]

Chaldea *See* BABYLON

Chebar A river or canal of Babylon beside which the exiles of Judah were settled after the downfall of Jerusalem. It is mentioned in the visions of Ezekiel. [*Refs.* Ezekiel 1: 1, 3; 3: 15; 10: 15, 20.]

Cherub The plural of this Hebrew word is *cherubim*. These symbolic creatures were usually portrayed with human or animal faces and with wings. They were thought of as angelic servants of God with the special task of guarding holy places and objects. Cherubim are mentioned in poetry and vision as guardians of the Ark, the mercy-seat, and other furnishings of Tabernacle and Temple. In Christian art a cherub is usually shown as a child with its wings about its head. [*Refs.*

Genesis 3: 24. Exodus 25: 18-22. 1 Kings 6: 23-9. Psalm 80: 1. Hebrews 9: 5.]

Chinnereth *See* GALILEE, SEA OF

Chittim *See* CYPRUS

Christ Christ is the Greek form of the Hebrew word *Messiah* and means 'the anointed one'. Some Jewish writers, especially in the days between the Old and New Testaments, thought that God would send their people a king of David's line who would deliver them from suffering and oppression and would bring about God's kingdom. They called him the Anointed One, the Messiah, or the Christ. The title is found throughout the N.T. applied to Jesus. It is not much used, however, in the Gospels of Matthew, Mark and Luke. Jesus did not seem to claim the title for himself, and when Peter, at Caesarea Philippi, declared 'You are the Christ', Jesus strictly charged his disciples not to use that word of him. Certainly, in his life of service and suffering and in the manner of his death, Jesus did not fulfil the popular hopes for a Christ who would powerfully be 'great David's greater son'. In the Gospel of John, however, the title Christ is used openly of Jesus, and other N.T. writings repeat it almost like a proper name, without any real sense of its original Jewish meaning. [*Refs.* Matthew 2: 4; 16: 16-20; 26: 63; 27: 17. Mark 1: 1; 8: 29; 14: 61. Luke 2: 11; 3: 15; 4: 41; 9: 20. John 1: 41; 6: 69; 20: 31. Acts 2: 36. Romans 5: 6, 8.]

Chronicles, 1 and 2 These two books in the original Hebrew formed part of a longer work which included our books of Ezra and Nehemiah. They are to be found among the Writings of the Jewish Scriptures, of less importance than the *Torah* ('Law') and the Prophets. The closing words of 2 Chronicles 36: 22-3 and the opening words of Ezra 1: 1-3 are the same, linking the books and showing the same writer at work. He is usually known as 'the chronicler', and he was probably a Levite of the Temple in the days when some faithful Jews had returned to restore Jerusalem after the Exile in Babylon.

A good deal of the narrative in 1 and 2 Chronicles is parallel to the writing in 1 and 2 Samuel and 1 and 2 Kings. Other lost source books are mentioned, e.g. the Chronicles of Samuel the seer, the Chronicles of Nathan the prophet, the Chronicles of Gad the seer, in 1 Chronicles 29: 29 and the story of the prophet Iddo in 2 Chronicles 13: 22.

An outline of contents is:

(a) 1 Chronicles 1-10: Lists of the ancestors of the people of Israel from the time of Adam onwards, with special mention of the Jews who returned from Babylon to rebuild the Temple.

(b) 1 Chronicles 11-29: Stories of David, and in particular how he planned to build a house for the Lord in Jerusalem.

(c) 2 Chronicles 1-9: Solomon and the building and dedication of the Temple.

(d) 2 Chronicles 10-36: Stories of the decline and fall of Judah.

The books contain much detail about the worship of the Temple and the duties of priests and Levites, and the writer was especially interested in music, praise and thanksgiving. The chronicler's purpose through all his writing is clear. His people have come back from Exile purged of political and military ambition. They are to dedicate themselves to God and his service, particularly through their religious practices. The chronicler's devotion to the Temple is absolute, and he sets down the story of Israel as the nation who were chosen to be a worshipping people, faithful in every detail of ritual. His aim in writing is that his people should fulfil their ancient covenant with God at Sinai: to be 'a kingdom of priests and a holy nation'.

Cilicia Part of the coastal plain in the south of Asia Minor, a Roman province in N.T. times. Solomon imported horses from Cilicia (known as Kue in the O.T.). The chief city was Tarsus, Paul's native place. Paul visited Cilicia on his missionary journeys. Cilicia was famous for goats' hair cloth, known in Latin as *cilicium*. [*Refs.* Acts 15: 41; 21: 39; 22: 3.] *See also*: TARSUS

Cities of Refuge These were places of sanctuary provided by

O.T. law for people who had committed murder unintentionally and had to flee from the tribal code of 'a life for a life'. They could remain unharmed in a city of refuge. [*Refs.* Numbers 35: 11. Joshua 20: 1-6.]

Cleopas One of the two disciples who met the risen Jesus on the road to Emmaus on the first day of the week after the Crucifixion. [*Ref.* Luke 24: 18.]

Colossae A city of Phrygia in Asia Minor mentioned by Paul at the beginning of his Letter to the Colossians. Some of the leading Christians of Colossae were Philemon, Onesimus, Tychicus and Archippus. [*Ref.* Colossians 1: 2.]

Colossians, The Letter of Paul to the Colossae was a town on the bank of the river Lycus in Asia Minor and is mentioned with two nearby towns, Laodicea and Hierapolis, at 4: 13 of the Letter. Colossians 1: 4, 8 and 2: 1 suggest that Paul had not visited the Christians in these places but that he had certainly been told of their faith and love. The link with the believers at Colossae appears to have been the faithful Epaphras [1: 7].

There are two main problems regarding this Letter. The first is whether it was written from Ephesus during Paul's extended stay there on his third missionary journey [Acts 19: 1, 10, 22]. Timothy was mentioned then as well as in this Letter, and Colossae was only about 100 miles from Ephesus.

The letter to Philemon, which is connected with this one, suggests that Paul hopes to come to Colossae to visit his friends there, and we get the impression that the distance is not great and that the visit may be soon. On the other hand, this piece of writing is one of the 'letters from prison'—namely, Colossians, Philemon, Ephesians, Philippians, and there is no direct reference in the Acts of the Apostles to Paul being in prison in Ephesus. Perhaps the mysterious phrase in 1 Corinthians 15: 32, 'I fought with beasts at Ephesus' refers to a time of imprisonment there. Certainly Paul does speak of being frequently in prison for the faith and this Letter bears witness to his confinement and letters [4: 3, 10, 18].

More probably the Letters to the Colossians and to Philemon

were written from Rome during Paul's imprisonment there
[Acts 28: 30].

The other problem is that for more than a century Bible
scholars have doubted whether the Letter to the Colossians
is by Paul at all. The ideas it contains, the style and language are unlike some of the writings more certainly attributed to him. Computer analysis rejects it as unauthentic on
account of the number of non-Pauline words it contains.
The attack on the heresy known as gnosticism in Colossians
1-2 seems to be later than Paul's time. It may be argued,
however, that the Letter contains some of Paul's mature
thinking, towards the end of his life. And he may have used
a secretary who worked from notes, which would account
for some difference in the language.

The occasion for the Letter is this: Epaphras has come to
Paul in prison, bringing him news of the Christians in Colossae.
Onesimus is also there, and various other friends and helpers,
including Timothy, Aristarchus, Mark and Luke. Tychicus, 'a
beloved brother and faithful minister and fellow servant in
the Lord', is about to return to Colossae, taking with him
Onesimus the slave who belongs to the household of Philemon
in that town. So Paul sends this Letter at the hands of Tychicus
to urge the Christians in Colossae to be faithful to Christ and
his cross in the face of false teaching.

A brief outline of the Letter is:

(a) Colossians 1: 1-2: Greetings from Paul and Timothy, and
    blessing.
(b) Colossians 1: 3-14: News of the Christians in Colossae
    and a prayer for them.
(c) Colossians 1: 15-20: An early Christian hymn.
(d) Colossians 1: 21 to 2:7: 'continue in the faith...just as
    you were taught.'
(e) Colossians 2: 8-23: A warning against false teachers of
    philosophy. Paul insists on the centrality of Christ and
    the cross.
(f) Colossians 3: 1-17: Purity of behaviour.

(g) Colossians 3: 18 to 4: 1: Advice to wives, husbands, children, fathers, slaves, masters.

(h) Colossians 4: 2-6: Advice about prayer.

(i) Colossians 4: 7-17: Greetings and information about various Christian friends and fellow-prisoners.

(j) Colossians 4: 18: Paul's signature and blessing.

Commandments The Ten Commandments, as they are usually known, form part of the code of Law which the o.t. traces back to Moses and sets down as the basis of Israel's faith and life. They are the opening statement of Exodus 20-3, and are also found in a parallel passage in Deuteronomy 5: 6-21. Although many of the so-called Mosaic laws belong to a later age, scholars today believe that the Decalogue, or 'ten words', does indeed come from Moses the leader and law-giver of the Hebrews during the wilderness wanderings. That is not to deny similarities to other law codes of early times, such as the famous Code of Hammurabi.

The original Ten Commandments were perhaps simply expressed thus:

You shall have no other gods before me.

You shall not make a graven image, or any likeness.

You shall not take the name of the Lord your God in vain.

Observe the sabbath day, to keep it holy.

Honour your father and your mother.

You shall not kill.

You shall not commit adultery.

You shall not steal.

You shall not bear false witness against your neighbour.

You shall not covet anything that is your neighbour's.

It is important to note that the Ten Commandments are not set down as wise advice or social regulations or a consensus of opinion. They are unconditional, declared to be divine, and prefaced by the words: 'I am the Lord your God, who brought you out of the land of Egypt, out of the house of bondage.' These commandments are of God, not to be adapted, modified or argued about, but to be obeyed. This understanding of them is reinforced by the tradition that the Ten Commandments were given to Moses at the holy Mt. Sinai and that they were written by the finger of God on the two tablets of stone which were carried in the sacred Ark of the Covenant as the children of Israel journeyed towards the promised land.

The core of the commandments is to be found in the summary which the Jews call the Shema (from the Hebrew word for 'Hear'), namely, 'Hear, O Israel: The Lord our God is one Lord; and you shall love the Lord your God with all your heart, and with all your soul, and with all your might.' (Deuteronomy 6: 4-5). These are the words quoted by Jesus as the first of all the commandments. [*Refs.* Exodus 20: 1-17; 31: -18 to 32: 16; 34: 27*f*. Deuteronomy 5: 6-12; 6: 4-5. Mark 10: 19; 12: 28*f*.]

Corinth The greatest trading city of ancient Greece, with two harbours and a vast sea trade linking the eastern and western Mediterranean. Corinth was a market place for the goods of the Mediterranean world, and also for new ideas. Paul stayed there with Aquila and Priscilla, working with them at the trade of tent-making and arguing in the synagogue every sabbath. The Jews brought him before the Roman tribunal on account of his teaching.

Corinth was proverbially one of the most vicious cities in the Roman empire, yet it became a centre of the Christian faith in N.T. times. Paul wrote his Letters to the Corinthians to the Church there. [*Refs.* Acts 18: 1. 1 Corinthians 1: 2. 2 Corinthians 1: 1.]

Corinthians, The First and Second Letter of Paul to the Acts 18: 1 tells of Paul's coming to Corinth, the great seaport city at the heart of the Mediterranean. These writings reveal his intimate concern for the Christian development of the Church there. The first point to note is that Paul probably wrote four letters to the Christians in Corinth. This may be deduced from such references as 1 Corinthians 5: 9 'I wrote to you in my letter', indicating a previous letter, and also 2 Corinthians 2: 3-9 and 7: 8-12 which apparently refer to a severe letter rebuking the Corinthians. We have no knowledge now of these two other letters apart from Paul's references to them here. We may assume, however, that Paul's correspondence with the Church in Corinth can be divided thus:

Letter *A*. Mentioned in 1 Corinthians 5: 9-13. Written to warn the Christians in Corinth about moral behaviour. It may be remembered that Corinth was notorious in the whole Mediterranean world for immorality and vice. Believers in Christ are to live by utterly different standards.

Letter *B*. The First Letter to the Corinthians of our N.T. Its contents are:

(a) 1 Corinthians 1: 1-9: Greetings and thanksgiving.

(b) 1 Corinthians 1: 10 to 4: 21. An appeal to the Christians of Corinth to heal the dissensions among themselves caused by party strife and cliques. No one is to say 'I belong to Paul', or 'I belong to Apollos', or 'I belong to Cephas'. They all belong to Christ.

(c) 1 Corinthians 5: 1-8: Paul rebukes a case of incest.

(d) 1 Corinthians 5: 9-13: Reference to the previous letter.

(e) 1 Corinthians 6: 1-8: Paul tells them not to indulge in law-suits.

(f) 1 Corinthians 6: 9-20: 'Glorify God in your body'.

(g) 1 Corinthians 7: 1 to 11: 34. Replies to a letter from the Church in Corinth apparently asking about marriage, sexual problems, and the difficulties that arise for Christians in a pagan community. At 11: 23-5 we have the oldest account of the central sacrament of the Church, the Eucharist or Holy Communion.

(h) 1 Corinthians 12: 1 to 14: 40. A discussion of the variety of spiritual gifts, the parable of the body with its many members, the hymn of love as the most excellent way of all, and a warning against being misled by 'speaking with tongues' without interpretation.

(i) 1 Corinthians 15: The earliest statement about the central importance of the resurrection of Christ in Christian belief: 'If Christ has not been raised, your faith is futile.'

Paul goes on to discuss the spiritual body as distinct from the perishable, physical body.

(j) 1 Corinthians 16: Information about the collection of money to aid the Christians in Jerusalem and of Paul's travel plans, references to Timothy and Apollos and other Christians, and final greetings.

Letter *C*. The 'painful' or severe letter mentioned in 2 Corinthians 2: 3-9 and 7: 8-12. 2 Corinthians 13: 1 infers that Paul paid a visit to Corinth, and wrote Corinth after Letter B, noted what was happening in Corinth, and wrote this letter of rebuke.

Letter *D*. The Second Letter to the Corinthians of our N.T. Its contents are:

(a) 2 Corinthians 1: 1-7: Greetings and thanksgiving.

(b) 2 Corinthians 1: 8 to 6: 13: Paul tells of his own belief, behaviour, and plans—an 'apology' for his ministry.

(c) 2 Corinthians 6: 14 to 7: 1: A comment on purity of life—a fragment which is identified by scholars with part of Letter A.

(d) 2 Corinthians 7: 2-16: The visit of Titus to Paul and the message he brought from Corinth. Paul rejoices that all is well among them.

(e) 2 Corinthians 8: 1-24: Paul tells of the liberality of the Churches of Macedonia and appeals for a like generosity from the Corinthian Christians.

(f) 2 Corinthians 9: 1-15: Repeats the theme of (c).

(g) 2 Corinthians 10: 1 to 12: 21. Paul tells of his sufferings as an apostle, and boasts of his work for the Lord.

(h) 2 Corinthians 13: The test of a faithful Christian.

It is reasonable to suppose that Letters A, B, C, were written while Paul was staying in Ephesus (1 Corinthians 16: 8, 19). Letter D, our 2 Corinthians, was written from Macedonia. The letters come from the years A.D. 52-4. They tell more clearly than any other N.T. writings of the daily life of Christians in a heathen community. Their quality of living and Christ-like love shone in the pagan world of the day. They tell us also a great deal about the humanity of Paul as well as his suffering for the sake of his Lord.

Cornelius A Roman centurion of the Italian Cohort stationed at Caesarea on the coast of Palestine. Cornelius was sympathetic to the Jewish faith and customs. Following a vision, he sent for Peter who told him about Jesus Christ and baptized him and his household. Cornelius was thus an early Gentile convert to the Christian faith. [*Ref.* Acts 10.]

Cornerstone A specially strong foundation stone laid at the corner of a building or a wall. Such stones could be seen at the base of the walls of Jerusalem. An old saying found in the Bible speaks of 'the stone which the builders rejected has become the chief cornerstone'. In the N.T. the writers apply this proverb to Christ as 'the chief cornerstone' of the Church. [*Refs.* Psalm 118: 22. Mark 12: 10. Acts 4: 11. Ephesians 2: 20. 1 Peter 2: 5-7.]

Council The name given in the N.T. to the *Sanhedrin*, or court of the Jews, which met in the Temple area in Jerusalem to interpret and administer the sacred Law and to deal with breaches of it. The Council was made up of seventy-one members including the high priest, former high priests, members of leading priestly families, Pharisees and scribes. The Gospels describe the composition of the Council in terms of 'high priest, chief priests and the elders and the scribes'. Members mentioned by name here and there in the Gospels are Annas, Caiaphas, John and Alexander Nicodemus and Joseph of Arimathea. The chairman was the reigning high priest.

It would appear from the somewhat confused Gospel accounts of the arrest and trial of Jesus that he was brought before the Council, or a section of it, and accused of blasphemy. But, although the council could and did pronounce the verdict of guilty, they had no power to carry out the death sentence. Only the Roman authorities could do that, and so Jesus was delivered to Pilate for sentence. In the Acts of the Apostles we find the disciples of Jesus, particularly Peter and John, brought before the Council for speaking and teaching in the name of Jesus. They were arrested, imprisoned, interrogated and threatened. Stephen, the first Christian martyr, was taken before the Council on a charge of blasphemy, condemned to death and stoned. Paul the apostle also had to face the Council because he spoke about 'the resurrection of the dead'.

The Council eventually lost its place of meeting, its traditional members and its authority with the downfall of Jerusalem in A.D. 70. [*Refs.* Matthew 26: 57*f*. Mark 14: 53*f*; 15: 1. Luke 22: 66*f*. John 11: 47*f*. Acts 4: 5*f*; 5: 21*f*; 6: 12, 15; 22: 30; 23: 1*f*.] *See also*: TRIAL OF JESUS

Covenant A covenant is literally an agreement between two or more people. There are many examples in the O.T. of covenants between individuals or tribal groups. Abraham made a covenant with Abimelech, the king of Gerar, about a well of water. Jonathan swore a covenant with David because he loved him as his own soul. Ahab, king of Israel, made a covenant with Benhadad of Syria about trade between their two countries. Marriage was considered a covenant between man and wife. A covenant was usually sealed in some way, by the exchange of gifts, by a handshake, a kiss, by sharing a meal together, by eating salt, by setting up a stone or pillar as witness to the bond, by swearing the covenant in a sacred place. The idea of covenant was to establish brotherhood, with sworn loyalty one to another. The most solemn of all seals was the seal of blood. To break a covenant was the most grievous of offences. [*Refs.* Genesis 21: 27, 31-2; 31: 44-50. 1 Samuel 10: 1; 18: 3-4; 23: 18. 1 Kings 20: 34. 2 Kings 10: 15; 23: 3. Ezra 4: 14. Psalm 41: 9. Malachi 2: 14.]

The idea of a Covenant between God and individuals and between God and his chosen people is a constant theme throughout the Bible, particularly in the O.T. A Covenant with Noah is mentioned, and with his descendants and 'every living creature of all flesh that is upon the earth'.

The rainbow in the cloud is God's 'sign of the Covenant'. There is also a Covenant between God and Abraham, with circumcision as the sign of it, and between God and the tribes of Israel under Joshua at Shechem. The setting up of the royal house of David is thought of as a Covenant. But the supreme Covenant of O.T. is centred on Mt. Sinai where, through his servant Moses, God declares that he has chosen Israel to be 'a kingdom of priests and a holy nation'. The people pledge their obedience to the Covenant: 'All that the Lord has spoken we will do, and we will be obedient.' Both parties have rights and obligations: the people are to walk in God's ways, keep his commandments, and obey his voice; the Lord, for his part, will set them high above all nations that he has made, in praise, and in fame and in honour. Moses seals the Covenant by throwing blood on the altar which he has set up and upon the people.

The Sinai Covenant is the dominant feature of Hebrew religion and is mentioned countless times in the pages of the O.T. The very name of our English O.T. means 'Old Covenant'. The Lord who chose them, set his love upon them, and brought them out of Egypt, is Israel's God. They are for ever his people. God and Israel are one family. The Ten Commandments and subsequent laws of the *Torah* are thought of as 'the book of the Covenant', sacred, never to be broken. The box containing the stones on which the Commandments were inscribed was known as 'the Ark of the Covenant'. The prophets of Israel's later history constantly remind their people of the sacred bond which unites God and his chosen people. A recurring theme of the Book of Amos is Israel's unfaithfulness to the Covenant. Hosea portrays the relationship in the theme of marriage. The ultimate downfall of Israel and later Judah and Jerusalem is traced to the fact that they have been unfaithful and have broken the Covenant. Prophets such as Jeremiah, Ezekiel and Isaiah of Babylon think of the forgiving God who will one day faithfully restore the broken relationship and make a new Covenant with his wayward people.

The N.T. writers, particularly Paul and the author of Hebrews, see the 'new covenant' fulfilled in Christ. The words of Jesus at the Last Supper convey the idea that 'this cup is the new covenant in my blood'. Through the death of Christ, God and his 'new Israel' are made one, and the blood of Christ is the sign and seal of that renewed Covenant. It is expressed not in the letter of a written law but through the Spirit which gives life. The Lord's Supper is a continuing symbol of the restored relationship of God's family. [*Refs*. Genesis 9: 8-17; 15: 17-18; 17: 1-10. Exodus 19: 4-6; 24: 3-8. Deuteronomy 5: 1-5. Joshua 24: 25-7. 2 Samuel 23: 5. Psalm 25: 10; 103: 17-18. Isaiah 54: 5; 61: 8. Jeremiah 31: 31-4. Ezekiel 16: 8, 60-3. Hosea 2: 19-23. Amos 3: 1-2. Matthew 26: 27-8. Mark 14: 24. Luke 1: 72. 1 Corinthians 11: 25. Corinthians 3: 6. Hebrews 8: 6*f*; 13: 20.]

Creation There are two accounts of the Creation in the book of Genesis. The first is in Genesis 1: 1 to 2: 4a. It was written down by a priestly writer some time after the Exile, but it contains earlier themes familiar in Jewish worship, and some of the details of the story have affinities with much older Babylonian myths of the Creation. The aim of this account is to state in sublime language the Jewish belief that God was the creator of all things in heaven and earth. This creation story is not scientific, nor was it ever intended to be. For example, the earth is mentioned before the sun, and light is described on the first day of Creation, sun, moon and stars on the fourth. The picture of the universe we find in this opening passage of Genesis is often called 'three-storied'—that is, 'heaven above, earth beneath, and the water under the earth'. It is not our understanding of the universe today. But the writer's purpose was not to give a step by step account of the order of the Creation, however orderly his story may seem to be. Rather was it to declare that everything in the universe is the outcome of the thought and will and word of God. The whole cosmos in the Bible story depends on God and is upheld by him. The last act of all is the making of man in the image and likeness of God. Mankind is thus placed as the crown of creation. Man is to fill the earth and subdue it and to have dominion over every living thing that moves upon the earth.

The story closes with the ordering of the sabbath as a blessed and holy day, thus setting the seal of divine approval on that most characteristic feature of Judaism. The whole passage is poetical in form and religious in purpose.

The other, more primitive, account of the Creation is Genesis 2: 4b-25, which describes how the Lord God planted a garden in Eden with every tree that is pleasant to the sight and good for food, and put man there to till the garden and look after it. The Lord God also created the beasts of the field and birds of the air, all, like man, of the dust of the earth. Finally, the Lord God caused a deep sleep to fall on the man, took a rib from his side, and made woman to be a helper fit for man. The writer is not concerned with a picture of the universe as a whole. He sets Man in the scene of his earthly life. In the sweat of his face he must toil to eat his bread all the days of his life until he returns to the dust from which he was taken and shaped.

Neither story of the Creation is concerned with details of history or geography or any other proper study of science. Both of them use myth and symbolism, as do some of the Psalms which belong to the same tradition. The Creation stories are a poetical and dramatic prologue to Israel's sacred history. [*Refs.* Genesis 1: 1 to 2: 4a; 2: 4-25. Deuteronomy 5: 8. Psalm 8: 1-4.]

Crete An island in the middle of the Mediterranean famous in ancient times for its Minoan civilization and stories of the pagan gods. In the O.T. Crete is called Caphtor, and it was thought to be the original home of the Philistines. Paul sailed past Crete as a prisoner on his way to Rome. [*Refs.* Deuteronomy 2: 23. Amos 9: 7. Acts 27: 7.]

Crucifixion The act of putting to death on a cross. When the term The Crucifixion is used it refers to the death of Jesus at Calvary. This method of capital punishment was used by many nations in ancient times, including the Romans who ruled Palestine in the time of Jesus. Mark's Gospel tells how, after trial and ill-treatment at the hands of the council of the Jews,

Jesus was led away to Pilate the Roman governor for final judgment. This took place early in the morning of the day we call Good Friday. Pilate had Jesus scourged and delivered him to be crucified. The soldiers clothed Jesus in a purple cloak, put a crown of thorns on his head, and mocked him. Then they returned his own clothes to him and led him out for crucifixion outside the walls of Jerusalem. On the way they compelled a passer-by, Simon of Cyrene, to carry the cross-bar. Jesus was crucified between two robbers at a place called Golgotha (Calvary) at the third hour of the day, that is, at nine o'clock in the morning. According to Roman custom the charge against him was written out and fastened to the cross. It read: 'The King of the Jews'. Mark records that there was darkness from noon until three o'clock. At that hour Jesus cried out with a loud voice and breathed his last.

Other Gospel accounts add their own details to the story, particularly in giving differing sayings of Jesus from the cross, seven in all. Later pious interpretation has no doubt added Christian meanings to every moment of the Crucifixion. The event of the death of Jesus on the cross has been dated as between A.D. 28 and 33. No more precise date can be given. Throughout later history the cross has been the most sacred of all symbols of the Christian faith. [*Refs.* Matthew 27: 24-54. Mark 15: 1-39. Luke 23: 1-49. John 19: 1-37.] *See also*: GOLGOTHA

Cubit An ancient measure of length, between eighteen and twenty-two inches, a man's arm from elbow to finger tips. The O.T. uses the cubit often in describing measurements of the Temple and its furnishings. [*Refs.* Deuteronomy 3: 11. 1. Samuel 17: 4. 1 Kings 6: 2. Nehemiah 3: 13. Matthew 6: 27.]

Cyprus An island in the eastern Mediterranean. In the O.T. it is called *Chittim* or *Kittim*. Cyprus was famous in ancient times for its copper mines. It was the homeland of Joseph called Barnabas, the friend and companion of Paul. These two men visited Cyprus on their first missionary journey, taking John Mark with them. [*Refs.* Jeremiah 2: 10. Acts 4: 36; 13: 2-6; 15: 39.]

Cyrene A Greek city in North Africa where large numbers of Jews were settled in N.T. times. Simon, who was compelled to carry Jesus' cross, came from Cyrene, and there were Christians there in the early days of the Church. [*Refs*. Mark 15: 21. Acts 6: 9; 11: 20; 13: 1.]

Cyrus Cyrus the Great was founder of the Persian empire and its ruler 548-529 B.C. He conquered Babylon in 539 B.C. and proclaimed that the exiled Jews might return to Jerusalem to rebuild the Temple. Isaiah of Babylon, the Jewish prophet whose oracles are found in Isaiah 40 to 55, spoke of Cyrus as God's 'shepherd' and as the Lord's 'anointed' servant.

A famous clay cylinder now in the British Museum tells of the conquests of Cyrus, 'king of the world, great king, mighty king, king of Babylon'. His empire lasted for two hundred years. The simple tomb of Cyrus bore this inscription: 'O man, whosoever thou art and whencesoever thou comest, for I know that thou wilt come, I am Cyrus, and I won for the Persians their empire. Do not, therefore, begrudge me this little earth which covers my body.' [*Refs*. 2 Chronicles 36: 22-3. Ezra 1: 1-8. Isaiah 44: 28; 45: 1.] *See also*: PERSIA

D

Damascus The capital of Syria and probably the oldest inhabited city in the world. It is situated on the river Abana in a fertile, well-watered plain near the foot of Mt. Hermon. Damascus was a meeting-place of important caravan trade routes in the ancient world. In N.T. times there was a large colony of Jews there and it was on the road near Damascus that Saul of Tarsus was converted. The 'street called Straight' is still to be seen. [*Refs.* Genesis 12: 2. 2 Samuel 8: 5-6. 2 Kings 5: 12; 16: 10. Acts 9: 1-22.]

Dan (1) One of the twelve tribes of Israel said to be descended from Dan the son of Jacob. [*Ref.* Genesis 30: 5-6.] (2) The most northerly town in Palestine, as in the proverbial phrase 'from Dan even to Beersheba' which speaks of the boundaries of the promised land which the children of Israel thought of as their home. Dan was near the headwaters of the river Jordan. King Jeroboam I of Israel set up a shrine at Dan with a golden image of a bull-calf and a priesthood to serve there. [*Refs.* 1 Kings 4: 25; 12: 28-30.]

Daniel, The Book of The Book of Daniel is found among the Writings of the Hebrew Scriptures. It is a work of historical fiction, not to be taken literally, the leading characters being an invention and the setting imagined as if in the days of the Exile. The story belongs, in fact, to the time when Antiochus Epiphanes was persecuting the Jews in Jerusalem, culminating in the Maccabaean revolt of 167 B.C. Antiochus forbade the keeping of the Sabbath, his soldiers put to the sword Jewish women who kept the custom of circumcising their infant sons, all copies of the Jewish Scriptures were seized and burned, the Temple was desecrated, heathen altars were erected up and down the land and pig's flesh offered upon them. The final insult to the Jews was that an altar to Zeus the Greek god was erected at the place of the most sacred altar in the Temple. Many Jews at this time gave up their faith and followed Greek customs. Others, who resisted, suffered persecution and many were put to death. 'And they shed innocent blood on every side of the sanctuary, and defiled the sanctuary...and on the fifteenth day of Chislev, in the hundred and forty and fifth year, they builded an abomination of desolation upon the altar, and in the cities of Judah on every side they builded idol altars.. And many in Israel were fully resolved and confirmed in themselves not to eat unclean things. And they chose to die, that they might not be defiled with the meats, and that they might not profane the holy covenant: and they died.' (1 Maccabees 1; *cf* Daniel 11: 31).

Such was the background of the times in which the book of Daniel was written. It is an apocalyptic work, a type of 'underground literature', full of hidden meanings and symbols, written to encourage the Jews to stand fast to their faith in a time of terror and distress. Seemingly set in the bygone days of Nebuchadrezzar, it refers in fact to current events. The first six chapters contain tales of faithful Daniel and his Jewish companions in the land of Babylon who steadfastly refuse to eat forbidden food, bow to heathen gods or conform to foreign customs. Their faith sees them survive all ordeals such as the burning fiery furnace and the den of lions and they triumph in the end over all their foes. The message of these chapters is clear to those who can read and understand their secret meaning: they are to endure persecution and be true to their faith—'Dare to be a Daniel', in fact.

Chapters 7-12 contain various visions of Daniel in which diverse beasts and figures symbolize the imperial powers which have persecuted the Jewish people through the years. Babylonians, Medes, Persians, Greeks are all mysteriously portrayed, but in the end their power is broken, and 'the kingdom and the domin-ion and the greatness of the kingdoms under the whole heaven shall be given to the people of the saints of the Most High' (i.e. the Jews). 'Their kingdom shall be an everlasting kingdom, and all dominions shall serve and obey them' (7: 27).

The author is unknown. The book was written partly in He-brew and partly in Aramaic, which in itself is an argument for a date in the second half of the second century B.C. As well as being the great apocalyptic book of the O.T., the pages of Daniel introduce the significant phrase 'son of man' (7: 13), the idea of resurrection (12: 2) and the angel figures Gabriel (8: 16) and Michael (10: 13). Unfortunately, in more recent years the Book of Daniel has become a happy hunting-ground of those who profess to read hints and portents of contemporary disasters in the beasts, horns, numbers and symbols which fill its pages.

Darius (1) Darius the Great was king of Persia c. 522-486 B.C. at the time when the Jews were in Exile in Babylon. He contin-ued the tolerant policy of Cyrus and allowed the Jews to re-build the Temple in Jerusalem. [*Refs.* Ezra 5: 7-17; 6: 1-15. Haggai 1: 1; 2: 10. Zechariah 1: 1; 7: 1.] (2) Darius the Mede is mentioned a number of times in the story of Daniel, but in this context he is not to be regarded as a historical person. [*Refs.* Daniel 5: 31; 6: 1; 9: 1.]

David There is only one David in the whole Bible, and his name appears more than a thousand times as the ideal king of He-brew history. It is impossible to tell how much of the O.T. mate-rial is fact and how much is legendary and idealized. We are told in the David stories that he was the son of Jesse of Bethle-hem and anointed by Samuel, the man of God, to be successor to Saul, the first king of Israel. David was a shepherd: 'he was ruddy, and had beautiful eyes, and was handsome'. He was also 'skilful in playing, a man of valour, a man of war, prudent in speech, and a man of good presence, and the Lord is with him'. It was David who was reputed to have killed the Philistine giant Goliath with a stone from his sling, who became Saul's armour-bearer and captain over the men of war, who became the beloved friend of Jonathan, and married Saul's daughter, Michal. Because of the jealousy of the king, David had to flee the court and become an outlaw and leader of lawless men. On the deaths of Saul and Jonathan, in battle with the Philistines, the men of Judah made David their king and later he was chosen as ruler by all the tribes of Israel. He took Jerusalem as his capital and reigned there for thirty-three years. David broke the Philistine power, united the country, brought the Ark of the Covenant to Jerusalem, establishing it as the religious centre. A number of tales are told of his magnanimity as well as his treachery, his lust for Bathsheba, the foolish spoiling of his son Absalom which led to the young man's rebellion and death, the loyalty he inspired in his men, and his poetic gifts as 'the sweet psalmist of Israel'. Jewish tradition thought of him as the king of their golden age who 'administered justice and equity to all his people and who was a man after God's own heart'. His name is associated with many of the Psalms, and the oldest part of Jerusalem is known as 'the city of David'.

A great deal of this account comes from a court history which sought to glorify David as the ideal king. Nevertheless, there are human stories enough in the telling to let us see a man of outstanding ability, courage and charm, and a real leader of men. It is not surprising that in the bitterness and defeat of later days there arose the hope of a Messiah (which means 'the anointed one') who would be of the house and lineage of David, would restore Jerusalem, unite God's people Israel, and rule over them in a prolonged age of peace and plenty. Then it would be that God 'will make with you an everlasting covenant, my steadfast, sure love for David'. The N.T. writers take up this theme and seek to identify Jesus as 'son of David' in many references, though there is evidence that Jesus himself avoided such a title. The last word lies with the book of The Revelation where, in a vision of a new heaven and a new earth and a new Jerusalem, the risen and glorified Jesus who is the Christ (Messiah), is hailed as 'the root and offspring of David, the bright morning star'. [*Refs.* 1 Samuel 16: 1 to 1 Kings 2: 11 (here and there). 1

Chronicles 11: 1 to 29: 29 (here and there). Isaiah 9: 6-7; 11: 1-10; 55: 3. Jeremiah 23: 5-6; 33: 15-17. Ezekiel 37: 24-5. Matthew 1: 1; 20: 30-1. John 7: 42. Acts 13: 22-3. Romans 1: 3. Revelation 5; 22: 16.] *See also*: SAUL; JONATHAN

Dead Sea The Dead Sea is usually called the Salt Sea, the Sea of the Arabah, or the Eastern Sea in the O.T., but it is not mentioned in the N.T. at all. It is fifty-three miles long and ten miles across at its widest, and is the lowest stretch of water in the world. The waters of the Jordan and other rivers run into the Dead Sea, but there is no outlet except by evaporation under the hot sun. There are no fish, and, because it is so salty, the Sea is much more buoyant than the ocean. [*Refs*. Numbers 34: 3, 12. Joshua 3: 16. Ezekiel 47: 18. Joel 2: 20. Zechariah 14: 8.] *See also*: SODOM; GOMORRAH

Deborah The Hebrew name means 'a bee'. An Israelite prophetess and influential 'judge' mentioned in the book of Judges, who summoned Barak to gather the tribes to attack Sisera by the River Kishon. After the overwhelming victory, Deborah is referred to in song as 'a mother in Israel'. This vivid, savage war-song is usually known as The Song of Deborah and is certainly a very early work of Hebrew poetry. [*Ref.* Judges 4: 4 to 5: 31.] *See also*: KISHON

Decapolis The Greek word means 'ten cities'. The Decapolis was a group of cities built in the Greek style of the first century B.C., nine of the ten being east of the Jordan in an area extending from Damascus to the Dead Sea. Jesus visited the Decapolis and some of his healing acts occurred there. [*Refs*. Matthew 4: 25. Mark 5: 20; 7: 31.] *See also*: GADARA

Delilah A Philistine woman who enticed Samson to reveal the secret of his great strength and then betrayed him to the Philistine leaders. [*Ref.* Judges 16.]

Demas A fellow-worker with Paul who eventually proved unreliable and forsook the apostle. [*Refs*. Colossians 4: 14. Philemon 24. 11. Timothy 4: 10.]

Demetrius A silversmith in the city of Ephesus who made silver shrines of Artemis. He stirred up his fellow-craftsmen against Paul and his companions because Paul's preaching was threatening their livelihood. [*Ref.* Acts 19: 24-41.]

Demon *See* DEVIL

Derbe An inland town of Asia Minor visited and evangelized by Paul on his first and second missionary journeys. [*Refs.* Acts 14: 6, 20; 16: 1; 20: 4.]

Deuteronomy The name means 'the second law'. Deuteronomy is the fifth and final book of the Pentateuch. In spite of its position at the end of the 'five books of Moses', it is probable that Deuteronomy was the first of all the books written about Moses and his part in the shaping of the Jewish nation and the Jewish faith. In 2 Kings 22: 8 we read of the finding of 'the book of the law' in the Temple at Jerusalem in the reign of Josiah, king of Judah. The date was 621 B.C. Josiah read the book and embarked on a reformation based on this writing which completely transformed the religious customs of his time. It is believed that this 'book of the law' was the core of Deuteronomy which had probably been set down in the dark days of the reign of Manasseh when the faithful upholders of ancient religious traditions of Israel had to keep silent.

The book of Deuteronomy appears to be a sermon spoken by Moses before the people of Israel go in to take possession of Canaan. It ends with the account of Moses' death, within sight of the promised land. In fact, however, the writing plainly belongs to settled days in Palestine in a much later age. Deuteronomy shows not only the influence of the early covenant code but also the humanitarian and social teaching of the eighth-century prophets, Amos, Hosea, Isaiah and Micah. A tradition of settled monarchy is evident, as well as regular priesthood and the custom of animal sacrifice at the one central Temple in Jerusalem. All this takes in the gradual development of centuries.

The laws of Deuteronomy are noteworthy for their spirit of compassion and mercy, best summed up in the verses: 'And now, Israel, what does the Lord your God require of you, but to fear the Lord your God, to walk in all his ways, to love him, to serve the Lord your God with all your heart and with all your soul, and to keep the commandments and statues of the Lord, which I command you this day for your good?'

[Deuteronomy 10: 12-13]. This comes from a part of the book known as the Deuteronomic Code, which has been called the finest essence of the Jewish faith.

Deuteronomy is to be regarded as a preface to the story of Moses and the making of the people of God rather than as an epilogue. It is the key book of the O.T. in setting forth the highest ideals of Jewish faith, worship, and daily conduct. It is the O.T. law-book most often quoted in the Gospels. When Jesus summed up the whole Law in one sentence he did it in words from Deuteronomy: 'Hear, O Israel: The Lord our God, the Lord is one; and you shall love the Lord your God with all your heart, and with all your soul, and with all your mind, with all your strength' (Mark 12: 29-30. Deuteronomy 6: 4-5)

Devil In the N.T. the R.S.V. translation uses the word 'demon' where the A.V. and N.E.B have 'devil'. Both terms translate the Greek word which means 'evil spirit'. It was believed that diseases of body or of mind were caused by evil spirits, servants of Satan, which took possession of men and women and tormented their victims. The only way to make such a sick person well again was to exorcize the evil spirit, that is, to drive it out through the power of a holy name. Thus we read that Jesus exorcized evil spirits in God's name from a deranged man in the synagogue, an epileptic boy, a blind and dumb man, the sick daughter of the Syrophoenician woman, as well as many others 'afflicted with various diseases and pains, demoniacs, epileptics, and paralytics'. Jesus' primary task as a healer was to cast out demons, and thus reveal the coming of the kingdom of God. Mary, called Magdalene, is mentioned as one from whom seven demons had gone out, and the man who lived among the tombs in the country of the Gerasenes was named 'Legion' because many demons had entered him. Jesus commissioned disciples to go and heal, casting out demons in the name of God. [*Refs.* Matthew 4: 24. Mark 1: 23*f*, 34, 39; 3: 14; 6: 13; 7: 26, 29, 30. Luke 4: 41; 8: 2, 27, 30; 9: 1; 10: 17; 13: 32.] *See also*: SATAN

Diana The goddess of the hunt, sister of Apollo the sun god in Greek and Roman mythology. In the ancient world, however,

Diana was the same as Artemis, a goddess of fertility. Diana of the Ephesians was a large statue in the temple at Ephesus which was one of the seven wonders of the world. It showed the goddess with many breasts, the fertile earth-mother. Miniatures of the goddess and her shrine were made by the silversmiths of Ephesus to sell to pilgrims. Paul's preaching disturbed their craft and trade and there was a riot in the city. [*Ref.* Acts 19: 23-41.] *See also*: EPHESUS

Diaspora *See* DISPERSION

Didymus The Greek word for 'the twin'. A name applied in John's Gospel to Thomas, one of the twelve disciples of Jesus. [*Refs.* John 2: 16; 20: 24; 21: 2.]

Disciples The word disciple in the N.T. means 'learner', 'pupil', 'one who is taught'. It is commonly applied to the followers of Jesus, particularly to the twelve men he chose to be with him, to learn of him, and to be instructed so that he might send them out to teach and preach and heal. After the resurrection they were to be 'witnesses'. The chosen twelve are also referred to as apostles. The number twelve is no doubt a reminder of the twelve tribes of ancient Israel. The twelve chosen and appointed apostles of Jesus are to be the leaders of the new Israel. The lists of these men vary in the Gospels and Acts thus:

(a) Matthew 10: 2-4 'Simon, who is called Peter and Andrew his brother; James the son of Zebedee, and John his brother; Philip and Bartholomew; Thomas and Matthew the tax collector; James the son of Alphaeus, and Thaddaeus; Simon the Cananaean, and Judas Iscariot who betrayed him.'

(b) Mark 3: 16-19 'Simon whom he surnamed Peter; James the son of Zebedee and John the brother of James, whom he surnamed Boanerges, that is, sons of thunder; Andrew, and Philip, and Bartholomew, and Matthew, and Thomas, and James the son of Alphaeus, and Thaddaeus, and Simon the Cananaean, and Judas Iscariot, who betrayed him.'

(c) Luke 6: 14-16 'Simon, whom he surnamed Peter, and Andrew his brother, and James and John, and Philip and Bartholomew, and Matthew, and Thomas, and James the son of Alphaeus, and Simon who was called the Zealot, and Judas the son of James, and Judas Iscariot, who became a traitor.'

(d) Acts 1: 13 'Peter and John and James and Andrew, Philip and Thomas, Bartholomew and Matthew, James the son of Alphaeus, and Simon the Zealot and Judas the son of James.' (This was after the death of Judas Iscariot.)

Although the Gospel of John contains no such list, it does mention a 'Nathanael of Cana in Galilee' who does not appear under that name in the other groups (John 1: 44*f*; 21: 2).

It may be noted also that the above lists are not entirely identical, but vary from Gospel to Gospel; that a number of the chosen disciples cannot be identified apart from their mention here; and that some of them did not, in fact, become leaders in the early Church so far as we know. Various stories in the Gospels show that Simon Peter, James and John were in the 'inner circle' of the company of Jesus.

The word *disciple*, however, has a wider reference than the twelve men who became apostles of Jesus. Disciples of John the Baptist are mentioned a number of times in the Gospels, and disciples of the Pharisees. In the Gospels and Acts the name is also applied to others of the followers of Jesus, both men and women. Luke mentions seventy sent out by Jesus, two by two, to go ahead of him into every town and place where he himself was about to come, and 'many' disciples are mentioned by John. In the Acts the word disciple is one of the names given to the ever-growing company of believers in Jesus. It is applied, for example to Hebrews and Hellenists in Jerusalem, to Ananias at Damascus, Tabitha at Joppa, Timothy at Lystra, believers in Ephesus, and a household in Caesarea. [*Refs*. Matthew 5: 1; 9: 14. Mark 2: 18. Luke 5: 33; 6: 17; 10: 1, 17; 11: 1. John 1: 35-41. Acts 6: 1, 7; 9: 1, 10, 36; 11: 26; 16: 1; 19: 1; 20: 1; 21: 16.]

Dispersion The Diaspora or Dispersion is the name given to the 'scattering' of the Jews which followed the downfall of Jerusalem in 587 B.C. and their exile in Babylon. Many of the Jews of the Exile and their descendants did not return to Palestine. Throughout the Persian, Greek, and Roman periods they made their way to towns and cities all over the known world. They set up their synagogues, observed Jewish religious laws and customs, and took part in pilgrimages at time of festival to the Temple in Jerusalem.

In N.T. times there were Jewish settlements in all the lands round the Mediterranean and, in later ages, all over the world. These were, and are, the Jews of the Dispersion. The existence of the Dispersion helped to pave the way for the rapid spread of Christianity in the first century A.D. Paul of Tarsus was himself a Jew of the Dispersion. One thing which united their scattered communities was the Septuagint, their own version of their Scriptures in the Greek language, translated from the Hebrew by Jewish scholars in Alexandria in the third century B.C. More than one ancient historian has noted that 'this people has already made its way into every city, and it is not easy to find any place in the habitable world which has not received this nation and in which it has not made its power felt'. That comment on the Dispersion remains true to the present day. [*Refs.* John 7: 35. Acts 2: 9-11. James 1: 1. 1 Peter 1: 1.]

Dorcas A Greek name which means 'gazelle' and is the same as *Tabitha* in Aramaic. Dorcas was a woman disciple who lived at Joppa and was widely known for her good works and acts of charity, in particular the garments she made for the widows of the poor. When she died the Christians sent for Peter, who prayed and raised her to life. The story is reminiscent of the raising of Jairus' daughter by Jesus. [*Ref.* Acts 9: 36-42.]

Dove Turtledoves or young pigeons were by Jewish law the offering to be brought to the Temple by the poor. Doves were kept around the house from earliest times in Palestine. In the story of the flood, Noah sent out a dove as a messenger and the bird brought back a fresh olive leaf in its mouth. Hebrew poetry mentions the flight of the dove and its mournful crooning. Jesus pointed to its harmlessness. Symbolically, the dove portrays the spirit of God, as in the story of the baptism of Jesus. It is often carved on baptismal fonts in churches. [*Refs.* Leviticus 12: 6, 8. Matthew 10: 16. Mark 1: 10. Luke 2: 24.]

E

Eagle The eagle mentioned in the Bible was regarded as an unclean bird of prey by the Jews. It was probably often confused in Bible times with the vulture, which eats carrion. Other characteristics of the eagle are more admirable—its swiftness, its care for its young, its keen sight, its power to soar high in the sky. The eagle has been a favourite symbol of power for centuries: in Persia, Rome, Russia, Austria, Germany, and in the USA. In Christian tradition the eagle is a symbol of the Resurrection, and of St. John the evangelist. It is also an emblem of the inspiration of the Gospels. That is why a lectern in church is often in the shape of an eagle bearing the Bible on its outspread wings. [*Refs*. Leviticus 11: 13. Deuteronomy 32: 11. Job 39: 27-30. Proverbs 23: 5. Isaiah 40: 31.]

Ebedmelech The Ethiopian eunuch of the king's house in Jerusalem who rescued the prophet Jeremiah from the deep cistern where his enemies had put him. He threw down old rags and worn-out clothes to put under his armpits and then drew the prophet up with ropes. Jeremiah promised Ebedmelech that he would be saved when the city fell. [*Refs*. Jeremiah 38: 7-13; 39: 15-18.]

Ecclesiastes The word ecclesiastes is Greek and means 'the preacher'. The book forms part of the Wisdom literature among the Writings of Hebrew Scriptures. At the very beginning there is the hint that Solomon 'the son of David, king in

Jerusalem' is the author, but it is plain from the language and ideas that the book belongs in fact to some time after the Exile, probably as late as 250-200 B.C. It may have been attributed to Solomon because he was famous for wise sayings of a proverbial kind.

Vanity is the favourite word of the book and its main theme is expressed in the verse:

'Vanity of vanities, says the Preacher,
vanity of vanities! All is vanity'   (1: 2)

A great deal of the work concerns the frailty and futility of life. Human wisdom can only teach man to be philosophical about work, pleasure, wealth, health and strength. In the end all is vain, man must die. 'The race is not to the swift, nor the battle to the strong, nor bread to the wise, nor riches to the intelligent, nor favour to the men of skill; but time and chance happen to them all' (9: 11). There is a graphic and famous picture of old age in 12: 1-7.

Eden The well-watered garden land, full of trees, where Adam and Eve lived in the creation myth of the book of Genesis. Eden belongs to the realm of 'stories with a meaning' rather than to geography, but no doubt the tales of a green and fertile paradise arose in Mesopotamia. [*Ref.* Genesis 2; 3.]

Edom The name Edom means 'red'. The land of Edom lay south of the Dead Sea and stretched to the Gulf of Aqaba or Elath on the Red Sea. The Edomites were descended from Esau, the twin brother of Jacob, and thus closely related to the Israelites. Certainly their fortunes were intertwined in O.T. history, but in terms of bitter enmity. It is recorded that when Moses led the children of Israel through the desert he sought permission from the king of Edom for right of way through his territory. But Edom said: 'You shall not pass through.'

In the more settled days of the monarchy both David and Solomon were ready to fight for the rich copper and iron mines at Elath. Solomon built his sea-going fleet there, and used Elath for treasures imported from Africa and Arabia.

Israelite control of Edom was accompanied by grim slaughter which resulted in revolt and revenge in later days. According to the Psalmist the Edomites rejoiced savagely when Jerusalem fell to the Babylonians, and the prophet Amos called down doom on the ancient enemy 'because he pursued his brother with the sword, and cast off all pity'. The Book of Obadiah is largely a diatribe against Edom for her treatment of Judah in the day of her ruin. Joel and Ezekiel repeat the same theme. The ancient blood feud runs like a dark stain through the o.t. narrative.

In the N.T., Edom is known by the Greek form *Idumea*, but it extended further north and west, almost as far as Hebron in southern Palestine. Herod the Great was an Idumean and therefore despised by true Jews. [*Refs*. Psalm 137: 7. Ezekiel 25: 12-14; 35. Joel 3: 19. Amos 1: 6, 9, 11. Obadiah 1-14. Mark 3: 8.]

Egypt The country watered by the River Nile, in North Africa. A great deal of Egypt is desert, but the rich overflow of the Nile has annually brought fertile soil to the river valley and the wide delta. Throughout Bible times Egypt was noted as a source and storehouse of corn. Ancient Egypt was famous for wealth and trade as well as for the pyramids and monumental buildings which still remain as symbols of her religious beliefs.

The hungry Hebrew nomads went down to Egypt in time of famine from the days of Abraham, and eventually the Jacob clans settled there in the time of Joseph, whom the Pharaoh 'set over all the land of Egypt'. It was his task to store grain in the years of plenty and sell it in time of need. The Joseph saga tells that he married the daughter of Potiphera, priest of the sun god at On.

The book of Exodus begins in Egypt with stories of Moses, the Hebrew leader with an Egyptian name who was called by God to lead the Hebrew slaves from Egypt to Canaan. Many later references in Jewish writings mention Egypt as the place of captivity from which God brought his chosen people. Yet the Jews appear to have taken very little from Egypt in the way of law or custom.

The prophets in the time of the monarchy continually

warned kings and people not to seek military or political help from Egypt. Solomon was reproved for his marriage to a daughter of the Pharaoh. After the downfall of Jerusalem in 586 B.C., many Jewish refugees settled in Egypt, particularly around Alexandria, which became a centre of learning. It was there that the Greek translation of the O.T., known as the Septuagint, was prepared.

In the N.T., Matthew's account of the birth of Jesus tells of the flight of Joseph and Mary and the young child to Egypt to escape the wrath of Herod. [*Refs.* Genesis 10; 39-47. Exodus 1-14. 1 Kings 11: 1. Isaiah 30: 1-7. Jeremiah 42: 13-22. Matthew 2: 13-19.]

Elath, Eloth A town at the head of the Gulf of Aqaba, the northern arm of the Red Sea. The place is also known in the Bible as Ezion-geber. Solomon built a port there for his commercial fleet. He also established a mining centre for smelting and refining copper and iron from the nearby hills; this was the major source of his enormous wealth. Elath (the modern name for which is Elat) remains an important port for Israel today. [*Refs.* 1 Kings 9: 26-8; 10: 22.]

Elhanan *See* GOLIATH

Eli Eli was a priest of the shrine at Shiloh where the Ark was kept at that time. He was also a judge, but a weak one. It was to Eli that Hannah brought Samuel when he was a child, 'to serve the Lord'. When he was an old man and blind, Eli fell dead at the news that the Ark had been captured by the Philistines in battle with Israel. [*Refs.* 1 Samuel 3: 1, 13; 4: 11-18.]

Elias Elias is the Greek form of Elijah, and is the form used in the Gospels. [*Ref.* Mark 8: 28.]

Elijah The stormy prophet of Israel in the ninth century B.C. who rebuked the king of the northern kingdom and challenged the people to reject the Baal gods and return to the God of their fathers. Elijah appeared on the scene in the reign of Ahab and his Phoenician queen, Jezebel. The prophet is portrayed as a stern, lonely figure, a man of the desert clothed in haircloth with a girdle of leather round his waist, who was content to live in a cave or lie down under a broom tree. Many legendary stories surround him: the ravens brought him bread and meat morning and evening; at God's command he provided miraculously for a poor widow and her son and he brought the child back to life when he fell ill. These are homely tales, but Elijah's claim to fame in Jewish tradition springs from the fact that he was spokesman for the God of Israel at a time of apostasy which was nation-wide. King Ahab had not only married a foreign queen, he had also encouraged her Baal worship. The climax of the encounter between prophet and king came in the dramatic story of the sacrifice on Mt. Carmel when the prayers of the many prophets of Baal were of no avail, but the fire of the Lord fell at Elijah's word. The other memorable tale of Elijah is his fearless rebuke of Ahab when the king allowed Jezebel to steal for him the vineyard of the peasant Naboth whom the queen caused to be put to death. Elijah foretold doom for the whole house of Ahab.

Elijah has been remembered among the Jews from that day to this as pre-eminently the man of God who declared: 'Thus says the Lord!' So revered was he in later tradition that he is set down as one who never died. He chose Elisha as his disciple and successor, and the latter saw him carried up by a whirlwind into heaven. Jewish writing and teaching declare that Elijah will come again as God's messenger to announce 'the great and terrible day of the Lord'. So the o.t. closes, and thus he is mentioned in the n.t. under the Greek form of the name (Elias) in the a.v., in connection with John the Baptist and with Jesus. To this day the Jews remember Elijah at the Passover feast by leaving a vacant chair for the prophet and pouring out a cup of wine for him. Moses and Elijah are the two men of God who, more than any other of the prophets, influenced the Hebrew Covenant faith. [*Refs.* 1 Kings 17: 1 to 19: 21; 21: 1-29. 2 Kings 1: 1 to 2: 18. Malachi 4: 5-6. Matthew 11: 14; 16: 14; 17: 3, 10; 27: 47. Mark 6: 15; 8: 28; 9: 4, 11-13; 15: 35. Luke 1: 17; 4: 25; 9: 8. John 1: 21, 25. James 5: 17.]

Elisha A well-to-do farmer's son who became the disciple of Elijah the prophet and his anointed successor in ninth century Israel. He took up the mantle and the work of Elijah when the latter disappeared in a whirlwind to heaven. Many legends gathered about Elisha the man of God, though the tales are less dramatic than those which make Elijah the towering prophet of the O.T. Elisha appears as the helper of ordinary people as well as the counsellor of kings. It was to Elisha that Naaman the Syrian commander came to seek a cure for his leprosy. The miracles of Elisha were known far beyond the bounds of Israel and, even after his death, pious legend told how his very bones were able to restore a dead man to life. Elisha profoundly affected the course of Israel's history by sending a messenger to anoint Jehu when he was still a rebel against the house of Ahab. There is one mention of Elisha in the N.T. where the name in the A.V. is the Greek form Eliseus. [*Refs.* 1 Kings 19: 16-21. 2 Kings 2: 1 to 9: 3; 13: 14-21. Luke 4: 27.]

Elizabeth Wife of the priest Zechariah (or Zacharias) who lived in the hill-country of Judea. In her old age she gave birth to a son who became John the Baptist. Luke calls Elizabeth a kinswoman of Mary, the mother of Jesus. He writes of her and of the birth of her child in devotional poems at the beginning of his Gospel. [*Ref.* Luke 1: 5-80.]

Elymas A Jewish magician and false prophet who called himself Bar-Jesus ('Son of Jesus') and withstood Paul and Barnabas in the isle of Cyprus. He was struck blind for a time at Paul's command. [*Ref.* Acts 13: 6-12.]

Emmanuel, Immanuel The name means 'God with us'. In the O.T. Isaiah the prophet told Ahaz, king of Judah, whose capital city of Jerusalem was besieged by a coalition of Syria and Israel, that he had nothing to fear: 'A young woman shall conceive and bear a son and shall call his name Immanuel.' This was to be a 'sign' to the king. Before the child bearing this symbolic name was little more than an infant, the immediate enemy danger would disappear and Judah would be saved. Isaiah's message to the king was therefore 'trust in God'. It is possible that Isaiah was speaking of a child of the royal house of David.

In the N.T. the name has Messianic significance. Matthew applies the quotation from Isaiah to Jesus who is to be born of Mary. Unfortunately, however, where the words 'young woman' are used in the O.T., the version in Matthew appears as 'a virgin shall conceive', thus adding misquotation to the difficult doctrine of the virgin birth. [*Refs.* Isaiah 7: 14; 8: 8. Matthew 1: 23.]

Emmaus A village about seven miles from Jerusalem to which two disciples were walking on the day Jesus rose from the dead. They met Jesus on the road, held a conversation with him, and when they came to the village he stayed with them. At table he took the bread, blessed, broke and gave it to them, and they recognized him in that action. [*Ref.* Luke 24: 13-32.]

Epaphras A companion of Paul and 'beloved fellow-servant', the name is a shortened form of Epaphroditus. Epaphras was a native of Colossae and appears to have been the founder of the Church there. He visited Paul during his imprisonment in Rome and brought him news of the Church at Colossae. [*Refs.* Colossians 1: 7; 4: 12. Philemon 23.]

Epaphroditus A native of Philippi who visited Paul in prison in Rome, bringing gifts from the Church in Philippi. Apparently he became a fellow-worker with the apostle, who also calls him 'my brother' and 'fellow soldier'. Epaphroditus, however, fell seriously ill and Paul sent him home with warm praise 'for he nearly died for the work of Christ, risking his life to complete your service to me'. [*Refs.* Philippians 2: 25-9; 4: 18.]

Ephah A Hebrew dry measure of quantity. We might translate it as 'a basketful'. [*Refs.* Levitians 5: 11. Ezekiel 45: 11.] *See also*: ZECHARIAH, THE BOOK OF

Ephesians, The Letter of Paul to the This is one of the four 'letters from prison': to the Colossians, Philemon, Ephesians, and Philippians. Some scholars, however, find it difficult to believe that the Letter to the Ephesians was written by Paul. The apostle had stayed in Ephesus more than two years, according to Acts 19: 1-10. Yet this letter contains no personal greetings to friends in Ephesus, nor is there any mention of the place in the opening verse. The style of writing is not like other works of Paul, and many words and phrases are alien to him. Even in English translation we may note long sentences that are hard to understand, in contrast to the quick, graphic language of the Letter to the Galatians. The whole thing is more of a tract than a letter to Christians well known to the writer.

On the other hand, it is surely by someone who knew Paul's writings and teaching and whether by Paul or not, it certainly seems to have been written from prison. There are references at 3: 1; 4: 1, and 6: 20 to the writer's imprisonment. If by Paul, it may belong to about A.D. 60 when the apostle was under house arrest in Rome. If by an unknown writer, it may be later still, after Paul's death.

The general theme of the Letter is the unity of Jewish and Gentile believers in the Church of Jesus Christ. In short, there is one body and one spirit.

A brief outline of the contents is:

(a) Ephesians: 1-2: Greetings of a general nature, and the blessing.

(b) Ephesians 1: 3-23: Thanksgiving for Christ. 'In him we have redemption through his blood, the forgiveness of our trespasses, according to the riches of his grace which he lavished upon us' [7-8]

(c) Ephesians 2: 1 to 3: 13: The Gentiles are part of the Church along with the Jews—'you are no longer strangers and sojourners but you are fellow citizens with the saints and members of the household of God' [2; 19].

(d) Ephesians 3: 14-21: One of the great prayers of the early Church, and a doxology.

(e) Ephesians 4: 1-16: The gifts and the moral behaviour proper to those who are joined together in the body of Christ.

(f) Ephesians 4: 17 to 5: 20: The moral task of those who are created after the likeness of God: 'be kind to one another, tenderhearted, forgiving one another, as God in Christ forgave you' [4: 32].

(g) Ephesians 5: 21 to 6: 9: Detailed instructions concerning how wives and husbands, children and parents, servants and masters, are to behave one to another.

(h) Ephesians 6: 10-20: A picture of the Christian armed with the whole armour of God.

(i) Ephesians 6: 21-34: Final greeting, with mention of Tychicus, and the blessing.

Ephesus An important seaport in Asia Minor where east met west in the Mediterranean. Ephesus ranked as the capital city of the Roman province of Asia. The temple of Diana (or Artemis) was one of the seven wonders of the ancient world. According to Acts, Paul's preaching there brought harm to the craft of silversmiths who made and sold silver models of the shrine of Artemis to pilgrims and visitors. There was an uproar in the city as a result. Nevertheless, Ephesus became a prominent centre of the Christian faith. Paul stayed there at least two years, and Aquila and Priscilla, Timothy, and the author of The Revelation were all associated with the city at one time or another. [*Refs.* Acts 18: 19; 19: 1-41. 1 Corinthians 15: 32; 16: 9. 1 Timothy 1: 3. Revelation 2: 1.]

Ephod A piece of linen shaped like an apron which the high priest wore under his breast-plate when he took part in Temple services. It had shoulder straps and a belt, and was of richly-woven design and colour. The name was also used for a simple linen waist-cloth, worn by a servant at a shrine or by a king or a judge. Not much is known of the ephod, except from Biblical description. [*Refs.* Exodus 28. 1 Samuel 2: 18. 2 Samuel 6: 14.]

Ephraim The name refers to the Israelite tribe and to the place they inhabited in Canaan. According to Biblical tradition, Ephraim was the second son of Joseph and Asenath, the daughter of a priest of Egypt. The land allotted to Ephraim lay in the hill country at the centre of Canaan, and the people increased and prospered. Ephraim and Manasseh are named together as making up one tribe. Joshua, the servant and successor of Moses, was an Ephraimite. Their chief town was Shechem, taken as his capital by Jeroboam the Ephraimite who rebelled against Rehoboam, son of Solomon. Ephraim and the other northern tribes supported Jeroboam, and the latter set up a separate kingdom which he called Israel. From that time until its downfall at the hands of the Assyrians, the northern kingdom was often known as Ephraim. It was under this name that the prophets critized their people for being unfaithful to the Lord their God. [*Refs*. Genesis 41: 50-2; 48: 1, 5, 17-20. Numbers 13: 8. Joshua 16: 5-10. 1 Kings 11: 26; 12: 20, 25. Hosea 4: 17; 5: 9.]

Esaias Esaias is the Greek form of Isaiah. It is used in the N.T. because most of the O.T. names and quotations there came from the Greek Septuagint translation of Jewish scriptures. [*Ref.* Matthew 3: 3.]

Esau Son of Isaac and Rebekah and older twin brother of Jacob. Esau is described as his father's favourite, a skilful hunter and a man of the open air. Jacob tricked him for their father's blessing and had to flee before Esau's anger, but the brothers were later reconciled. Esau is said to be the ancestor of the people of Edom. [*Refs*. Genesis 25: 25-7; 27; 33: 1-15; 36: 9.]

Esdraelon *See* JEZREEL

Esther A Jewish heroine who has a book named after her in the O.T. The story tells how Esther became queen to Xerxes the Persian king (Hebrew name, Ahasuerus) and because of the king's favour towards her she was able to save her people from destruction planned by the wicked Haman.

The book of Esther is set in the days of Jewish captivity under Persian rule, with much local colour, but it is a work of historical fiction. It records ancient anti-Semitic feeling, as well as hatred, intolerance and revenge on the Jewish part. There is no mention of God in the book, and it is not quoted in the N.T. It was probably written in the nationalist Maccabean days, expressing the spirit of those times. The popular Jewish feast of Purim celebrates the events of the story, and the book of Esther is read twice in the synagogue during that festival.

Esther, The Book of The Book of Esther is included among the Writings of the Hebrew Scriptures, and is a work of historical fiction set in Persia in the days of the Exile. It was written with the patriotic purpose of encouraging Jews to be faithful to their nationality even in time of severe persecution. The story deals with anti-Semitism in ancient Persia and shows how Esther, the beautiful Jewish queen of the Persian king Ahasuerus (Xerxes), was able to save her people from wholesale slaughter in a time of racial intolerance. Indeed, she was able to turn the tables on her people's persecutors so effectively that the Jews were granted royal permission to slay their enemies, which they did wholeheartedly. There is no religious teaching in the book and no mention of God. Much of it is vindictive, vengeful and savage. Even in modern times, however, persecuted Jews in many lands have found encouragement in the Book of Esther and it is one of their favourite stories. They derive from it their sanction for the nationalistic annual festival of Purim.

Ethiopia Part of north-east Africa, also called Abyssinia. It was known to the Hebrews as *Cush*. There are references here and there in the O.T. to trade with Ethiopia. Moses is said to have had an Ethiopian wife. During the reign of King Asa a huge army of Ethiopians invaded Judah, but the king and his people did battle with them and utterly defeated them. It was an Ethiopian royal servant named Ebedmelech who rescued the prophet Jeremiah from a muddy cistern into which he had been flung. In the N.T. a notable Ethiopian treasurer to Queen Candace listened to the preaching of Philip the evangelist and was baptized by him. Ethiopians by their name and by proverb were a black-skinned people: 'Can the Ethiopian change his skin or the leopard his spots?' [*Refs.* Genesis 10: 6. Numbers 12: 1. 2 Chronicles 14: 9-13. Job 28: 19. Isaiah 45: 14. Jeremiah 13: 23; 38: 7-13. Acts 8: 27-39]

Eucharist *See* LORD'S SUPPER

Euphrates The largest river of western Asia. Some of the greatest civilizations of the ancient world grew up along its fertile banks, their memory marked by such names as Babylon, Carchemish, Ur, Mari. It was the Euphrates and the Tigris that made Mesopotamia a garden land, rich in grain and fruit. The Euphrates is mentioned in the Genesis Creation myth as one of the rivers of Eden. It is known in the o.t. as 'the river' or 'the great river'. [*Refs.* Genesis 2: 14. Deuteronomy 11: 24. Joshua 1: 4. 2 Samuel 8: 3; 10: 16.]

Eutychus A young man in the town of Troas who sat in a window while Paul was speaking. He went to sleep and fell to the ground from the third storey. Eutychus was taken for dead, but Paul went down and restored him to life. [*Ref.* Acts 20: 7-12.]

Eunice The mother of Timothy, whom Paul met in Lystra. Eunice was a Jewish-Christian whose husband was Greek. She brought up her son in the Christian faith. [*Refs.* Acts 16: 1. 1 Timothy 1: 5.]

Eve The name of the first woman, wife of Adam, and 'mother of all living', mentioned in one of the Creation myths of Genesis. Eve was beguiled by the serpent and persuaded Adam to eat the forbidden fruit of the tree in the midst of the garden. Because of their disobedience God drove them out of the garden of Eden. Eve was the mother of Cain and Abel. [*Refs.* Genesis 3; 4: 1-2.]

Exile The period spent by the Jews in captivity in Babylon. The soldiers of Nebuchadrezzar of Babylon besieged Jerusalem for more than a year and a half, and finally captured and destroyed the city in 587 B.C. They burned the gates and broke down the walls. Within the city they burned the Temple palace and great houses, and systematically plundered the treasures of gold and silver. The king and men of the court, priests of the Temple, craftsmen of Jerusalem, and people of Judah were led away to captivity in Babylonia, leaving only 'some of the poor people who owned nothing'.

In the land of Exile the Jews were able to build houses, keep farms, and engage in work in city and country according to their skills and crafts. They preserved their identity by meeting for worship, for remembrance of the religious rites and customs of their people, and to instruct their children in the beliefs and practices of Judaism. It is probable that the synagogue had its origin in this time of Exile, and in their coming together the Jews maintained their religious traditions. It was also a time of literary activity. The priests of the Temple had brought with them the written documents of their laws, history and ritual. Now they put together, adapted and edited this literary material to instruct and encourage their people. It is in this period of the Exile that we see the O.T. beginning to take shape. Two prophets, Ezekiel and Isaiah of Babylon, also spoke words of hope and promise of liberation to their fellow-exiles. This hope was in part fulfilled by the edict of Cyrus, conqueror of Babylon. In 538 B.C., Cyrus of Persia made a proclamation which allowed the Jews to return to Judah and to rebuild the Temple in Jerusalem. They were to be assisted by silver and gold, goods and beasts and free-will offerings for the house of God contributed by the Jews who chose to remain in Babylonia. Cyrus also restored to the returning Jews the Temple vessels of gold and silver which Nebuchadrezzar had carried away from Jerusalem.

Two Psalms express vividly the feelings of the Jews in the land of Exile. One which recalls the downfall of Jerusalem is Psalm 137.

'By the waters of Babylon
There we sat down and wept,
When we remembered Zion.'

The other, Psalm 126, tells of the feelings of those who had been exiles and who were now restored to Jerusalem:

'When the Lord restored the fortunes of Zion,
We were like those who dream.
Then our mouth was filled with laughter,
And our tongue with shouts of joy.'

[*Refs.* 2 Kings 23: 36 to 25: 21. Ezra 1. Psalm 126; 137. Isaiah 40: 1-11. Jeremiah 29: 5; 39: 1-10. Ezekiel 1: 1; 3: 15; 12: 1-7.]

Exodus Exodus means 'a way out' and it is the name given to the book of the O.T. which describes the going out of the Israelites from Egypt under the leadership of Moses. Exodus

is the second of the 'five books of Moses' known as the Pentateuch.

The narrative falls into three main parts:

(a) Exodus 1: 1 to 4: 31: Israel in Egypt, and the birth, train-
    ing, and call of Moses.
(b) Exodus 5-19: From Egypt to Mt. Sinai.
(c) Exodus 20-40: The giving of the Law at Mt. Sinai, the
    Covenant, and the making of the Tabernacle.

It is impossible at this date to discover the exact sequence of
events of the Exodus or to trace accurately the route across the
desert, except to say that the latter was probably by way of the
Bitter Lakes or 'Sea of Reeds', which is the correct translation
of the Hebrew words *Yam Suph*. There is no certainty either
about the site of Mt. Sinai. What actually happened is lost in the
past. The Book of Exodus tells of the making of a nation; no
part of Scripture means more to the Jews; their religious beliefs
and customs to this day are rooted in it. But the traditions and
legends of people and places have come down through the centuries by word of mouth, and the re-telling of their past has
been a religious recital full of wonder and reverence rather than
a plain account of history. As in other parts of the Pentateuch
confusion is sometimes caused by two parallel stories from ancient sources being woven into one without regard for historical accuracy. The account of the crossing of the Sea of Reeds in
Exodus 14 is an example of this.

The most important part of the Book of Exodus tells of the
giving of the Law at the sacred mountain and of the Covenant between God and his chosen people. Many of the religious, moral and social laws belong to a later age and to a
settled, farming community rather than to nomadic desert
tribes. Nevertheless, it is probable that the Ten
Commandments in simple form go back to the time of Moses. The ritual laws concerning the Ark of the Covenant, the
making of the Tabernacle and the clothing and duties of the
priests (Exodus 25-31) show the work of writers during or
soon after the Exile in Babylon. At that time the Temple was

in ruins and the central pattern of sacrifice and worship in Jerusalem destroyed. In compiling the literature which was to remind the Jewish people of their past and to renew their dedication to God for present and future, the priestly editors made much of the Tabernacle in the wilderness in the days when their people were first called by God and entered into covenant with him to be 'a kingdom of priests and a holy nation'. It is the whole theme of the Book of Exodus.

Ezekiel A prophet of the sixth century B.C. in Judah who was also a priest of the Temple. Ezekiel was carried into Exile in Babylon when Nebuchadrezzar deported the first group of leaders of Jerusalem in 597 B.C. He must therefore have been a man of some importance in the Jewish priesthood. It was by the river (or canal) of Chebar that he had his visions of God which are set down in the Book of Ezekiel. Apparently Ezekiel had his own house to which the elders of Judah used to come. Like many a prophet, he was aware that people heard him but did not really listen and obey: 'You are to them like one who sings love songs with a beautiful voice and plays well on an instrument, for they hear what you say, but they will not do it.' Ezekiel's visions and allegories are elaborate and strange indeed, suggested often by the symbolic creatures of Babylonian art. It was Ezekiel's teaching about devotion to the Temple and its worship which shaped the life of the restored Jerusalem when some of the exiles eventually returned to Judah. [*Refs.* Ezekiel 1: 1-3; 3: 15, 24; 8: 1; 14: 1; 33: 30-3.]

Ezekiel, The Book of The third of the great prophetic books among the 'Latter Prophets' of the Hebrew Scriptures. Ezekiel was a priest of the Temple and a prophet at the time of the Jewish Exile in Babylon. The book which bears his name consists mainly of visions full of the most elaborate symbolism and imagery. It proclaims Ezekiel's 'word from the Lord' that Jerusalem shall be restored and that an ideal community shall return there to be a kingdom of priests and a holy nation. The book may be outlined thus:

(a) Ezekiel 1-24: Visions before the downfall of Jerusalem

declaring the doom of the last days of city and Temple. There are numerous allegories and parable-pictures, e.g. the flying wheels [1: 15-21], the picture-brick [4: 1-3], the barber's razor [5: 1-2], the exile's baggage [12: 3-7], the eagles with great wings [17: 1-10], the signpost (21: 18-23], the boiling pot [24: 3-14].

(b) Ezekiel 25-32: Prophecies about other nations round about.

(c) Ezekiel 33-9: Ezekiel, the watchman for the house of Israel, speaks of the restoration of Jerusalem. There is a vivid picture of false shepherds in contrast with God, the faithful shepherd who seeks out his sheep and rescues them, feeds them with good pasture, cares for the lost, the strayed, the crippled, the weak, and watches constantly over his flock to keep them safe (34). Most famous of all is the vision of the valley of dry bones brought to life and set upon their feet by the Spirit of God (37).

(d) Ezekiel 40-8: Contains the visions of the Temple rebuilt and restored to its former glory. The glory of the Lord fills the Temple and the people who come there are to be holy, exclusive, dedicated to the proper ritual of worship. No foreigner is to set foot in the sanctuary. 'And the name of the city henceforth shall be The Lord is There' (48: 35). The narrow religious nationalism of these chapters sets the pattern for what became of Judaism after the Exile.

Ezion-Geber *See* ELATH

Ezra A member of a Jewish priestly family who was in exile in Babylonia in the reign of Artaxerxes, king of Persia. Ezra was also a scribe skilled in the law of Moses, and he returned to Jerusalem with a company of priests, Levites, singers and Temple servants, taking with them offerings of silver and gold from the Persian king and from the Jewish people in exile, as well as some of the Temple vessels for use in Jerusalem. This return probably took place when Nehemiah was governor in Jerusalem. Certainly the book of Nehemiah tells that all the people gathered into the square before the Water Gate to hear Ezra the priest read from the book of law. He stood on a wooden pulpit made for the purpose and read from early morning until midday so that the men and women heard and understood. Ezra strictly gave orders that those Jews who had married foreign women were to put away their wives and children. He also re-instituted the Feast of Booths among the people who had returned from the land of the captivity.

The book of Ezra appears to contain autobiographical memoirs, particularly in chapters 7-9. 'Ezra the priest, the scribe of the law of the God of heaven' was, probably more than anyone else, the man who shaped post-exilic Judaism with its central obedience to the Law in all the details of daily life. [*Refs.* Ezra: 7-10. Nehemiah 8.]

Ezra, The Book of The Book of Ezra makes up one volume with Nehemiah in Hebrew Scriptures, and forms part of the Writings. It is also linked with 1 and 2 Chronicles and was written by the same writer, usually known as 'the chronicler'. Evidence of this is in the fact that the opening words of Ezra 1: 1-3 and the ending of 2 Chronicles 36: 22-3 are the same. The Book of Ezra tells of the time when some faithful Jews returned from Exile to Jerusalem after the edict of Cyrus set them free. The contents are: (a) Ezra 1-6: The decree of Cyrus, the return of the exiles, the re-building of the Temple. (b) Ezra 7-10: The work of Ezra.

The book is sometimes in the third person, sometimes in the first person, as if to make the work of Ezra more vivid. There is still scholarly argument about when Ezra came to Jerusalem, before or after Nehemiah. But it is safe to say that while Nehemiah rebuilt the walls of the holy city and brought about orderly government, it was Ezra who established the ritual of worship in the Temple and made it the heart of Judaism. He proclaimed the Law which was to be kept and laid down strict religious regulations for the future. The most notable of these was that the returned exiles who had married foreign wives were to put them away. Here we see the beginning of Jewish exclusiveness as a people.

F

Fair Havens A small bay on the south coast of Crete where the ship on which Paul was a prisoner found shelter in rough weather. [*Ref.* Acts 27: 8-12.]

Feasts *See* BOOTHS; PASSOVER; PENTECOST

Felix Felix was the Roman governor of Judea appointed by the emperor Claudius. Paul appeared for trial before him at Caesarea, following a riot in Jerusalem. Felix was widely known as a cruel ruler, but he listened to Paul's confident defence of his conduct. He eventually adjourned the hearing, ordered that Paul should be kept under open arrest, and allowed his friends to visit him. But when Nero recalled Felix two years later Paul was still a prisoner. [*Refs.* Acts 23: 24-35; 24.]

Festus Porcius Festus was the Roman governor of Judea appointed by the emperor Nero to succeed Felix. He heard Paul's defence at Caesarea, and suggested sending him to stand trial at Jerusalem, in the presence of the leading Jews. But Paul appealed to Caesar, and the governor's verdict was: 'to Caesar you shall go'. [*Refs.* Acts 24: 27; 25: 1-12.]

First-Born In ancient Hebrew custom the first-born son inherited a double share of his father's property and he took on the leadership of the family or clan. That is the point of the Jacob and Esau stories, where the sons of Isaac were twins, but Esau should have inherited the right of leadership because he was the first-born. Jacob coveted this birthright and eventually won it by trickery.

The O.T. mentions the Canaanite practice of sacrificing the first-born son in fertility rites. Jewish law speaks of the first-born male, of man or beast, as being sacred to God. The animals were to be sacrificed as an offering. The sons were to be 'redeemed', or bought back, by making an offering in their place.

The first-fruits of harvest were also included in the sacrificial system, and the wool of the sheep. When Mary and Joseph brought the child Jesus to the Temple to 'present him to the Lord' they were obeying the law of the first-born. They redeemed their son with the offering of 'a pair of turtledoves or two young pigeons' as the law required. [*Refs*. Genesis 25: 29-34. Exodus 13: 2,11-16. Deuteronomy 18: 4; 21: 15-17. Micah 6: 7. Luke 2: 22-4.] *See also*: MOLECH

Flood The story of the Flood or Deluge in Genesis 6 to 9 tells how God saw the wickedness of man, was sorry that he had ever made him, and decided to blot out man and every living creature from the face of the earth. Noah, however, found favour in God's sight and was told to build an ark to preserve himself and his family as well as male and female, two by two, of every animal and bird and creeping thing. The rains came, the Flood swept over the earth, until at last the waters abated and the ark came to rest on the mountains of Ararat.

Stories of this kind are common in the folklore of the ancient world, and no doubt the Genesis tale comes from a Babylonian source. The Gilgamesh epic, for example, contains many details which resemble the narrative of Noah. Modern archaeology has found out that the Flood stories are not mere fiction. There were overwhelming deluge disasters in the Tigris-Euphrates area in ancient times which may well have given rise to the folk-tales. The Bible writers make of the Flood epic a tale with many meanings, principally of the over-ruling power of God the creator and of his eternal covenant with the creature he has made. [*Refs*. Genesis 6-9. Matthew 24: 38. Luke 17: 26-7.]

Frankincense A white, fragrant gum from trees of Arabia, Africa and India which was used for making incense and the oil for anointing priests. The transport of frankincense and other spices was an important part of the camel caravan trade of the East for centuries, and it brought great wealth. Frankincense is mentioned as one of the treasures offered by the wise men from the East at the birth of Jesus, as told in Matthew's Gospel. [*Refs.* Exodus 30: 34-7. Leviticus 2: 1. Isaiah 60: 6. Matthew 2: 11.]

Frontlet A leather band worn round the forehead with a tiny bag between the eyes containing scraps of parchment with sacred writing on them. [*Refs.* Exodus 13: 16. Deuteronomy 6: 8.]

G

Gabriel An archangel, the traditional messenger of God. Gabriel appeared to Daniel to interpret his visions, to Zacharias to foretell the birth of John, and to Mary to announce that she would bear a son who was to be called Jesus. [*Refs.* Daniel 8: 15-18; 9: 21-7. Luke 1: 11-19, 20-38.] *See also*: ANGEL

Gadara One of the towns of the Decapolis, south-east of the Sea of Galilee. The exact site is uncertain. In that district Jesus healed a man with an unclean spirit. Matthew's account mentions two demoniacs. [*Refs.* Matthew 8: 28-34. Mark 5: 1-20. Luke 8: 26-39.]

Galatians, The Letter of Paul to the The main problem which has interested scholars is whether this letter was written to the Churches of South Galatia which Paul had founded on his first missionary journey with Barnabas, that is, at Iconium, Lystra and Derbe (Acts 14), or whether it is addressed to Christians in North Galatia, a region which Paul did not apparently visit at all. The details of the argument need not concern us here, except to say that if we accept the South Galatian theory we must date the letter about A.D. 48, and this places it first among Paul's writings, earlier even than 1 Thessalonians.

One thing is clear, the Christians to whom Paul was writing were Gentiles, formerly heathen (Galatians 4: 8). The reason for the letter is that they are deserting the Gospel Paul so recently preached to them and allowing themselves to be misled by teachers who pervert the Gospel of Christ.

A brief outline of the letter is:

(a) Galatians 1: 1-5: Greetings and a blessing.

(b) Galatians 1: 6 to 2: 21: Paul defends the truth of the gospel he has preached to them, and his own authority as an apostle. With a good deal of personal detail he tells how he defended his proclamation of Christ to the Gentiles as well as to the Jews, even face to face with Peter.

(c) Galatians 3: 1 to 5: 12: The Christian believer is the heir by faith, not by the law. The Galatians must not listen to trouble-makers who seek to make them submit to works of the Jewish law, including circumcision. 'For freedom Christ has set us free; stand fast therefore, and do not submit again to a yoke of slavery.' Christian freedom is expressed by faith, not by works.

(d) Galatians 5: 13 to 6: 10: Freedom, however, must not be used to satisfy the flesh, but through love they must be servants of one another. Paul urges his readers to walk in the Spirit and to avoid all forms of immorality, which are the works of the flesh. In complete contrast, 'the fruit of the Spirit is love, joy, peace, patience, kindness, goodness, faithfulness, gentleness, self-control'. Those who live by the Spirit are free from the law.

(e) Galatians 6: 11-18: A personal ending, in which Paul briefly repeats the main points of his argument—if you want marks on your body, let them be not the marks of circumcision, but the marks of the cross of Christ. Paul himself bears these. Finally, the blessing.

The main theme of Paul's letter to the Galatians is twofold: that the gospel is for Gentiles as well as Jews, and that men are set free through faith in Jesus Christ. This letter is a manifesto of Christian liberty, and no writing of Paul's more passionately and sympathetically sets forth the gospel he constantly proclaimed. If we wish readers to understand Paul we must say 'Begin here'.

Galilee Hill-country in the north of Palestine, rich in orchards and vineyards and with fertile fields. Because of its position,

Galilee was overrun time and again by invading armies from the north. Not surprisingly, with its mixed population, it came to be known as 'Galilee of the nations', or 'Galilee of the Gentiles'. At the time of Jesus, Galilee was ruled by Herod Antipas, and the Galilean accent was distinctive. All but one of the chosen disciples were Galilean, the first being fishermen from the side of the Lake or Sea of Galilee. Nazareth and Capernaum were towns of Galilee. [*Refs*. 1 Kings 9: 11. 2 Kings 15: 29. Isaiah 9: 1. Matthew 4: 15, 23; 26: 69-73. Mark 14: 70. Luke 23: 6. John 7: 41.]

Galilee, Sea of A fresh-water lake in the north of Palestine fed by the Jordan. In the O.T. it is called *Chinnereth*. In the N.T. it is also known as the Lake of Gennesaret and the Sea of Tiberias, or just 'the lake' or 'the sea'.

The Sea of Galilee is thirteen miles long and about seven and half miles wide, and it lies 700 feet below sea-level. There are mountains to east and west and the water is often troubled by violent storms. The Sea of Galilee is frequently mentioned in the ministry of Jesus and so are a number of the towns round or near its shores: Capernaum, Bethsaida, Chorazin, Magdala, Gadara. [*Refs*. Numbers 34: 11. Mark 1: 16; 4: 35-41. Luke 5: 1; 8: 22. John 6: 1, 16.]

Gamaliel A liberal Pharisee and doctor of the Law who was a member of the *Sanhedrin* or Council of the Jews. Gamaliel was a teacher of Saul, later known as Paul. During the trial of Peter and the other disciples before the Council, Gamaliel spoke for tolerance and caution. [*Refs*. Acts 5: 34-40; 22: 3.]

Gath One of the five chief Philistine cities on the coast of Palestine. Gath was the home of Goliath, famous as the opponent of David. The Ark of the Covenant, captured by the Philistines, was kept there for a time. David took the city of Gath when he was king. It was later seized by the Syrians and it eventually disappeared from history. [*Refs*. 1 Samuel 5: 8; 17: 4. 2 Samuel 1: 20. 2 Kings 12: 17. 1 Chronicles 18: 1.]

Gaza One of the five cities set up by the Philistines on the coast of Palestine. The story of Samson mentions the place. Gaza was a great trade centre throughout Bible times, controlling the rich caravan routes to Egypt, Arabia and Damascus. Gaza is mentioned once in the N.T. in the encounter between Philip and the Ethiopian. [*Refs.* Genesis 10: 19. Judges 16: 1-3, 21. 1 Kings 4: 24. Acts 8: 26.]

Genesis The Greek word genesis means 'beginning' or 'origin'. The name was given to the first book of the O.T. (and of the Bible) because it contains the stories of the creation of the world and the origin of the Jewish people. Genesis is the first of the 'five books of Moses' known as the Pentateuch, the most important collection of Scripture in Judaism.

The contents are:

(a) Genesis 1: 1 to 3: 24: Two accounts of the creation of the world, the story of Adam and Eve and the garden of Eden.

(b) Genesis 4-5: The descendants of Adam.

(c) Genesis 6 to 11: 26: Noah and the Flood and the tower of Babel.

(d) Genesis 11: 27 to 50: 26: The patriarchs and their families, Abraham, Isaac, Jacob, Joseph.

Much of the material of the Book of Genesis began as 'oral tradition', i.e. stories handed down by word of mouth among the tribes which came to make up the Jewish nation. Poetry, myths, sagas and legends about sacred places and notable leaders were eventually woven together with great skill to set down in writing what the Jews believed about the beginning of the world, God's Covenant with their forefathers, and the continuing faith of their people. Some of these tales and traditions were gathered together in the southern kingdom of Judah after the time of Solomon. Others belonged to Israel, the northern kingdom. Double accounts here and there in the narrative indicate different sources. The accounts of the Creation and of the Flood owe a good deal to Babylonian epics. The strongest literary influence in the composition of the book is that of Jewish priestly writers during the Exile and after. They were concerned to trace back to earliest times such Jewish religious customs as the keeping of the Sabbath, the rite of circumcision, the taboo against eating meat with blood in it. Yet another interest was to point to the importance of certain shrines associated with the early fathers of their people, Bethel, for example, and Salem. The priestly compilers and editors were more concerned to teach something about God and Man than merely to record history. No doubt there are real people and real places here, but the stories about them have been idealized. It is important, therefore, in reading the Book of Genesis to look for religious meanings rather than for scientific or historical facts. The Creation stories declare the writers' belief that God made the world and the patriarch tales continually insist that the same God guides the destiny of his chosen people.

Gennesaret A fertile place on the west side of the Sea of Galilee, south of Capernaum. The name was also used of the Sea itself. [*Refs*. Matthew 14: 34. Mark 6: 53. Luke 5: 1.]

Gentiles A name given by the Jews to all people who are not Hebrews. Sometimes in the Bible the writer speaks of the Gentiles as being heathen people who are beyond God's concern, quite different from his chosen people, Israel. But other writers thought of the Jewish mission to be 'a light to lighten the Gentiles'.

In N.T. times Galilee was known as 'Galilee of the Gentiles' because so many of its inhabitants were foreigners. Strict Jews did not enter the house of a Gentile and would not eat with them. Jesus, by contrast, met and helped a number of Gentiles. The attitude of the Christian Jew to the Gentile was a matter of controversy in the early Church. Paul was the first Christian missionary deliberately to turn to the Gentiles with the good news of Jesus. [*Refs*. Deuteronomy 7: 6. Isaiah 9: 1. Matthew 4: 15; 8: 5-13; 15: 21-8. Luke 2: 32. Acts 10: 28; 26: 17-18.]

Gergenses Gergesa, which is mentioned only by Matthew (A.V.) cannot be identified as a place. It is almost certain that the place should be Gadara, as in other versions of Matthew (R.S.V. and N.E.B.) and in the parallel stories in Mark and Luke. [*Refs*. Matthew 8: 28. Mark 5: 1. Luke 8: 26.] *See also*: GADARA

Gethsemane The place at the foot of the Mount of Olives, across the Kidron valley from Jerusalem, where Jesus went with his disciples to pray on the night of his betrayal and arrest. John's Gospel says there was a garden there. The traditional site is among olive groves. [*Refs.* Matthew 26: 36. Mark 14: 32. John 18: 1.]

Gideon One of the heroes of the Book of Judges, also known as Jerubbaal. He led his people against the Midianites who invaded Canaan from the Arabian desert on camels. The Israelites had to take to caves on the mountain tops, and the Midianites, like locusts, ate up their crops. Gideon took a stand against the Baal worship which had infected his town and even his own family. He carefully selected a fighting force of the men of Israel, attacked the camp of the Midianites by night, and drove them headlong from the land, pursuing them beyond the Jordan. The men of Israel begged Gideon to be their king, but Gideon refused: 'I will not rule over you, and my son will not rule over you; the Lord will rule over you.' [*Ref.* Judges 6-8.]

Gilboa A range of mountains in the north of Palestine which overlooks the pass from the plain of Jezreel to the Jordan valley. It was here that Saul, the first king of Israel, and his sons died in battle with the Philistines. [*Refs.* 1 Samuel 28: 4; 31: 1. 2 Samuel 1: 21. 1 Chronicles 10: 1, 8.]

Gilead A well-watered hilly area to the east of Jordan, famous in O.T. times for its flocks of sheep and its balm or resin from the trees which grew there. The proverbial 'balm of Gilead' was used for healing, embalming, and as a cosmetic. It formed an important article of trade. Elijah the prophet came from Gilead. [*Refs.* Genesis 37: 25. Joshua 17: 5. 1 Kings 17: 1. Song of Solomon 6: 5. Jeremiah 8: 22.]

Gilgal The word means 'circle of stones'. Gilgal is the name of a number of ancient places in the O.T., usually of military or religious importance. Joshua pitched camp at Gilgal when the Israelites first crossed the Jordan into Canaan and set up twelve standing stones there. The name also appears in the traditions of Samuel and Saul. It was at Gilgal that the people of Israel made Saul their king and there later Samuel rejected him. When Saul disobeyed Samuel's orders, the prophet cut Agag king of the Amalekites to pieces at Gilgal. Later prophets condemned Gilgal as a place of heathen worship. [*Refs.* Joshua 4: 19-20. 1 Samuel 11: 14-15; 13: 4-15; 15: 33. Hosea 4: 15; 9: 15. Amos 4: 4. Micah 6: 5.]

Gog and Magog The title 'Gog of the land of Magog' is used by Ezekiel of a mysterious, probably symbolic enemy of Israel, against whom God 'will summon every kind of terror'—sword, pestilence, bloodshed, torrential rains, hailstones, fire and brimstone. It is impossible to recognize a known historical figure. The Book of Revelation mentions Gog and Magog as 'the nations which are at the four corners of the earth' whom Satan deceives and leads to battle. [*Refs.* Ezekiel 38: 2, 18*f.* Revelation 20: 8*f.*]

Golgotha The Aramaic name for the place where Jesus was crucified. The word means 'skull' and the Latin name Calvaria has the same meaning. [*Refs.* Matthew 27: 33. Mark 15: 22. John 19: 17.]

Goliath The Philistine giant from Gath whom David slew with a stone from his sling. Another story says it was Elhanan, also from Bethlehem, who killed Goliath. Perhaps the tale was taken from him to add to the hero stories which grew up about David in later days. [*Refs.* 1 Samuel 17. 2 Samuel 21: 19.]

Gomorrah *See* SODOM

Goshen Part of Egypt where the shepherd clan of Jacob settled in the time of Joseph. [*Ref.* Genesis 46: 28-34.] *See also*: NILE

Greece Sometimes called Javan in the O.T. and Achaia in the N.T. Greek influence on Palestine was seen from the time of Alexander the Great onwards. His soldiers and their successors brought the Greek language, ideas, buildings, dress, games, customs and the Greek way of life to the East. [*Refs.* Genesis 10: 2, 4. Isaiah 66: 19. Ezekiel 27: 13. Acts 20: 2.] *See also*: GREEK

Greek The Greek language in which the N.T. was written was not the refined classical Greek of Attic civilization familiar to us in the poets, philosophers and dramatists of ancient Greece. It was the *koine*, the common, idiomatic, spoken tongue of everyday life in the Mediterranean world, the dialect of the home and the market-place, the highways and the harbours. The conquests of Alexander the Great and his successors had spread the Greek language, culture and customs over a wide empire, including Palestine. Galilee, for example, was known as 'Galilee of the Gentiles', many Palestinian towns and buildings were of Greek design, the names of places and people—the name Jesus for example—are reminders of the pervasive Greek influence. The Hebrew Scriptures had been translated into Greek for the many Jews who could no longer read nor understand their ancient language. Since the common Greek tongue was spoken everywhere, the gospel of Jesus Christ was able to spread very rapidly once the apostles shook themselves free of the bands of Judaism. Peter, Paul, and many others carried the good news of Jesus along the highways and seaways of the Roman empire, preaching and teaching in a language spoken and understood by the Jews of the Dispersion as well as by the Gentiles of the great cities of the Graeco-Roman civilization. Mark's Gospel was written in this koine and the other Gospels and the letters of Paul use the same commonly understood tongue, each writer adding his own individual grace of style. [*Refs.* John 19: 20. Acts 19: 10; 21: 37.]

H

Habbakuk A prophet named as author of the Book of Habakkuk in the O.T. He was perhaps a musician of the Temple, and spoke a few years before the fall of Jerusalem, at the turn of the seventh century B.C. The theme of the Book of Habakkuk is whether God is indeed in control of history in a time of a holocaust of evil. The Chaldeans are on the march and nothing apparently can stand in their way: 'They sweep by like the wind and go on, guilty men, whose own might is their god.' Why does God, almighty and pure, allow this? The only answer to Habakkuk's question seems to lie in the future, and in the abiding integrity of the human spirit: 'the righteous shall live by his faith'. It was this phrase that Paul took up in his day and expounded in his teaching about 'justification by faith'. Later, during the sixteenth century, at the time of the Reformation, it became the watchword of Martin Luther. [*Refs.* Habakkuk 1: 1, 11 ; 2: 4. *Romans* 1: 17. *Galatians* 3: 11.]

Habakkuk, The Book of The Book of Habakkuk is found among the 'Latter Prophets' of the Hebrew Scriptures and is one of the twelve minor prophets of our O.T. Nothing is known of the man Habakkuk apart from the title of this prophetic work. The date of writing is unknown, but internal evidence reveals that the Temple still stood: 'the Lord is in his holy temple; let all the earth keep silence before him' (2: 20). It probably belongs to the same time as Jeremiah, not long before the downfall of Jerusalem.

This short book consists of prophetic oracles in poetic form in chapters 1 and 2 and a psalm in chapter 3. The theme is not unlike that of Job and some of the Psalms: why does God allow wrong-doers to flourish and the righteous to suffer? Habakkuk takes his stand as a watchman on a tower looking for some answer from God to Man's cry from the heart: 'Thou who art of purer eyes than to behold evil and canst not look on wrong, why dost thou look on faithless men, and art silent when the wicked swallows up the man more righteous than he?' (1: 13). The only answer to the mystery comes in the words: 'the righteous shall live by his faith' (2: 4).

Hades *See* HELL

Hagar The Egyptian maidservant of Sarah, wife of Abraham. Hagar bore a son to Abraham when Sarah was childless. But when Sarah's own son, Isaac, was born, Hagar and her child Ishmael were cast out to be wanderers in the desert. The story belongs to the legends and traditions of the patriarchs, safe-guarding the purity of the racial stock. Ishmael is claimed by Moslems as the ancestor of the Arabs, who also call Abraham their 'father'. [*Refs.* Genesis 16: 1, 3-16; 21: 8-21.]

Haggai, The Book of The Book of Haggai is one of the 'Latter Prophets' of the Hebrew Scriptures and is to be found among the twelve minor prophets of our O.T. It consists of five brief fragments of addresses urging the rebuilding of the temple in Jerusalem. Unlike many prophetic writings, dates are here clearly given. These passages refer to the year 520 B.C., in the second year of the reign of Darius of Persia. We know nothing about this post-exilic prophet Haggai apart from his connection with the rebuilding of the Temple. Ezra 5: 1 mentions him and his contemporary Zechariah as prophets who stirred up the people of Jerusalem to the work.

The book, which is a prose work, is important for our knowledge of conditions in Palestine after the return from Exile. It was a time of great unrest throughout the whole empire of Darius and there are references here to 'the shaking of the nations'. In the land of Judah drought, poor harvests, a high cost of living are all interpreted by Haggai as punishments from God because the people have not put first things first. The Temple still lies in ruins. Haggai stirs up Zerubbabel the governor and Joshua the high priest to take the lead in the restoration of the house of the Lord. The foundation was laid in the month of December 520 B.C. From that moment Haggai foresees divine blessing on the restored remnant of Israel, with Zerubbabel the descendant of David as their anointed king.

Hallelujah A Hebrew word meaning 'praise Yahweh' or 'praise the Lord'. It is found at the beginning or end of many of the Psalms. [*Refs.* Psalms 111-113; 146-150. Revelation 19: 1-6.]

Hannah The mother of the prophet Samuel. The childless Hannah prayed for a long time in deep distress and vowed that if God gave her a son she would 'give him to the Lord all the days of his life'. In due course Samuel was born and, when he was still a child, Hannah kept her promise. She brought him to the shrine at Shiloh to serve the Lord there. [*Ref.* 1 Samuel 1.]

Hanukkah *See* TEMPLE

Haran A city in northern Mesopotamia associated with the stories of Abraham, Isaac, Jacob and their kinsfolk. Haran was a centre of nomadic trade and a place of moon-god worship in Semitic times. Hebrew tradition tells how it was from Haran that Abraham set out at the call of God to become the father of a great nation. Isaac's wife Rebekah and Jacob's wives Leah and Rachel came from near Haran, thus maintaining the patriarchal connection with their original homeland in Mesopotamia.

The name Haran is also given to a brother of Abraham and father of Lot. [*Refs.* Genesis 11: 31-2; 12: 4, 24, 28-9.]

Heave Offering Literally it means an offering which was 'heaved' or 'lifted up'. The sacrificial gift from the vineyard and especially the animals brought to the shrine or temple were symbolically offered to God by being 'lifted up'. The heave offering was eaten by the priests as part of their share in these holy offerings. [*Refs.* Exodus 29: 20-8. Leviticus 7: 34. Numbers 18: 11.]

Heaven A general name for the wide sky above the earth where the sun shines by day and moon and stars by night, across which the winds blow and the clouds move. Poetic biblical descriptions of heaven use the terms 'firmament', 'a tent spread to dwell in', 'the storehouse of the rain, hail and snow, from which fire flashes and the thunder sounds forth', 'the abode of the angels'. In all lands and literature heaven is also spoken of as the dwelling-place of the unseen, almighty, ever-present God or gods.

One sense of the name occurs in the opening words of the Bible: 'In the beginning God created the heavens and the earth' (Genesis 1: 1). Solomon's prayer suggests the other sense of the mystery of God's omnipresence.

'Behold, heaven and the highest heaven cannot contain thee' (1 Kings 8: 27). The ancient world came to think of a number of heavens, one beyond the other. God's throne was set in the highest heaven on all, yet no heaven of heavens could ever contain him.

Jewish tradition forbade the direct naming of the Almighty, so the word heaven sometimes stands for the person of God. Thus in the N.T. the phrase 'the kingdom of heaven' is used by Matthew as a reverent substitute for 'the kingdom of God'. For the most vivid, colourful and materialistic description of the heaven of apocalyptic vision nothing can match the final book of the Bible, the Revelation to John. [*Refs.* Genesis 1: 1, 8; 7: 11. Joshua 2: 11. 1 Kings 8: 22-30. Job 38: 22*f*. Psalm 2: 4; 11: 4; 14: 2; 104: 2. Isaiah 40: 22. Jeremiah 23: 24. Matthew 3: 2; 5: 3, 10. Revelation 12; 15; 21: 1.]

Hebrew The name sometimes given to the men and women of Israel in the early stories of their race, as, for example, in the accounts of Abraham, Joseph and Moses. The racial origins of the Hebrews are obscure, but they belonged to the wandering Semitic tribes who came out of Arabia and spread throughout the Fertile Crescent. [*Refs.* Genesis 14: 13; 39: 14, 17. Exodus 1: 15-16; 2: 6. John 19: 20. 2 Corinthians 11: 22.]

Also the Semitic language spoken by the Hebrews and in which most of the O.T. was originally written. The Hebrew language began to be replaced by Aramaic after the return from the Exile. In N.T. times the Jews of Palestine spoke Aramaic or Greek, though the sacred Scriptures were still read in the original tongue in the synagogues. A translation in Aramaic was usually given so that the common people could understand. The text of the O.T. has come down to us in Hebrew except for a few late passages.

Hebrews, The Letter to the In older versions of the Bible, such as the familiar A.V. of 1611, this N.T. book is attributed to Paul. From early times, however, it has been generally agreed that it was not written by Paul, is not addressed especially to Hebrews, and is not in the form of a letter. The question of authorship has evoked a variety of guesses: Barnabas, Priscilla, Apollos, Luke, Silas are only some of the names suggested. The work has none of the usual features of a letter except, perhaps, in the greetings at the close. It is rather in the form of a sermon, addressed to Christians threatened by persecution. No one knows who the 'Hebrews' were, but they are not to be thought of as Jews. Rather they were 'the new Israel of God', and as such might be found in any of the great cities of the Mediterranean world. A hint at 13: 24, as well as the continual mention of oppression, suggests that the destination of the book may be Rome, the capital of the Empire. The writer was apparently a second or third generation Christian (2: 3), one who knew the Greek language well and was familiar with Greek thought. This would suggest that the book may have been written in Alexandria in Egypt which, both before and after the downfall of Jerusalem, was the main centre of the Greek-speaking Jewish population and culture outside Palestine.

The author uses a great deal of O.T. imagery to encourage his oppressed readers to be pilgrims in the way of faith. Perhaps the most characteristic, as well as the best-known passage in this difficult book, is the roll-call of men of faith from Abel onwards who have endured every affliction and remained steadfast. They are given as examples to the reader, who, inspired by such martyr witnesses, is to persevere, 'looking to Jesus the pioneer and perfecter of our faith, who for the joy that was set before him endured the cross, despising the shame, and is seated at the right hand of the throne of God' (12: 2). A title for the whole book might well be 'The Christian Pilgrim's Progress'. The other main theme is also closely associated with the 'pilgrim' idea, namely the Tabernacle or sacred tent in the days of Israel's wanderings in the desert. The ideal figure is the pilgrim, his shrine is the tent. An outline of the contents is:

(a) Hebrews 1: 1-4: A clear statement that, although God revealed himself 'in many and various ways' to our fathers by the prophets, his final revelation is in his Son, who 'reflects the glory of God and bears the very stamp of his nature' .

(b) Hebrews 1: 5 to 4: 13: A passage full of o.t. quotation and imagery to reinforce his opening argument that the Son is 'the heir of all things'. Jewish-Christian readers and hearers would be reminded of the long heritage of their faith from Abraham, fulfilled in Jesus.

(c) Hebrews 4: 14 to 6: 20: The writer applies the title 'a great high priest' to Jesus, and deals with the choice, work and duties of the high priest. Christ is one 'who in every respect has been tempted as we are, yet without sinning' and who can, like the high priest, enter into the inmost shrine of God as a forerunner on our behalf.

(d) Hebrews 7: 1 to 10: 18: A full and detailed account of the work of Christ in terms of the high priesthood: 'He has no need, like those high priests, to offer sacrifices daily, first for his own sins and then for those of the people; he did this once and for all when he offered up himself.' A careful description of the liturgy of the Tabernacle in the wilderness follows, familiar and meaningful to Jewish-Christian readers, as is the mention of the 'first covenant' and 'the new covenant'.

(e) Hebrews 10: 19-39: The reader is urged to be faithful 'since we have confidence to enter the sanctuary by the blood of Jesus'.

(f) Hebrews 11: 1 to 13: 21. The roll-call of the faithful. 'Faith is assurance of things hoped for.' The faithful believers 'desire a better country, that is, a heavenly one'. Many examples are given from Hebrew history, both famous and humble, of a great cloud of witnesses. The perfect pioneer of all is Jesus. The readers are urged to endure, as sons of God the father. A code of Christian ethics is set forth: compassionate concern for strangers, for those in prison, for the ill-treated. Marriage is to be upheld, love of money is condemned, obedience to leaders is enjoined, faithfulness to Christ comes before all. The writer ends with an ascription of praise.

(g) Hebrews 13: 22-5: A brief personal message and greeting, finally the blessing.

Hebron A very ancient city of Canaan often mentioned in early O.T. history. Hebron lay in a well-watered valley in the hills about nineteen miles south-west of Jerusalem. It appears in the stories of Abraham, who camped there and built an altar to the Lord. When Sarah died at Hebron, Abraham bought a cave in which to bury her there. The cave of Machpelah became a hallowed burial place in Hebrew tradition for there also were buried Abraham, Isaac and Rebekah, Jacob and Leah. In later Israelite times Hebron was one of the cities of refuge. It was also David's first capital, the place where the men of Judah anointed him as their king, and where most of his family was born. At Hebron, his birthplace, Absalom raised his rebellion against David his father and proclaimed himself king. [*Refs.* Genesis 13: 18; 23: 2, 19; 49: 31; 50: 13. Joshua 20: 7. 2 Samuel 2: 1, 11; 3: 2-5; 5: 1-5; 15: 7-12.]

Hell The place of the dead or abode of departed spirits. In ancient Hebrew thought it was believed that the dead went to an underworld of shadows and misery. The grave, as it were, was the gateway to wretchedness. The Hebrew term was Sheol and its Greek equivalent Hades. Another name was 'the pit' or 'the bottomless pit'. Hell was not only the place to which all mortals must go at the last, it was also utterly cut off from God: 'My life draws near to Sheol. I am reckoned among those who go down to the pit; I am a man who has no strength, like one forsaken among the dead, like the slain that lie in the grave, like those whom thou dost remember no more, for they are cut off from thy hand' (Psalm 88: 3-5). Yet in this belief the Book of Psalms can contradict itself, for: 'If I ascend to heaven, thou art there! If I make my bed in Sheol, thou art there!' (Psalm 139: 8).

By N.T. times hell was more specifically the place for the wicked after death, as Paradise was the abode of the righteous. The symbolism of fire of judgment connected with hell was no doubt suggested by Gehenna, which was Jerusalem's rubbish-dump in the valley of Hinnom, a place of continual flames and destruction. [*Refs.* 2 Samuel 22: 6. Psalm 116: 3. Isaiah 14: 15; 38: 18. Matthew 5: 22. Luke 16: 23. Revelation 1: 18; 20: 13-14.] *See also*: HINNOM

Hermon A range of mountains, part of the Anti-Lebanon, more than 9,000 feet above sea level at its highest point and covered with snow the whole year round. Hermon was regarded as the northern boundary of the homeland of ancient Israel. The Jordan rises at its foot and gathers its waters from the melting snows of the mountain peaks. Hermon is mentioned in Hebrew psalms and poetry for its majesty and beauty. In the N.T. it may have been the 'high mountain' which was the scene of Jesus' Transfiguration. [*Ref.* Deuteronomy 3: 8. Joshua 12: 1. Psalm 89: 12; 133: 3.]

Herod The name of a large and much inter-married line of kings, governors and tetrarchs who ruled over parts of Palestine for a hundred and fifty years. The Herod family were Idumaean in origin, not Jewish, although they claimed to adopt that faith by circumcision and the observance of Jewish religious customs. The whole dynasty, male and female alike, were renowned for cruelty, lust and extravagance, and they were hated by the Jewish people. The Herods of the N.T. were (1) Herod the Great. He was helped to power by the Romans at a time of appalling slaughter of the stubborn Jews of Jerusalem, and was allowed to call himself 'king'. Herod the Great ruled over the Jews from 37 to 4 B.C. and was the king mentioned in the birth stories of Jesus in the Gospels of Matthew and Luke. Herod was strong in conquest and in rule, and he tried to seek the favour of his subjects by planning the restoration of the Temple, a magnificent building of Greek design. To pay for it the Jews were most harshly taxed. The Temple was begun about 20 B.C. but it was not completed until after the time of Jesus, only a few years before it was destroyed by the Romans in the downfall of Jerusalem. Herod the Great had ten wives and his family life was made dramatic by intrigue and murder. He had a passion for building—theatres, sports grounds and an ornate palace as well as the Temple and the port of Caesarea which he named in honour of Augustus Caesar who had set him in his seat of power. It was said of Herod the Great that he 'stole along to his throne like a fox, he ruled like a tiger and died like a dog'. It was Gentile flatterers who named him 'the Great'. His Jewish subjects thought of him as 'the Edomite slave'. Josephus, the Jewish historian, calls this Herod 'the most barbarous tyrant who ever sat on a throne'. [*Refs.* Matthew 2: 1*f*. Luke 1: 5.] (2) Herod Antipas, tetrarch of Galilee and Peraea in the time of Jesus, ruled from 4 B.C. to A.D. 39. He was the son of Herod the Great and a Samaritan woman, and therefore no true Jew. Antipas is mentioned a number of times in the Gospels. This is the Herod whom Jesus called 'that fox'. He was a son of his father in treachery, cruelty, lust and greed. His divorce and subsequent marriage to Herodias, who was not only his niece but also the former wife of his half-brother, infuriated the Jews and, according to the Gospels, brought a rebuke from John the Baptist. It was Herod Antipas who had John put to death. Luke tells how Jesus, under arrest, was sent by Pilate to Herod for questioning because he was a Galilean. The wily Herod mocked Jesus and sent him back to Pilate for final sentence. Like his father, Antipas had a craze for building. One of his towns was Tiberias on the Sea of Galilee, built in honour of Tiberius Caesar, the Roman emperor of his day. Eventually Herod Antipas was banished to Gaul by the Romans in A.D. 39. [*Refs.* Matthew 14: 1*f*. Mark 6: 14*f*; 8: 15. Luke 3: 1,19; 9: 7, 9; 13: 31; 23 7*f*.] (3) Herod Archelaus, son of Herod the Great and ethnarch ('leader of the people') of Judea, Samaria and Idumaea from 4 B.C. to A.D. 6. He was the brother of Herod

Antipas. Archelaus was as notorious for cruelty as his father before him. For once, the Jews and the Samaritans united to complain to the emperor about him. Archelaus was removed from power and exiled, and a Roman governor or procurator was put in his place to supply rule over Judea. [*Ref.* Matthew 2: 22.] (4) Herod, son of Herod the Great and half-brother of Herod Antipas. He is mentioned only in passing in the Gospels in connection with his marriage to Herodias. [*Refs.* Matthew 14: 3. Mark 6: 17. Luke 3: 19.] (5) Herod Philip, son of Herod the Great and half-brother of Herod Antipas. He was tetrarch of Ituraea and Trachonitis. Like his father before him, Philip had a craze for building. He rebuilt Caesarea Philippi which he named in honour of 'the Caesar of Philip', that is, the emperor Tiberius. [*Ref. Luke* 3: 1.] (6) Herod Agrippa I, grandson of Herod the Great. He is named in the Acts of the Apostles as a persecutor of the early Church. He killed James the brother of John 'with the sword', and had Peter arrested. Under the authority of Rome, he ruled over territory in Palestine almost as wide as the kingdom of his grandfather. The same chapter in Acts tells of his horrible death. [*Ref.* Acts 12: 1*f.*] (7) Herod Agrippa II, son of the above and great-grandson of Herod the Great. Paul was brought before him at Caesarea to be questioned in the presence of Festus the governor. Agrippa II was the last ruling member of the Herod dynasty. [*Refs.* Acts 25: 13 to 26: 32.]

Herodians A political party of leading Jews who supported Herod Antipas, the ruler of Galilee from 4 B.C. to A.D. 39. They joined with the Phari in their plots to destroy Jesus. [*Refs.* Matthew 22: 16. Mark 3: 6; 12: 13.]

Herodias The wife, first of Philip the son of Herod the Great, then of his brother, Herod Antipas of Galilee. She was herself a granddaughter of Herod the Great, so she married first one uncle then another. Herodias was offended by John the Baptist's severe reproof of her morals. Her daughter Salome danced before Herod Antipas and pleased the king so much that he offered her any gift she might ask. Prompted by her mother, she asked for the head of John the Baptist. [*Refs.* Matthew 14: 3-11. Mark 6: 17-28.]

Hezekiah King of Judah who reigned 716-687 B.C. He was the
son of Ahaz, who was regarded by the Bible writers as an evil
king because he submitted to the Assyrians and indulged in
heathen practices. Hezekiah came to the throne at the age of
twenty-five and he reigned twenty-nine years in Jerusalem. Unlike his father, he is mentioned with approval: 'he did what was
right in the eyes of the Lord, according to all that David his
father had done'. Hezekiah destroyed the symbols of heathen
worship in Jerusalem, and this earned him the highest praise
of the historian of his times: 'he trusted in the Lord the God of
Israel; so that there was none like him among all the kings of
Judah after him, nor among those who were before him.' Apparently he was able to resist the power of Assyria for a time.
Then Sennacherib, king of Assyria, laid low the fortified cities
of Judah and besieged the capital, Jerusalem. Hezekiah had to
pay a heavy tribute of gold and silver. Under the advice of Isaiah
the prophet, however, Hezekiah resisted Assyria and prayed to
the Lord God of Israel. Mysteriously, disease broke out in the
Assyrian camp and destroyed thousands of their men, so the
siege was lifted and the remnants of the Assyrian army departed.
Thus Jerusalem was saved. The event is graphically described
in 2 Kings 18-20 and in a parallel passage in Isaiah 36-9.
  King Hezekiah was also famous in Jewish history for the
conduit which his engineers made to bring water by tunnel
into the city of Jerusalem. His son was Manasseh, of evil fame.
[*Refs.* 2 Kings 16: 20; 18: 1 to 20: 21. 2 Chronicles 29-32. Isaiah
36-9.] *See also*: SILOAM, ZEPHENIAH

High Priest The high priest was the chief representative of the
Jewish people before God and Man. Tradition declared that
Aaron, the brother of Moses, was the first of the high priests and
that each succeeding high priest should be of his line. The written law shows that the high priest was set apart from all ordinary
men and from other priests by his clothing, his duties, and his
whole way of life. He wore 'a breastpiece, an ephod, a robe, a coat
of chequer work, a turban and a girdle' of the finest linen, and
'gold, blue, purple and scarlet stuff'. The breastplate was adorned

with precious stones with the names of the twelve tribes of Israel engraved on them. The robe had alternate pomegranates and bells around its skirt. Fastened to the front of the turban was a plate of pure gold with the words: 'Holy to the Lord'. The high priest was to observe strict rules of purity. He must not let his hair hang loose, or rend his clothes, nor was he to go near any dead body. The high priest alone might go into the most sacred and awesome part of the Temple, the inmost shrine or 'holy of holies'. He went there on one day of the year, the Day of Atonement, to make offering for the priests and for the whole people.

Although the term 'high priest' appears in books such as Exodus and Leviticus which refer back to the time of Moses, it is unlikely that the title was in fact used before the Exile. After the return to Jerusalem, however, the high priest was regarded as the political as well as the religious head of the Jewish nation. Whereas once a king had ruled over them, the 'anointed one' was now the high priest. In the two centuries before Christ there were frequent changes in the office of high priest, and they were no longer of the line of Aaron. They were put in office as political appointments by conquerors of Palestine such as the Romans, and they exercised considerable worldly power by intriguing with their overlords. Thus the high priests of the N.T., Annas and Caiaphas, are mentioned for their political power and expediency rather than for their holiness and purity of life. [*Refs.* Exodus 28: 1-39; 29; 39: 1-31. Leviticus 8: 6-13; 16: 2-5 29-34; 21: 10-24. Matthew 26: 3-4, 57, 62-5. Mark 14: 53-64 Luke 3: 2; 22: 54. John 11: 49-53; 18: 13*f*. Acts 4: 6; 5 17*f*.; 9: 1; 23: 2*f*.] *See also*: PRIEST; ERHOD; TEMPLE

Hilkiah The high priest of the Temple in the time of King Josiah of Judah. He found the book of the Law in the Temple and brought it to the king who read it and began the reformation of religion throughout the land. [*Ref.* 2 Kings 22: 8-13.]

Hinnom A valley on the west and south of Jerusalem. The Greek name is Gehenna. The name has evil associations in the Bible because the valley was the scene of the sacrifice of children to Molech in O.T. times. Jeremiah and others cried out against the heathen custom. Later the valley became a rubbish dump, continually on fire. The filth and flames and foul smoke suggested the picture of punishment for wickedness which the word *hell* brings to mind. [*Refs*. 2 Kings 23: 10. 2 Chronicles 28: 3; 33: 6. Jeremiah 7: 30-1 32: 35.]

Hiram The name of a line of kings of Tyre, the Phoenician port on the northern coast of Palestine. The most famous King Hiram was a friend and ally of King David and supplied him with carpenters and masons and timber to build his palace in Jerusalem. In the time of Solomon, Hiram continued the contract for cedar and cypress of Lebanon in exchange for quantities of wheat and oil every year and twenty towns in the land of Galilee He also sent skilled workmen and an architect (also named Hiram) to build the Temple and palace, as well as men who were familiar with the sea to man Solomon's fleet of trading ships. [*Refs*. 2 Samuel 5: 11. 1 Kings 5: 1; 9: 11. 1 Chronicles 14: 1.]

Hittites A non-Semitic people frequently mentioned early in the Bible as inhabitants of Canaan and encountered by the Hebrews in their conquest of the promised land. Modern excavation has revealed that the Hittites once possessed a wide and powerful empire centred on Asia Minor. There is evidence that the Hittites spread east to plunder Babylon and south-east into Canaan to do battle with Egyptian armies. Biblical Hittites are mentioned as inhabitants of Canaan in the time of Abraham, who bought a field and a cave from them as a burying-place for his wife Sarah. A famous tale of King David tells of his sin against Uriah the Hittite when he took Uriah's wife, Bathsheba. Solomon's many wives included Hittite women. Solomon also traded horses from the Hittites of Asia Minor for chariots which he imported from Egypt. The influence of the Hittites on the Hebrew settlers in Canaan was such that the prophet Ezekiel referred to the mixed blood of the people of Jerusalem thus: 'Your father was an Amorite, and your mother a Hittite.' [*Refs*. Genesis 15: 20; 23; 3-20. Exodus 13: 5. Joshua 1: 4. Judges 3: 5. 2 Samuel 11: 2-27. 1 Kings 10: 28-9; 11: 1. Ezekiel 16: 3, 45.]

Hivites The Hivites were a tribe in Canaan before the Hebrew invasion and are frequently mentioned in Bible lists as enemies to be overcome. [*Refs.* Genesis 34: 2. Exodus 3: 8, 17. Deuteronomy 7: 1. Joshua 3: 10; 9: 1; 11: 19. 2 Samuel 24: 7. 1 Kings 9: 20.]

Horeb *See* SINAI

Horns of the Altar The horns of the altar mentioned frequently in the O.T. were projections at the corners of the altar which was used for burnt offerings in the Tabernacle, both in the wilderness and later in the Temple in Jerusalem. Part of the rite of animal sacrifice was to put the blood on the horns of the altar. The blood of beasts and of men, it must be remembered, was sacred according to Hebrew thought. The original purpose of the horns is unknown, but they came to symbolize refuge for murderers fleeing from retribution who 'took hold of the horns of the altar' and were not to be touched until they came to proper trial. [*Refs.* Exodus 29: 12; 30: 10; 38: 2. Leviticus 4: 7; 8: 15; 16: 18. 1 Kings 1: 50; 2: 28.]

Hosea Not much is known of Hosea beyond the book which bears his name. He was a prophet in the northern kingdom of Israel in the second half of the eighth century B.C., during the reign of Jereboam II. [*Ref.* Hosea 1: 1.]

Hosea, The Book of Hosea was a prophet of Israel during the second half of the eighth century B.C., at a time of turmoil in the northern kingdom. The book is one of the 'Latter Prophets' of the Hebrew Scriptures and is the first of the twelve minor prophets of the O.T. The general theme of the book is a warning of the judgment of God on a people who have forsaken his covenant and law: 'they sow the wind, and they shall reap the whirlwind' (8: 7). At the same time there runs all through the work the yearning love of God for his wayward children: 'It was I who taught Ephraim to walk, I took them up in my arms' (11: 3).

Chapters 1-3 tell of Hosea's tragic marriage to Gomer who bore him three children and then left him to go after her lovers. At last Hosea brought her back and installed her again as his wife, faithless though she had been. These chapters may be historical or they may be an allegory. There is no doubt that they provide a picture of God's faithful dealings with faithless Israel. The whole book is full of images of the most tender human relationships, husband and wife, father and child, spoiled by wilfulness and sin and restored by unwearying compassion and love. There is nothing so tender in the whole of the O.T. But there is no suggestion that forgiveness and restoration are easy. Love redeems, but it suffers. To put it in historical terms, Israel's Baal worship and idolatry through many a year is seen by Hosea as a betrayal of the covenant which will bring about her downfall as a nation. Beyond the day of doom, however, the prophet is aware of God's steadfast love which will somehow bring healing to his people.

The short oracles which make up the book of Hosea are rich in country metaphors. The poet-prophet's imagery takes in the beasts of the field, the birds of the air, the creeping things of the ground, the fish of the sea. Lion and dove, wild ass, heifer and lamb, leopard and bear, all are mentioned, as well as the work of the shepherd and of the farmer—seed-time, ploughing, harrowing, reaping, threshing. The early mist of morning, the dew on the grass, smoke rising in the air, grapes and figs, the vine on the hillside, weeds in the furrows, reeds and thorns and thistles, the parching east wind, the clouds in the sky, all bring the countryside vividly before us.

Hosanna A Hebrew word which means 'Save, we pray thee!' It occurs as a cry of greeting in the Gospels on the occasion of Jesus' entry into Jerusalem on the back of a donkey. Probably the Gospel writers had in mind the words of Psalm 118: 25*f* where Hosanna occurs in the Hebrew text. The cry was associated with the waving of green branches at the Feast of Tabernacles, when the words of Psalm 118 were sung. Indeed, the name Hosannas was given to the actual 'branches of palm trees, and boughs of leafy trees, and willows of the brook'. [*Refs.* Leviticus 23: 40. Matthew 21: 9. Mark 11: 9, 10. John 12: 13.]

I

Iconium A city in the central plain of Asia Minor visited by Paul on his first and second missionary journeys. A great many people there, Jews and Greeks, became believers in Jesus. But others drove Paul and Barnabas out of the place, pursued the apostles to Lystra, and stirred up the people there to stone Paul. Nothing daunted, Paul later returned to Iconium and encouraged the Christians there to stand fast in their faith in spite of persecution. [*Refs*. Acts 13: 51; 14: 1-6, 19-23; 16: 2. 11.]

Idumea *See* EDOM

Immanuel *See* EMMANUEL

Isaac Son of Abraham, born to Sarah in her old age. According to the patriarchal stories Abraham did not wish his son and heir to marry a woman of Canaan, so he sent his steward to Mesopotamia to seek a wife for Isaac from among their own people. Thus Rebekah came to Canaan to become Isaac's wife and mother of Esau and Jacob. A number of the Isaac stories in Genesis are a duplication of the Abraham legends. [*Refs*. Genesis 17: 19; 21: 3; 24: 4. Exodus 3: 6.] *See also*: ABRAHAM

Iscariot The name applied to Judas the traitor, disciple of Jesus, probably means 'the man from Kerioth' but the place is now unknown. Judas was perhaps the only one among the disciples who did not belong to Galilee. [*Refs*. Matthew 10: 4. Mark 3: 19. Luke 6: 16.]

Isaiah Isaiah, the son of Amoz and sometimes called 'First Isaiah' or 'Isaiah of Jerusalem', was a prophet of the eighth century B.C.

whose oracles are contained in the book named after him, chapters 1-39. He lived through the reigns of Uzziah, Jotham, Ahaz and Hezekiah, the kings of Judah. From his prophecies we may judge that he was of the royal circle in Jerusalem, familiar with the politics of the court and of the Temple, and a citizen of some importance. But it is as a prophet that he is supreme. He advised King Hezekiah to stand firm against the threat of Sennacherib of Assyria. Almost all the oracles of Isaiah are in poetic form, and they deal with the corruption of the times and the oppression of the poor as well as with the hope of an ideal ruler who is to come, a son of David, a Prince of Peace. [*Refs.* 2 Kings 29: 2*f*. Isaiah 1: 1; 2: 1; 37: 2.] *See also*: HEZEKIAH

Isaiah, The Book of In Hebrew Scriptures Isaiah is the first book of the 'Latter Prophets'. It is the longest among the prophetic books of the O.T. and certainly one of the greatest. The first thing to note is that its sixty-six chapters belong to three quite different periods of Israel's history and are by different writers. Only the first part, chapters 1-39, is connected with the prophet we know as Isaiah of Jerusalem. The rest comes from a much later date.

Isaiah 1-39: This work belongs mostly to the second half of the eighth century B.C. and is associated with the prophet Isaiah of Jerusalem who lived and spoke for more than forty years through the reigns of Uzziah (Azariah), Jotham, Ahaz and Hezekiah, kings of Judah. It is a mixture of prose and poetry, containing prophetic oracles as well as some autobiographical and historical material. Oracles are inspired utterances, set down here in poetic form, and often introduced by such words as 'The Lord said' or 'Hear the word of the Lord'.

The background of events is the time of the great advance of the all-conquering Assyrians and intrigue among the smaller nations such as Israel and Judah which were threatened by the imperial power. Isaiah the prophet was a man of the Jerusalem court and advised the king in the name of God. His words were faithfully preserved by a circle of disciples, probably learned by heart at first and constantly repeated and set down in writing some time later. There is evidence in this collection of the words of Isaiah of later material which has been added by editors to the utterances of the Judah. Here is a brief outline of these chapters:

(a) Isaiah 1-5: Oracles addressed to Judah and Jerusalem warning the people against being unfaithful to the Lord their God. Note especially the parable of the vineyard, a ballad song found in 5: 1-7.

(b) Isaiah 6: An autobiographical fragment about the young prophet's vision in the Temple at Jerusalem in the year that King Uzziah died.

(c) Isaiah 7-12: Isaiah's message to King Ahaz about his foreign policy towards Syria and Israel. Oracles about Assyria and about the hope of an ideal leader of God's people. Note the passages which are often read at Christmas time: 9: 2-7 and 11: 1-9.

(d) Isaiah 12-23: Prophecies about foreign nations. This collection of poems belongs to a different period.

(e) Isaiah 24-7: These chapters belong to a much later age than Isaiah of Jerusalem, long after the Exile.

(f) Isaiah 28-35: More oracles about Jerusalem, warning the leaders of the city about their blindness and hypocrisy. They are 'rebellious children' in their political plotting, forgetting to keep their trust in the Lord. Chapter 32: 1-5 is a Messianic poem about the ideal king, and the famous poem of the return to Jerusalem in chapter 35 belongs to some time after the Exile.

(g) Isaiah 36-9: These chapters form an historical appendix mainly in prose, telling of the unsuccessful siege of Jerusalem by Sennacherib, king of Assyria in the days of Hezekiah of Judah. It is much the same as the narrative in 2 Kings 18: 13 to 20: 19.

The theme of the special note in the message of Isaiah of Jerusalem is that God is the Lord of all history and of all peoples. He cries out for justice and righteousness among men. In several passages the early church thought of Isaiah as an ancient witness to the coming of Christ.

Isaiah 40-55: These chapters come from a time more than 150 years after Isaiah of Jerusalem. The author is unknown, but because his writings were put together in one scroll of Hebrew Scripture with the work of the earlier prophet, he is usually known as Second Isaiah, or Deutero-Isaiah, or simply as Isaiah of Babylon. The background of the poems is the time of Exile in Babylon. Jerusalem is in ruins, the Temple has been destroyed, the Jewish people are captives in an alien land. But this prophet of the Exile proclaims their coming deliverance. God will bring about a second Exodus even more wonderful than the first. Remarkably, he will do it by the hand of Cyrus, the Persian emperor who is to be the 'shepherd' of Israel, the 'anointed servant' of God's purpose to deliver his people. In poem after poem the prophet declares the sovereignty of Israel's God. He alone is Creator of the ends of the earth and all-powerful. Beside him the idols of Babylon are no gods at all, simply bits of wood and metal and clay which men have shaped for themselves. God the Redeemer will tenderly bring his own people homeward to Jerusalem: 'He will feed his flock like a shepherd, he will gather the lambs in his arms, he will carry them in his bosom, and gently lead those that are with young.' All the ends of the earth will see it, and will marvel. Such is the message of these passages which are among the most splendid in the whole of the o.t. The spirit of hope and joy in deliverance has been caught and expressed in Handel's Messiah.

Embedded in these chapters are four poems known as the Servant Songs: Isaiah 42: 1-4; 49: 1-6; 50: 4-9; 52: 13 to 53: 12. They are markedly different in theme, for they speak of suffering and sorrow. No one can tell who the Servant was meant to be. Since the words are in the past tense it might seem that the writer is thinking of an historical figure who suffered greatly among his people—the prophet Jeremiah, for instance. Others have thought that the Servant portrays an idealized Israel or a remnant of the nation made pure by suffering. The Christian interpretation has been to see in these mysterious passages a foretelling of the life and work of Jesus, particularly his passion and death. Such a meaning cannot be taken too literally, however. It would be more appropriate to say that Jesus fulfilled the ideas depicted in the Servant Songs and found his vocation in vicarious suffering.

Isaiah 56-66: These chapters are usually called Third Isaiah or Trito-Isaiah. They would appear to be by yet another hand than the earlier poems of chapters 40-55. The background is different once again. The Jewish people have returned to Jerusalem from the land of Exile but they are enduring many difficulties, particularly at the hands of hostile foreigners, and the Temple has not yet been restored. It is thought that these poems are the work of a disciple, or a group of disciples, of Second Isaiah. There is some concern about details of worship, sabbath-keeping and fasting, for instance, as well as signs of a narrow nationalism. On the other hand the authentic note of joy in a renewed Zion is found in chapters 60-2, echoing the theme of Second Isaiah. But there is a spirit of disillusionment in the air. The glory of the Lord has not been revealed. We may note that when Jesus spoke in the synagogue in Nazareth he read from Isaiah 61: 1-3 and announced that passage as the charter of his life's work. (*See* Luke 4: 16-21.)

Ishbosheth After the death of Saul in battle with the Philistines at Mt. Gilboa, his surviving son Ishbosheth intrigued for power. Aided by Abner, the commander of Saul's army, he set himself up as king over the tribes of Israel. Judah, however, refused allegiance and followed David. Joab, who was David's right-hand man, slew Abner in a private quarrel, leaving Ishbosheth greatly weakened. Two of his own raiding captains slew him while he lay asleep in bed at the hour of the noonday siesta and carried the head of Ishbosheth to David, hoping, no doubt, for his favour. David, however, expressed horror that they had 'slain a righteous man in his own house upon his bed', and had them put to death for their crime. The political outcome was that all the tribes of Israel swore loyalty to David as their king. [*Refs.* 2 Samuel 2: 8-11; 3: 27-30; 4: 1-12.]

Ishmael The son of Abraham and the Egyptian woman Hagar, who was Sarah's maidservant. Ishmael was born when Sarah was childless. When Sarah gave birth to Isaac, however, Abraham cast out Hagar and the boy Ishmael to be wanderers in the desert. The story is told to safeguard the true religious and racial inheritance through Isaac and his descendants.

There is a tender side to the Ishmael tales which points to God's concern for the outcast. Tradition suggests that Ishmael became the ancestor of twelve tribes of Arabia. To this day the Moslems claim him as their forefather. In Paul's Letter to the Galatians Abraham's two sons, Ishmael and Isaac, are contrasted in an allegory. [*Refs.* Genesis 16; 21; 25: 12*f*. Galatians 4: 21*f*.] *See also*: HAGAR; ISHMAELITES; KEDAR

Ishmaelites The desert traders mentioned in the story of Joseph, who travelled with a caravan of camels bearing gum, balm, and myrrh from Gilead to Egypt. Joseph's brothers sold him to the Ishmaelites for twenty shekels of silver. In another account they are called Midianites. A reference in the Book of Judges says they wore golden earrings. Hebrew traditions declared them to be the descendants of Ishmael, outcast son of Abraham and Hagar. [*Refs.* Genesis 37: 25-8. Judges 8: 24.]

Israel The name is used in several ways in the Bible: (1) It is the name given to Jacob in the story of his wrestling with a messenger of God at Peniel. Jacob, or Israel, is set down in the early narratives of the Hebrew people as the father of twelve sons from whom were descended 'the twelve tribes of Israel'. The titles 'children of Israel', 'people of Israel', or simply Israel apply to the Hebrew tribes on their Exodus journeys, and their entry and settlement in the promised land. [*Refs.* Genesis 32: 28; 46: 8*f*; 49: 2-28.] (2) Israel is also the name given to the Northern Kingdom of ten tribes which broke away after the death of Solomon. Their rebel cry was:

'What portion have we in David?
We have no inheritance in the son of Jesse.
To your tents, O Israel!
Look now to your own house, David.'

The first king of the Northern Kingdom was Jeroboam, who had led the revolt. The fortunes of Israel and Judah are thereafter recorded side by side in the books of Kings, until the downfall of Israel at the hands of the Assyrians in 721 B.C. and of Judah before Babylon in 587 B.C. [*Refs.* 1 Kings 12: 1-20. 2 Kings 17: 6, 20, 23.] (3) The title Israel is applied continually in a religious rather than a political sense to the holy nation chosen by God to be his peculiar people— 'a people holy to the Lord your God' who are chosen 'out of all the peoples that are on the face of the earth'. This is the most frequent use of the word in the Bible. [*Refs.* Exodus 19: 6. Deuteronomy 6: 4*f*; 7: 6. Psalm 14: 7. 49: 7. Luke 1: 16, 54, 68. Acts 2: 36. Galatians 6: 16.]

J

Jabbok A tributary of the Jordan flowing from the east and joining it about twenty-three miles north of the Dead Sea. The river Jabbok was regarded as a tribal boundary in O.T. times. A ford of the river was the scene of the wrestling between Jacob and a mysterious stranger, and also of his reunion with his brother Esau. [*Refs*. Genesis 32: 22. Deuteronomy 3: 16. Joshua 12: 2.]

Jabesh-Gilead A town in the hill country east of Jordan. When the Ammonites threatened to gouge out the right eyes of the men of Jabesh-Gilead and thus disgrace them, they appealed for help to Saul. In great anger Saul raised a muster of Israelite fighters and did battle with the Ammonites, destroying them. When Saul and his sons later fell in battle at Mt. Gilboa the victorious Philistines stripped them of their armour, beheaded Saul and fixed his body to the walls of a town. When the men of Jabesh-Gilead heard of it they bravely went across the Jordan by night and took the bodies of Saul and his sons back to their own town for solemn burial. David praised them for their loyalty and courage. [*Refs*. 1 Samuel 11: 1-11; 31: 11-13. 2 Samuel 2: 5-6.]

Jacob Jacob was the grandson of Abraham, the first of the patriarchs, twin-son of Isaac and his wife Rebekah, and the traditional ancestor of the children of Israel. The Jacob stories of the Book of Genesis no doubt include camp-fire tales and legendary material. Nevertheless, the portrait of Jacob they enshrine is of a real man, crafty, skilful, intelligent, self-reliant, and yet devout. Jacob as a young man is portrayed as a sheperd, 'a quiet man, dwelling in tents' and his mother's favourite. His name means 'trickster' or 'supplanter.' He deceived his brother Esau to win the coveted birthright, fled from his wrath to the ancestral land of Haran, and had a vision of God at Bethel. In Haran he found work as a sheperd with his uncle Laban and fell in love with his older sister Leah. After his return with all his household to Canaan his old age was saddened by the supposed loss of his son Joseph. The story ends with the reunion of father and son in Egypt and the settlement of Jacob and his family, their cattle and all their goods in the land of Goshen, where at last he died. Various traditions are interwoven in the stories of Jacob. One tells that the name of Israel was given to Jacob after he had wrestled all night at the ford of Jabbok with a mysterious messenger of God. The Hebrew people of the Exodus have for ever after known themselves as 'the children of Israel'. [*Refs.* Genesis 25: 26 to 50: 14.] *See also*: ANGELS

Jairus The ruler of a synagogue who begged Jesus to come and heal his only daughter, about twelve years of age, who was dying. Jesus went to the ruler's house and restored the girl. [*Refs.* Mark 5: 22-4, 35-43. Luke 8: 41-2,49-56.]

James (1) James, the Galilean fisherman, son of Zebedee and brother of John, was one of the twelve disciples who left his work to follow Jesus. His name is always mentioned with John, and Jesus gave the brothers the surname Boanerges, that is, 'sons of thunder'. Along with Peter and John, James appears to have been in the inner circle of Jesus' company, with Jesus at Simon Peter's home in Capernaum, at the house of Jairus the ruler of the synagogue, on the Mount of Transfiguration, on the road to Jerusalem, and at Gethsemane. James was put to death by Herod in the early days of the Church. [*Refs.* Matthew 10: 2. Mark 1: 19, 29; 3: 17; 5: 37; 9: 2; 10: 35, 41; 13: 33. Luke 5: 10; 6: 14; 9: 54. Acts 1: 13; 12: 2.] (2) James the brother of Jesus, who is menioned only in passing in the Gospels, but appears in the Acts of the Apostles and in Pauline writings as an important leader of the early Church. James was chairman of the council of apostles and elders which met in Jerusalem to decide whether the Gentiles had to be circumcised before they could be received into the faith. It was James who gave judgment for that council. [*Refs.* Matthew 13: 55. Mark 6: 3. Acts 12: 17; 15: 13; 21: 18. 1 Corinthians 15: 7. Galatians 1: 19; 9, 12.]

James, The Letter of This short N.T. writing begins as if it were a letter by someone called James, but is, in fact, more like a series of notes on conduct and good behaviour. It is impossible to say who wrote it, or when. There are a number of men called James in the N.T. Tradition has always mentioned James the brother of Jesus as the author. But he was put to death in A.D. 62 and, in any case, the polished Greek found here is not likely to be the work of a Galilean peasant. This letter, addressed to the Church at large, came from some time a generation later. At first sight it is not an especially Christian piece of writing based on faith in Christ crucified and risen. Rather it is a collection of homilies inspired by the teaching of the Gospels and by the kind of ethical instruction given to catechumens in the Church of the first century. The author is a Jewish-Christian writing for believers who are familiar with the Jewish moral law. Luther, who put 'faith' at the heart of his preaching, branded the letter of James 'a right strawy epistle'. Nevertheless, it has many things to say which appeal to the modern reader as aspects of 'practical Christianity'. Christian faith and works are not to be separated. This letter stresses 'works', it is true, but claims: 'I by my works will show you my faith.'

A brief outline of the contents is:

(a) James 1: 1: Introduction and greeting.

(b) James 1: 2-12: Trials are there to test your faith. 'Blessed is the man who endures trial...he will receive the crown of life.'

(c) James 1: 13-18: All good things come from God.

(d) James 1: 19-27: A group of maxims about right speaking and right doing.

(e) James 2: 1-13: Christians are to show no partiality among rich or poor.

(f) James 2: 14-26: Faith without works is dead.

(g) James 3: 1-12: Counsel to teachers: 'the tongue is a little member and boasts of great things'.

(h) James 3: 13-18: The true wisdom which comes from above, 'pure, then peaceable, gentle, open to reason, full of mercy and good fruits'.

(i) James 4: 1-12: Human passions breed strife. 'Who are you that you judge your neighbour?'

(j) James 4: 13-17: The future is all in God's hands.

(k) James 5: 1-6: Condemnation of the rich, especially the way they behave to their fellow-men.

(l) James 5: 13-20. 'Be patient, therefore, brethren, until the coming of the Lord.'

(m)James 5: 13-20. The practice of prayer among members of the Church who suffer, are sick, or fall into sin.

Javan *See* GREECE

Jebusites The original Canaanite inhabitants of Jerusalem from whom David captured the fortress and made it his capital city. [*Refs.* Exodus 3: 8. Numbers 13: 29. Judges 1: 21. 2 Samuel 5: 6-9.]

Jehoiachin The second last king of Judah and son of Jehoiakim. His name also appears as *Jeconiah*, *Jechoniah*, and *Coniah* in different versions of the O.T. Jehoiachin came to the throne on the death of his father when he was eighteen and reigned in Jerusalem only three months. The army of Nebuchadrezzar besieged Jerusalem in 597 B.C. and Jehoiachin gave himself up. He went into Exile in Babylon along with 'his mother, his servants and his princes and his palace officials', as well as mighty men of valour, craftsmen and smiths of the land of Judah. The Temple and palace treasures were carried off as booty. Strangely enough, Jehoiachin appears to have been well treated in the land of exile. We hear of him again being freed from prison in Babylon in the thirty-seventh year of his stay there. He was given a position of honour, lived at court, and ate at the royal table for the rest of his life. [*Refs*. 2 Kings 24: 8-17; 25: 27-30. Jeremiah 24: 1; 27: 20; 52: 31-4.] *See also*: ZERUBBABEL.

Jehoiada The name of several men in the O.T., the most famous being the chief priest of the Temple in Jerusalem in the time of Queen Athaliah of Judah. Jehoiada encouraged a conspiracy against the queen to save the life of the infant Joash, son of Ahaziah. When the boy was seven years old, Jehoiada had him brought secretly to the Temple under close guard. Joash was proclaimed king, anointed and crowned, and by command of Jehoiada, Athaliah the queen was taken out and slain. Jehoiada then made a covenant between the Lord and the king and the people, and he instigated a purge of the pagan Baal worship which had grown up in Jerusalem. It was written: 'And Jehoash (Joash) did what was right in the eyes of the Lord all his days, because Jehoiada the priest instructed him.' One of his works, under the guidance of Jehoiada, was to set up a chest with a hole in the lid to receive offerings of money brought to the altar of God. The money was used for the repair of the Temple. The Book of Chronicles records that Jehoiada the priest died at a great age and was buried in the city of David among the kings, 'because he had done good to Israel, and towards God and his house'. [*Refs*. 2 Kings 11: 1 to 12: 16. 2 Chronicles 23; 24: 2, 15-16.]

Jehoiakim The third last king of Judah, son of Josiah, and puppet king of the Pharaoh Neco of Egypt who put him on the throne of Jerusalem. Jehoiakim had to levy heavy taxes from his people to pay the Pharaoh in silver and gold. It was during his eleven-year reign that the prophet Jeremiah gave warning of the attack from the north in the shape of Nebuchadrezzar of Babylon. He also spoke against Jehoiakim's heathen practices. Jeremiah told Baruch his scribe to write his words of warning in a scroll and deliver it to the king. The latter, however, cut the scroll in pieces and threw them in the fire. When

Nebuchadrezzar did eventually attack Jerusalem, Jehoiakim capitulated, but later rebelled. The outcome was that raiders attacked Judah and Jehoiakim perished. According to an oracle of Jeremiah, he was dragged beyond the gates of Jerusalem and given the burial of an ass. [*Refs.* 2 Kings 23: 34-6; 24: 1-6. Jeremiah 7: 18, 30-1; 22: 18-19; 25; 26; 36: 1-26.]

Jehoram or Joram (1) The son of Ahab who succeeded his brother Ahaziah as king of Israel and who reigned for twelve years. He was the king mentioned in the cycle of Elisha stories to whom Naaman the Syrian captain came, seeking a cure for his leprosy. Joram was wounded in battle with the Syrians, and was put to death by Jehu, an Israelite army commander who was encouraged in his rebellion by the prophet Elisha. [*Refs.* 2 Kings 1: 17; 3: 1; 5: 6; 8: 28 to 9: 28.] (2) A king of Judah, son of Jehoshaphat and roughly contemporary with (1) above. They are mentioned together in 2 Kings 8: 16. Jehoram of Judah reigned eight years in Jerusalem and his wife was Athaliah, the daughter of Ahab and Jezebel, who was as evil an influence in the southern kingdom as her mother had been in Israel. According to 2 Chronicles, Jehoram died in great agony of an incurable disease of the bowels, 'and he departed with no one's regret'. [*Refs.* 1 Kings 22: 50. 2 Kings 8: 16-18. 2 Chronicles 21: 1-20.]

Jehoshaphat The name of several men in the old Testament, in particular a ninth-century B.C. king of Judah who reigned twenty-five years in Jerusalem. According to the extended account in 2 Chronicles, Jehoshaphat strongly fortified the cities of Judah, gained great wealth for himself and his kingdom, and made peace with the northern kingdom of Israel, including a marriage alliance with the royal house of Ahab. The writers note approvingly that Jehoshaphat 'sought the God of his father and walked in his commandments'. In his reign he sent priests and Levites to teach the people the law of the Lord: 'they went about through all the cities of Judah and taught among the people'. He also appointed judges throughout the land with the instruction: 'Consider what you do, for you judge not for man but for the Lord; he is with you in giving judgment.' The shorter record of 1 Kings notes that Jehoshaphat sent a fleet to Ophir for gold, but the ships were wrecked at Ezion-geber. [*Refs.* I Kings 22: 41-50. 2 Chronicles 17: 1 to 21: 1.]

Jehu An army commander of Israel in the ninth century B.C. who was anointed king by order of Elisha the prophet and told to destroy the house of Ahab. Jehu and his men drove in their chariots to the palace at Jezreel and fought against King Joram of Israel and his nephew Ahaziah of Judah. Jehu drew his bow with his full strength and shot Joram between the shoulders, killing him. His men pursued Ahaziah and killed him also. Jehu went on to put Jezebel the queen to death and then the sons of Ahab, all his great men, his close friends, and his priests. He also summoned the worshippers of Baal to a solemn assembly and slaughtered them all, destroying the house and symbols of Baal at the same time. Jehu reigned over Israel in Samaria for twenty-eight years. He is remembered proverbially as a fast or furious driver. [*Ref.* 2 Kings 9-10.]

Jephthah A mighty warrior and one of the most important of the 'judges' mentioned in the Book of Judges. His tribe recalled him from the desert to be their leader in war against the Ammonites. Jephthah's tragedy was that he made a vow to God that he would sacrifice whatever came out of the door of his house when he returned victorious from battle. When he came home triumphant it was his daughter, an only child, who came out to meet him with music and dancing. Jephthah kept his vow and offered her as a burnt-offering. [*Refs.* Judges 11: 1-11, 29-40.]

Jeremiah The book of Jeremiah gives us a good deal of personal inforrnation about this great prophet of the seventh century B.C. Jeremiah belonged to Anathoth, a town a short distance from Jerusalem, and he began to prophesy in the reign of King Josiah of Judah, about the year 626 B.C. He was probably very young at the time, if we are to judge by his own words: 'Ah, Lord God! Behold I do not know how to speak, for I am only a youth' (1: 6). All his life Jeremiah appears to have been a reluctant prophet, partly because he was by nature shy, partly because his message was one of doom for his own nation. His life was bound up with the fate of Jerusalem. His people's wounds were his wounds. He wept over Jerusalem, his grief beyond healing, his heart sick within him. Although he was called by God to stand publicly in the market-place, at the gate of the temple, in the court of the king, Jeremiah would have preferred to hide himself away: 'O that I had in the desert a wayfarer's lodging place, that I might leave my people and go away from them!' (9: 2). He had to endure threat and physical attack from the priests, prophets and people of Jerusalem; he was put in the stocks; his life was in danger from his own townsmen. Little wonder that he cursed the day he was born.

It was Jeremiah's destiny to be heard but not believed by the rulers and citizens of his own day. He proclaimed clearly and specifically that king and people would go into captivity in Babylon. Sword, famine, pestilence was the future for Jerusalem, and the city would perish in flames. The popular prophets defied Jeremiah with the words: 'No evil shall come upon you.' Jeremiah's advice to King Zedekiah, son of Josiah, was to surrender to Nebuchadrezzar of Babylon and submit to the yoke of defeat and exile. This was his word from the Lord. In God's good time, the prophet proclaimed, the people of Judah would be allowed to return to their own land and live in peace, none daring to make them afraid. Jeremiah's letter to Jews already in Exile was one of peace. They were to seek the good of the land in which they found themselves, and at last they would be brought back to Judah and given a future and a hope. As proof of his conviction, even though he was in prison in the darkest days of the city's siege, Jeremiah bought a field in his native Anathoth, looking to the future when 'houses and fields and vineyards shall again be bought in this land'.

When Jerusalem was eventually entered by the Babylonians in 587 B.C., Nebuchadrezzar gave special orders about Jeremiah: 'Take him, look after him well and do him no harm, but deal with him as he tells you' (39: 12). Eventually we find Jeremiah in Egypt in the company of other refugee Jews and, so far as we know, he died there. The Book of Jeremiah is by no means a chronological account of the prophet's life and times and words. Nevertheless, enough can be discerned from its pages to form a clear picture of the most memorable of all the prophets of Hebrew tradition.

Jeremiah, The Book of The second of the prophetic books among the 'Latter Prophets' of Hebrew Scriptures. Many people regard Jeremiah as the greatest prophet of the o.t., perhaps because we know more about the man himself than about any of the others, perhaps because he lived through the most disastrous period of Hebrew history and shared the agony of the defeat and downfall of Judah and Jerusalem. The Book of Jeremiah is a collection of prophetic oracles concerning Jerusalem, its king, its priests and prophets, magistrates and merchants, and its ordinary people. Here and there a bit of autobiography reveals what Jeremiah was doing and what he had to endure by way of rejection and punishment for his words of warning during the forty years of his prophetic work. Chapter 36: 1-32 suggests that Jeremiah dictated a great deal of his message to his secretary and disciple, the faithful Baruch. The whole book, therefore, might be described as the memoirs of Jeremiah set down by Baruch with various oracles added here and there as in an anthology of poems. We can divide the book thus:

(a) Jeremiah 1-25: The book begins with a fragment of autobiography and goes on to poetic oracles (inspired speeches) about the land of Judah and the threat of invasion from the north. Jeremiah's 'word of the Lord' is that 'out of the north evil shall break forth upon all the inhabitants of the land' (1: 14). Judah has been even more faithless than Israel, and her downfall is near. 'A lion has gone up from his thicket, a destroyer of nations has set out; he has gone up from his place to make your land a waste; your cities will be ruins without inhabitant' (4: 7).

Chapter 7 tells how Jeremiah stands at the gate of the

Temple in Jerusalem and warns the passers-by that the outward show of worship and animal sacrifice will not save them. True to the spirit of the eighth-century prophets, especially Hosea, he proclaims moral obedience in terms of justice, honesty and compassion. In poem after poem Jeremiah laments the inevitability of God's judgment. The people of Judah will not listen: 'Can the Ethiopian change his skin or the leopard his spots?' (13: 23). He attacks the tame prophets who belong to the court and who soothe the men of Jerusalem with smooth words: 'They have healed the wound of my people lightly saying "Peace, peace", when there is no peace' (6: 14). There are memorable stories with a meaning in Jeremiah's description of the potter working at his wheel (18: 1-6), the breaking of a potter's flask as a symbol of destruction (19: 1-12), the spoiling of a linen waist-cloth (13: 1-11), the baskets of good and bad figs (24: 1-10). And there is the prophecy that one day, beyond this time of doom and disaster, God will send his people a king of the house of David who will reign with justice and righteousness in the land (23: 5-0).

(b) Jeremiah 26-45: These chapters continue the account of Jeremiah's warnings to king, priests, prophets and people even at the very time of attack by Nebuchadrezzar and his Babylonian army. They tell of Jeremiah's imprisonment for his seemingly traitorous talk, and of the encounters between prophet and king. Jeremiah came to believe that the catastrophe of the Exile was not merely a divine punishment but was also the only hope for the Jewish people that they might learn the lesson of their wrongdoing and repent of it far away from the sham worship of the Temple in Jerusalem. The faithful Lord God would then forgive and save his people and bring them home to their own land. He will thus 'turn their mourning into joy' (31: 13). There will be a new convenant, no longer on tablets of stone, but written upon the heart (31: 31-4).

(c) Jeremiah 46-51: These chapters are made up of poetic oracles against foreign nations, some of them, perhaps, added to the book at a later date.

(d) Jeremiah 52: An historical appendix, identical with 2 Kings 24: 18 to 25: 30; telling of the siege; downfall and sacking of Jerusalem.

Jeremiah has been known proverbially as 'the gloomy prophet', particularly because the burden of his message is one of woe at the time of his nation's agony. But through his words that speak of doom and judgment there sounds also the steady note of hope. See especially chapters 30-3. Jeremiah takes no delight in condemnation. He is full of compassion in his identification with his fellow Jews. Perhaps he is the foremost of all the spokesmen for God of ancient times not only because of his passion and power, but also because he is the most piteous of the prophets.

Jericho An ancient city in the Jordan valley known as 'the city of palms' and frequently mentioned in the O.T. accounts of the Hebrew invasion of Canaan. Jericho lay below sea-level, about five miles west of Jordan, near where the river enters the Dead Sea. To the invading Hebrews it was a key fortress which must be overcome before they entered the hill country of Canaan. The Book of Joshua contains the legendary account of the downfall and total destruction of Jericho and its 'devotion' to God with all its inhabitants and possessions. Religious tradition states that the place was never to be rebuilt: 'Cursed before the Lord be the man that rises up and rebuilds this city, Jericho.' It was noted as one of King Ahab's crimes that in his days he allowed the rebuilding to take place, accompanied by human sacrifice. Archaeologists have revealed that Jericho is one of the oldest places of human habitation in Palestine. The site has been used for building again and again, long before and long after the coming of the Israelites under Joshua. It is associated in sacred memory with the last moments of Elijah the prophet. Zedekiah, the last king of Judah, was captured at Jericho when he fled from Jerusalem after its downfall at the hands of Nebuchadrezzar. In the N.T. Jericho is mentioned in the parable of the good Samaritan, and it was there that Jesus gave sight to Bartimaeus the blind beggar and went to stay at the house of Zacchaeus the rich tax-collector. [*Refs.* Deuteronomy 34: 3. Joshua 2; 6. 1 Kings 16: 34. 2 Kings 2: 5-18. Jeremiah 52: 8. Mark 10: 46. Luke 10: 30; 18: 35; 19: 1.]

Jeroboam (1) Jeroboam I was the son of Nebat, and overseer of forced labour in the time of Solomon, and was encouraged by the prophet Ahijah to rebel against the king. Solomon tried to kill him, but Jeroboam fled to Egypt and returned at the accession of Rehoboam to lead the people. The discontented northern tribes made him king, leaving Rehoboam with only Judah and Benjamin. Jeroboam built Shechem as his capital and set up golden calves for worship at Bethel and Dan. He also instituted pagan practices and a priesthood of his own devising in imitation of the ritual in Jerusalem. There was war between Rehoboam and Jeroboam continually, that is, between Judah and Israel. Jeroboam was for ever remembered in the O.T. records as one of the most wicked kings of all Israel's history because of his heathen worship and particularly because of the shrines at Bethel and Dan. Other kings were judged in comparision with 'Jeroboam the son of Nebat, which he made Israel to sin'. [*Refs.* 1 Kings 11: 26-40; 12: 2-33. 2 Kings 3: 3; 17: 21-3.] (2) Jeroboam II was the son of King Jehoash of Israel in the eighth century B.C. He reigned forty-one years in Samaria, the northern capital, but there is very little directly about him in the O.T. except the editor's comment that 'he did what was evil in the sight of the Lord'. In fact, Jeroboam II was a powerful and prosperous king, as we may in part discern from the prophecies of Amos and Hosea who spoke during his reign. The rich, at least, were rich, with fine houses, ornate furnishings, plenty to eat and drink, and elaborate religious festivals. Their wealth, however, was built upon oppression of the poor of the land, and it was their selfish luxury, immorality, and complete disregard of the convenant which the prophets condemned. [*Refs.* 2 Kings 14:

16, 23-9. Hosea 1: 1; 4: 1-3. Amos 1: 1; 2: 0-8; 7: 10-15; 8: 4-15.]

Jerubbaal *See* GIDEON

Jerusalem The most famous holy city in the world, held in reverence by Jews, Christians and Moslems. Jerusalem is first mentioned in the O.T. as a hill stronghold of the Jebusites. It was captured by David, who made it his capital for the whole country. The 'city of David' also became the religious capital of the tribes of Israel when David brought the Ark of the Covenant there. His son Solomon confirmed its importance by extending its area and by building a palace for himself and the Temple to house the Ark. Thus Jerusalem remained the royal and holy city throughout the reigns of successive descendants of the house of David in spite of frequent threat of attack and even siege. Its position, distant from the sea and from natural highways, with deep valleys on either side, made the walled fortress city seem impregnable and gave the Jews a false sense of security, especially when some prophets declared that the city in which the Lord delighted could never be overthrown. Its water supply, too, first by natural spring and later by the Siloam tunnel, hewn by King Hezekiah's workmen, made Jerusalem difficult to capture except by prolonged siege. Josiah, king of Judah, greatly strengthened its religious significance by destroying all local shrines and making the Temple the one place of prayer and sacrifice for all his people. Thus the city set on a hill became, and remained, a place of pilgrimage. It was the central sacred place where such prophets as Isaiah, Jeremiah, Haggai and others proclaimed their word from the lord. Its walls, towers, gates and streets were celebrated in song and poem.

Jerusalem, however, was destroyed by Nebuchadrezzar of Babylon in 587 B.C., a never-forgotten date in Hebrew history. The royal house, priests and leading citizens were led away to exile. The Temple was burned to the ground and gates and walls broken down. Later, when Cyrus allowed the Jews to return, the Temple was rebuilt on a much smaller scale, and in the time of Nehemiah the walls, towers and gates were restored. In N.T. times the Temple of which we read was the third, a building of Greek design planned and commissioned by Herod the Great. But Jerusalem was to know no abiding peace. The long drawn out agony of Roman attack culminated in the siege of Jerusalem by the soldiers of Vespasian and Titus. Starvation at last brought about the city's downfall in A.D. 70 and the Romans destroyed the place and put the Temple to the flames.

Jerusalem's story in more modern times has not been peaceful or happy. It has been fought over by Christians, Arabs and Jews. To the Jew it is still ideally the place where God has put his name, a beacon of light among the nations of men. To the Christian, Jerusalem has sacred associations because some of the events of Jesus' life occurred there and in particular because of the last dramatic days on his journey from the Mt. of Olives to the cross of Calvary. The final book of the N.T., the apocalyptic writing of the Revelation, pictures 'the holy city, new Jerusalem, coming down out of heaven from God, prepared as a bride adorned for her husband' (1: 2).

Today, a number of branches of the Christian faith have churches in Jerusalem, the most famous of which is the Church of the Holy Sepulchre. A Moslem mosque on the site of the ancient Temples is known as the Mosque of Omar or the Dome of the Rock. The Jews remember at the Wailing Wall the ancient glories of the city which in their daily prayers they refer to as 'their highest joy'. [*Refs.* Joshua 15: 8. 2 Samuel 5: 6-9; 6: 12*f*. 1 Kings 6-7. 2 Kings 23; 25: 1-9. Ezra 1: 2*f*. Nehemiah. Psalm 122; 125: 1-2; 137: 1-6. Isaiah 2: 2-3; 65: 18-19. Matthew 21: 10. Mark 10: 32*f*. Luke 2: 22*f*; 19: 28*f*; 24: 47. John 12: 12. Acts 1: 8. Revelation 21: 2.] *See also*: ZION; TEMPLE

Jesse The grandson of Ruth and Boaz, Jesse was a prosperous farmer of Bethlehem who had eight sons, the most famous of them being David. Jesse's name appears in the 'family tree' of Jesus in both Matthew and Luke. [*Refs.* 1 Samuel 16: 1; 17: 12. Isaiah 11: 1. Matthew 1: 5. Luke 3: 32.]

Jesus Jesus of Nazareth has been the central figure of the most widespread religion of the past two thousand years, yet almost nothing is known of his earthly life. We can confidently state that he lived in Palestine in the time of Herod Antipas, tetrarch of Galilee, and that he was crucified under Pontius Pilate. Beyond that, we have only the devout literature of his disciples and followers, and we see and hear Jesus only through their record. Our lack of historical information is due in part to the fact that to his disciples Jesus was not a memory but a living Lord, and when they came to set down his story they presented him not as the Jesus of past history but as the Christ of their living faith.

Two of the Gospels, Matthew and Luke, tell that Jesus was born in Bethlehem, and they set down some legendary tales of his birth and infancy. The other two, Mark and John, take up their story at the beginning of Jesus' ministry in Galilee. All four speak of him as Jesus of Nazareth. The name *Jesus* was quite common, being the Greek form of the Hebrew *Joshua*, meaning 'God is salvation'. It would appear that about the age of thirty Jesus became known as a teacher and preacher after John the Baptist had been put in prison. He gathered about him a group of disciples and their friends and relatives, though it is impossible to identify many of these with certainty, except perhaps Peter, Andrew, James and John, the Galilean fishermen. There followed a time of travel up and down Galilee where, it is claimed, Jesus attracted great crowds through his gifts of teaching and healing. His words are described as 'good news' and his deeds as 'mighty works', but the Gospel writers' way of describing them, and their religious interpretation of them, often obscure what was spoken and done. Jesus taught in the synagogues and in the open air. The common people may well have regarded him as a prophet, but the orthodox leaders of religion viewed him with increasing suspicion. One of the most remarkable things about this rabbi was that he mixed freely with men and women who were outcasts of society. A few places are mentioned in connection with one incident or another—Capernaum and Bethsaida by the Sea of Galilee, Jericho and Bethany on the road to Jerusalem. For the most part, however, we can neither make a map of his journeys nor a time-chart of events. We have to make do with 'a mountain', 'a desert place', 'a certain village', 'beside the sea', and with 'on the sabbath', 'at sundown', 'in the morning', 'after some days'.

After a time, perhaps because of official opposition to his teaching, or misunderstanding of his aims, Jesus seems to have withdrawn from public view to instruct his disciples. It is not clear how often he went up to Jerusalem, but the final journey is set down in some detail, from the entry on the back of a donkey (probably an act of prophetic symbolism) to the climax of the last supper, Gethsemane, the arrest, the hurried trial, and the Crucifixion at Calvary. Thereafter faith takes over, and he who was Jesus of Nazareth is hailed as Jesus the Christ, Lord and Saviour, Son of God. Historical fact fades away, and faith grows stronger and stronger. Thus it is impossible to put together an orderly account of the life of Jesus of Nazareth from the pages of the Gospels. It is equally impossible to deny that he was the most famous figure in the annals of recorded time. [*Refs*. The Gospels of Matthew; Mark; Luke; John.]

Jethro A shepherd-priest of the Kenites, a tribe of Midian. When Moses fled from the anger of Pharaoh after he had killed an Egyptian, he fell in with Jethro's clan and married his daughter, Zipporah. It was while he looked after Jethro's sheep that Moses saw the burning bush on Mt. Horeb and was aware of God speaking to him. Jethro is sometimes known as Reuel in the O.T. [*Refs*. Exodus 3: 1; 18: 1-12.]

Jews The word *Jew* literally means a member or descendant of the tribe of Judah. In Biblical literature it appears after the downfall of the northern kingdom of Israel, and is applied especially to the men and women of Judah who went into Exile in Babylonia. It came, however, to have a wider reference, not only to those who belonged to the southern kingdom, but to all of the Hebrew race who shared the religious faith, traditions and customs of the whole community of the children of Israel. Jews of the Dispersion were eventually scattered throughout the world, but they claimed a common bond of race and faith and looked to Jerusalem as their religious capital. Even today, without a Temple as a focal point, a Jew is a Jew by race and religion, wherever he may live. [*Refs.* 2 Kings 25: 25. Nehemiah 1: 2. Jeremiah 52: 28-30. Matthew 2: 2. Acts 2: 5. Romans 2: 28-9. Galatians 2: 14-15.] *See also*: DISPERSION

Jezebel A princess of Tyre and wife of Ahab the king of Israel, 869-850 B.C. She worshipped a Baal god and encouraged this cult in Israel, bringing hundreds of its priests and prophets from her native Tyre and ruthlessly persecuting the prophets of God. Elijah withstood her in the matter of Naboth's vineyard and in the religious contest at Mt. Carmel. In the end the house of Ahab was destroyed in Jehu's rebellion. Jezebel was flung from her high palace window and eaten by dogs. Her name remains as a synonym for female wickedness. [*Refs.* 1 Kings 16: 31; 18: 4, 19; 19: 1-2; 21: 1-25. 2 Kings 9: 30-7] *See also*: AHAB; NABOTH; ATHALIAH

Jezreel A fertile plain stretching from north of Mt. Carmel to the river Jordan, frequently mentioned in the O.T. It was also known by its Greek name Esdraelon. The hill fortress of Megiddo guarded a pass which led into the plain and overlooked one of the main highways of the middle east, from Egypt to Mesopotamia. Since roads in ancient times were used mainly for trade or war, we find that some of the most famous expeditions and battles in the history of Palestine took place where the pass of Megiddo led into the plain of Jezreel. It was by the River Kishon in Jezreel that Barak, inspired by Deborah, defeated the forces of Sisera. At Mt. Gilboa, on the edge of Jezreel, Saul and his sons perished in battle with the Philistines. King Josiah of Judah died in battle with the Egyptian Pharaoh Neco on the plain of Jezreel.

The name is also used for a town overlooking the plain where King Ahab had a royal palace. It was here that Naboth the peasant farmer was put to death by Jezebel the queen because she plotted to seize his vineyard and give it to Ahab. At Jezreel, Jezebel herself perished at the hands of Jehu. [*Refs.* Judges 4: 4-16. 1 Samuel 31: 1-7. 1 Kings 18: 46; 21: 1-16. 2 Kings 9: 15-37; 10: 11; 23: 29.] *See also*: MEGIDDO; ARMAGEDDON

Joab Commander of David's army and mentioned continually as the king's right-hand man. It is told that he became leader among David's men because he was the first to penetrate the stronghold of Zion which was held by the Jebusites. Joab murdered Abner who had been Saul's relative and army commander, and was rebuked by David for this treachery. But all through David's rise to power Joab was at his side, and led the fight on the field against Syrians, Ammonites, and all the foes of Israel. It was Joab who sought to heal the breach between David and his rebellious son Absalom, but when Absalom conspired against his father it was Joab who eventually killed him with his own hand. In the end Joab was himself killed by command of Solomon, son of David. [*Refs.* 2 Samuel 2: 13 to 1 Kings 2: 34.] *See also*: ADONIJAH

Joash The name occurs a number of times in the O.T., the most notable being Joash, or Jehoash, son of Ahaziah and eighth king of Judah. He was hidden away for safety as an infant when his grandmother Athaliah sought to destroy the family of Ahaziah and thus wipe out the royal line of David. In his seventh year Jehoiada the priest of the Temple brought the boy Joash out before the loyal troops and the people. He put the crown upon him, anointed him, and proclaimed him king. Athaliah was slain, and Joash became king in deed as well as by proclamation and popular acclaim. One of his first acts under the influence of Jehoida was to destroy a great deal of the Baal cult of the land, the images, altars and priesthood. For this he is noted as one who 'did what was right in the eyes of the Lord all his days, because Jehoiada the priest instructed him'. During his reign of about forty years in Jerusalem, Joash encouraged the repair of the Temple by means of freewill offerings put in a chest which stood beside the altar. In the end, however, Joash had to part with gifts and gold from the Temple treasury in tribute to the king of Syria, to save Jerusalem from attack. In an uprising Joash was slain by his own men, and was buried in the city of David. [*Refs.* 2 Kings 11-12. 2 Chronicles 23-4.]

Job, The Book of The Book of Job is to be found among the Writings in Hebrew Scriptures, but it is usually mentioned as the greatest of the three Wisdom books, Job, Proverbs and Ecclesiastes. It is a long poem with a prose prologue and epilogue on the subject of suffering. The comfortable teaching of a great deal of ancient literature was that God, or the gods, blessed good people in this world and punished the wicked. But the writer of the Book of Job looks around him and sees more truly that good people often suffer misfortune for no apparent reason, and he asks why. If God is all-powerful and just, why does he send trouble on the blameless and the righteous?

The poem is in the form of a debate between Job and his three friends, Eliphaz, Bildad and Zophar, who come to comfort him when he is afflicted by the loss of his possessions, death in his family, and disease in his own body. Job's first comment on all his troubles is: 'The Lord gave, and the Lord has taken away; blessed be the name of the Lord'. Eliphaz tells him that 'man is born to trouble as the sparks fly upward', and advises him to submit to the inscrutable dealings of God. Bildad asks: 'Does God pervert justice?' and Zophar accuses Job of some iniquity which has brought misfortune upon him. Job finds no comfort in any of them: 'no doubt you are the people, and wisdom will die with you'. He is aware that all their words are non-answers, and he is roused to a fury of despair that God gives no answer either. He is aware that 'man that is born of a woman, is of few days, and full of trouble'. The poem ends with a splendid section on the power of God in the universe, and at the last Job submits in complete trust. Then, as in all good folk-tales, his fortunes are restored to him.

The poem is difficult to read, as the various parts do not hold together well. Even the portrait of Job changes here and there. The problem of suffering which wise men have pondered in every age is not the only one that confronts us here. Job is perhaps the best example in all literature of the man of disinterested integrity. In the end he submits to life as it is. There is no solution to the mystery of existence, but God is God, infinite in wisdom. Man, his creature, is mortal and finite in understanding. To know that is to understand one's relationship to the living God.

The author of the Book of Job is unknown and the date uncertain, for there is no historical detail in it to give a clue to the background of the poem. Probably it comes from the time of the Exile or later. Apart from the importance of the main theme of the poem, there are parts of it which are delightful and majestic in their description of the wonders of nature. See, for example, chapters 38-41 with lines about the whirlwind, the sea, stars of the heavens, snow, rain, ice, frost, as well as the beasts of the field and the birds of the air, the young lions, goats, the wild ass, the horse and his rider, raven, ostrich, hawk and eagle, and the crocodile in 'his double coat of mail'.

Joel The name of a number of men in the O.T., in particular the prophet who is named at the opening of the prophetic book as Joel, the son of Pethuel. Nothing else is known of him. [*Refs.* Joel 1: 1. Acts 2: 16.]

Joel, The Book of The Book of Joel is found among the 'Latter Prophets' of Hebrew Scriptures and is one of the twelve minor prophets of our old Testament. Nothing is known about the prophet Joel apart from this short book, and there is no mention of a date. The work probably comes from some time after the Exile when some of the Jewish people returned to their homeland to rebuild their devastated towns and villages and their sacred Temple in Jerusalem.

The main theme of Joel 1: 1 to 2: 17 is a disastrous plague of locusts which swarms all over the land, devouring every growing thing. 'The fields are laid waste, the ground mourns' (1: 10). Joel speaks of this calamity as a sign of the coming day of the Lord—'a day of clouds and thick darkness!' He summons his people to repentance. Then comes a passage (2: 18f) which tells of the day of God's deliverance of his people, when he will bless the land with abundant rain and fruitful crops. In those days God will pour out his spirit on young and old, and he will restore the fortunes of Judah and Jerusalem.

The passage in 2: 28-32 is quoted in Acts 2: 16-21, where the writer sees the fulfilment of the prophecy in the coming of the Spirit of God at Pentecost.

John (1) The father of Simon Peter, according to the Gospel of John. The form Jona or Jonas is used in the A.V. Nothing else is known of him. [*Refs*. John 1: 42; 21: 15-17.] (2) John the Galilean fisherman, son of Zebedee and, with his brother James, among the first chosen disciples of Jesus. The two brothers are often mentioned together, and Jesus gave them the surname or nickname of Boanerges, which means 'sons of thunder'. Along with Peter and James, John was in the 'inner circle' of the twelve, and is mentioned in company with Jesus at Simon Peter's home in Capernaum, at the house of Jairus the ruler of the synagogue, on the Mount of Transfiguration, on the road to Jerusalem, and at Gethsemane.

It may also be that this John is 'the beloved disciple' mentioned in John's Gospel at the last supper and at the cross. The same anonymous disciple is mentioned as running with Simon Peter to see the empty tomb and later in the fishing boat on the Sea of Galilee.

John the fisherman disciple appears in the list at the beginning of the Acts of the Apostles and with Peter at the Temple when the latter healed the lame man in the name of Jesus Christ. They were both arrested by the Temple authorities and put on trial before the priestly council, but released with a warning. After the martyrdom of Stephen we find John again in company with Peter in Samaria to approve the spread of the Gospel there. Thereafter John disappears from the N.T. except where Paul mentions him as a 'pillar' of the Church in Jerusalem. [*Refs*. Matthew 4: 21; 10: 2. Mark 1: 19, 29; 3: 17; 5: 37; 9: 2, 38; 10: 35, 41. Luke 5: 10; 9: 49; 22: 8. Acts 1: 13; 3: 1, 3; 4: 13; 8: 14. Galatians 2: 9.]

John the Baptist The austere prophet of the desert who appears by the Jordan at the beginning of all the Gospel accounts of the ministry of Jesus and who is described by the Gospel writers as the forerunner of the Messiah. Luke sets down some legendary material concerning his birth, relating that John was the son of the aged priest Zechariah and his equally elderly wife, Elizabeth. The appearance of an angel, other wondrous signs, and a song of thanksgiving (the Benedictus) mark the significance of the child. Luke also links Jesus and John as cousins.

John the Baptist is presented as bearing a striking resemblance to Elijah of ancient Israel. His dress and austere life are the same 'he was clothed with camel's hair, and had a leather girdle around his waist, and ate locusts and wild honey'— as was also his message of judgment and wrath to come.

Jesus names him 'a prophet...and more than a prophet...Elijah who is to come'. In short, the writers of the Synoptic Gospels and, no doubt, the early Church, saw John as Elijah come again in fulfilment of God's promise, to warn and exhort and to be a herald of the kingdom of God. John's Gospel specifically denies the connection with Elijah, but calls John the Baptist 'the voice of one crying in the wilderness'.

John's public work was to preach 'a baptism of repentance for the forgiveness of sins'. Great crowds went out to hear him, to confess, and to be baptized in the Jordan. John's message was uncompromising: 'You brood of vipers! Who warned you to flee from the wrath to come? Bear fruits that befit repentance.' Matthew, Mark and Luke all record that Jesus was baptised by John. The fourth Gospel tells of John's tribute to Jesus—'Behold, the Lamb of God, who takes away the sin of the world!'—and adds the information that John had disciples, one of whom was Andrew, Simon Peter's brother, who became a follower of Jesus. Other references to the disciples of John the Baptist are scattered throughout the N.T. He was suddenly arrested by order of Herod Antipas and confined in the frightful fortress of Machaerus, on the shore of the Dead Sea. Because of the grudge Herodias had against him John was put to death. Almost twenty-five years later, the Christian leaders Priscilla and Aquila came across a follower of John the Baptist in far-off Ephesus, an Alexandrian Jew named Apollos. Thus far and memorably had his message spread.

The accounts of John the Baptist in our Gospels are inextricably bound up with traditions of the mission and message of Jesus. It must be realized, however, that John was a real and significant figure in his own right, not merely a 'prologue' to the story of Jesus. Josephus, the Jewish historian, pays tribute to him: 'Herod slew him, who was a good man and commanded the Jews to exercise virtue, both as to righteousness towards one another, and piety towards God, and so to come to baptism.' [*Refs.* 2 Kings 1: 8. Matthew 3; 9: 14; 11: 2*f*; 14: 1-12; 17: 11-13. Mark 1: 2*f*; 6: 14-29. Luke 1: 5*f*; 3: 1-20; 7: 18-30; 11: 1. John 1: 19*f*; 3: 23; 10: 40. Acts 18: 25; 19: 1-4.]

John, The Gospel of The Gospel according to John is the fourth and last of the Gospels in our N.T. and it differs in many ways from the writings of Mark, Matthew and Luke. The Synoptic Gospels use a great deal of common material in their outlines of the life and work of Jesus. The Gospel of John stands by itself and is like a portrait of Christ, the Son of God. In other words, it expresses throughout the way this writer sees Jesus and thinks of him.

This Gospel does not set out to give an outline story of the life of Jesus in Galilee and Jerusalem. A good deal of it is taken up with long soliloquies and prayers of Jesus, or dialogues with disciple friends or Jewish foes which are apparently set down to reveal Jesus' way of thinking rather than his actual words on any occasion. There are no parables of the kind we find in the other Gospels, perhaps because the whole Gospel of John is a parable about Jesus, that is, a story to which he gives meaning.

One significant difference in the Gospel of John is the word he uses for the so-called 'miracles' of Jesus. The Synoptic

Gospels use the Greek word *dunamis* (*cf.* dynamo, dynamic) to show the 'power' of God which is revealed in the 'mighty works' done by Jesus. John, on the other hand, uses continually the Greek word *semeion* which means 'sign'. He intends his readers to realize that the recorded deeds of Jesus point like a signpost to who he is. A modern scholar has called the whole work 'the book of signs'. No doubt the Gospel is more difficult to read than the others because of its constant use of symbolism or 'sign language'. The opening words of the very first chapter Jesus as 'the Word', and it goes on to use words such as 'life', 'light', 'truth'. The language of John is full of spiritual meaning. Thus we find him describing Jesus as 'the bread of life' (6: 35*f*), 'living water' (7: 37*f*),'the light of the world' (8: 12*f*),'the door of the sheep' (10: 7*f*), 'the good shepherd' (10: 11*f*), 'the resurrection and the life' (11: 25*f*), 'the way, and the truth, and the life' (14: 6*f*), 'the true vine' (15: 1*f*).

We must not think, however, that the Gospel of John is one long meditation on Jesus set against a vaguely Palestinian background, as insubstantial as an impressionist painting. There are vivid details all through the book which pin it down to time and place. There is accurate description in such phrases as: 'Cana in Galilee' (2: 1), 'Aenon near Salim, because there was much water there' (3: 23), 'a city of Samaria, called Sychar, near the field that Jacob gave to his son Joseph' (4: 5), 'the Sea of Galilee, which is the Sea of Tiberias' (6: 1), 'Bethany was near Jerusalem, about two miles off' (11: 18). It would appear that the writer knew the geography of Palestine very well. There is also, curiously, exact reminiscence in such details as: 'they stayed with him that day, for it was about the tenth hour' (1: 39), or 'there is a lad here who has five barley loaves and two fish' (6: 9), or 'it was winter, and Jesus was walking in the Temple, in the portico of Solomon' (10: 23), or 'he went forth with his disciples across the Kidron valley, where there was a garden' (18: 1). The author is apparently a Jew writing for a Greek-speaking world. He is careful to explain the meaning of Hebrew words: Rabbi means 'teacher' (1: 38), *Cephas* means 'Peter' (1: 42), *Siloam* means 'Sent' (9: 7), *Gabbatha* is 'The Pavement' (19: 13), *Golgotha* is called 'the place of a skull' (19: 17). Fact and meaning are closely interwoven. We hear first of the boy with the five barley loaves and two fish, and in a short time we find ourselves deep in dialogue between Jesus and the Jews on 'the true bread from heaven' (6). We have gross details of Jesus spitting on the ground and making clay of the spittle to anoint a blind man's eyes, set in the midst of a discussion about light and darkness and the spiritual meaning of 'blindness' and 'seeing'. The stark fact of the corpse of Lazarus is the occasion of a sermon on 'the resurrection and the life'. The homely mention of towel, water and basin, and the washing of the disciples' feet takes the place of the exposition of the Last Supper in the other Gospels. We might well call this book 'the Gospel of double meanings'.

This time-chart of the ministry of Jesus is not the same as in the other three Gospels. The cleansing of the Temple comes early in the story (2: 13*f*) instead of during the last visit to Jerusalem. The Synoptic Gospels suggest that the Last Supper was the Passover meal. John says that Jesus was put to death before Passover began (19: 14, 31.) The fourth Gospel also differs from others in centring most of the ministry of Jesus in and around Jerusalem.

(a) John 1: 1-18: The prologue: 'In the beginning was the Word.'
(b) John 1: 19-51: John the Baptist: 'Behold the Lamb of God!'
(c) John 2: 1 to 12: 50: The public ministry of Jesus: 'God so loved the world.'
(d) John 13: 1 to 17: 26. Jesus teaches his disciples: 'You call me Teacher and Lord; and you are right, for so I am.'
(e) John 18-20: An appendix to the Gospel added by another writer.

(*Note*: The story of the woman taken in adultery [7: 53 to 8: 11] is usually considered to be a later addition, not belonging to the original Gospel.)

Who wrote the fourth Gospel? Irenaeus, a Christian writer towards the end of the second century A.D., said that the author was John the fisherman of Galilee, 'the beloved disciple', and that the Gospel was written in Ephesus when he was an old man. Certainly John 21: 20, 24 seems to point to 'the disciple whom Jesus loved', but this last chapter is usually thought to be an appendix added later by another writer. The Gospel properly ends at 20: 31. The thought and style of writing suggest a date for the book about the end of the first century, too late, surely, for the fisherman John, though not too late for a younger disciple of his. The wisest thing is to say that the writer is anonymous. It is not clear whether this author knew the Synoptic Gospels, though, of course, he must have been aware of the traditions about Jesus: the fact that he was crucified and where and by whom, and other tales cherished and taught in the early Church. Books which seem to stand together in the N.T. as 'the writings of John' are the fourth Gospel, three epistles, and the Book of the Revelation, all of which bear this name. It is very doubtful if all are by the same writer, though there may be a link between the Gospel and the Epistles, and it is best to consider each book separately.

We may fairly assume that this Gospel is later than the Synoptic Gospels and crowns their achievement. Instead of being a vivid, anecdotal, story-filled handbook for believers by writers who were in touch with eye-witnesses to Jesus, it is a thoughtful commentary on the meaning of God in Christ for our human life. We are reminded of the way in which Plato gives us the essence of the teaching of Socrates, set forth in his own dialogues. The writer of the Gospel of John bears his own witness to the fact that 'God so loved the world that he gave his only Son', that love is the binding force of the fellowship of Christ's followers in life and in death, and that they are to abide forever in his love. The best summing-up of this Gospel and, indeed, of all the others, is in the writer's own words. 'These are written that you may believe that Jesus is the Christ, the Son of God, and that believing you may have life in his name' (20: 31).

John, The First and Second Letters of The N.T. writings which bear the name John include a Gospel, three Letters, and the Book of the Revelation. It is most unlikely that they are all by one writer, although there would seem to be a strong link of thought and language between the Gospel and the letters. Consider, for example, the repeated use of the words 'life', 'word', 'light', 'truth', 'world' and 'perfect love' in 1 John which reminds us of the Gospel of John. The writer of the letters cannot be identified, but he is at least mentioned as 'the elder' in the opening words of 2 and 3 John. No such identification appears in 1 John, but we may assume that all three letters come from the same hand.

The First Letter of John: 1 John comes from a time of conflict in the Church at large. A group of heretical Christians were teaching that Jesus never really appeared in flesh and blood as a human being. He only *seemed* to be real. This heresy was known as *docetism*, from the Greek word meaning 'seeming', and it spread far and wide in the Church towards the end of the first century A.D. This false teaching had to be strictly contradicted, because it denied the incarnation of Christ as well as the truth of the Resurrection. So the writer of 1 John continually warns his readers against liars, deceivers, false prophets, and antichrist.

An outline of 1 John is:

(a) 1 John 1: 1-4: Forcibly reminds the reader that God in Christ was a real human being—we saw with our eyes, heard with our ears, touched with our hands.

(b) 1 John 1: 5 to 2: 17: The docetists said they had no sin, yet they claimed to know God completely. The writer says this is impossible. A Christian is a sinner who knows it, confesses it, and is forgiven and cleansed. The docetists did not trouble about ethics; but right conduct is the hallmark of the true Christian. He who loves his brother abides in the Light.

(c) 1 John 2: 18-27: The writer attacks the heresy of docetism.

(d) 1 John 2: 28 to 3: 24: The love of the Father for the children of God. A meditation on the theme 'love one another' which we also find in the Gospel of John, especially at John 14: 21-4; 15: 1-17.

(e) 1 John 4: 1-6: A warning against false prophets. His readers are to discern between the spirit of truth and the spirit of error.

(f) 1 John 4: 7 to 5: 5: The key sentences of the whole letter lie here: 'Love is of God, and he who loves is born of God and knows God...if God so loved us, we also ought to love one another...we love because he first loved us.'

(g) 1 John 5: 6-21: True prayer in the name of the Son of God. 'This is the confidence which we have in him, that if we ask anything according to his will he hears us.'

The Second Letter of John: The Second Letter of John is very short, only thirteen verses of about three hundred words in all, but it is a real letter from 'the elder to the elect lady and her children'. The latter words probably mean a congregation of the Church and its members. The theme is the same as in the First Letter. There are deceivers going in and out among the people of God, 'men who will not acknowledge the coming of Jesus Christ in the flesh'. The writer counsels his readers to have nothing to do with them—do not give them any greeting or receive them into the house. The true commandment, as they have heard from the beginning, is to follow Love.

The Third Letter of John: This is also a real letter, addressed this time to Gaius, an individual member of the Church to which the Second Letter was sent. Again the message is brief. The writer gives thanks that Gaius and his fellow-Christians follow the truth and that they are hospitable to visitors. There has, however, been some trouble in the Church. A member called Diotrephes has refused to obey instructions and shuts the door against Christian missionaries sent by 'the elder'. The writer hopes to come soon and talk to Gaius face to face. Meanwhile he sends greetings: 'Greet the friends, every one of them.'

This brief letter throws light on the fellowship of the early Church, with its problems of discord as well as its bonds of love.

Jonah The name means 'dove'. Jonah the son of Amittai is the hero of the book that bears his name and tells his story. Apart from that nothing is known of him. The Greek form of the name is *Jonas*. [*Refs*. Jonah 1-4. Matthew 12: 39-41; 164. Luke 11: 29-32.]

Jonah, The Book of The Book of Jonah is one of the 'Latter Prophets' of the Hebrew Scriptures and is among the twelve minor prophets in our O.T. It differs from the other prophetic works in being in prose, and consists almost entirely of a straightforward tale. (Chapter 2: 2-9 is a later Psalm which interrupts the unity of the story.) It describes what happened to Jonah and what he did, instead of what he had to say as a prophet of God. It is important to realize that this short book is not a history, nor a literal account. It is a work of fiction, a story with a meaning, an O.T. parable. Nor, in spite of popular belief, does a whale appear in it.

The writer is unknown. He tells of the prophet Jonah who was told by God to go and prophesy against the great, wicked, foreign city of Nineveh. Jonah went off in quite the opposite direction, took ship westward from Joppa, was thrown overboard in a violent storm, and was swallowed up by a great fish. Three days later the fish vomited Jonah on dry land and he went on his way unwillingly to Nineveh at God's command. There, against all likelihood, the people listened to him and repented. This made Jonah very angry and he sat down to sulk, accusing God of being gracious, merciful and loving. God caused a castor oil plant to grow up to shade Jonah from the intense heat, but the plant was attacked by a worm and withered. Jonah pitied the plant and cried out that he might be allowed to die. Finally comes the 'moral' of the story. Jonah was full of pity for the plant by the wayside. Yet he had no mercy in his heart for the great city of Nineveh with all its thousands of people and their cattle.

The writer's aim in this pithy, good-humoured tale is to

protest against Jewish narrow-mindedness and intolerance towards other races. It is undoubtedly a late work, containing many Aramaic words and expressions, written some time after the Exile when the teaching of Ezra and Nehemiah had made the Jews of Jerusalem exclusive and inward-looking in their concern for the purity of their race and religion. In the Book of Jonah the universal fatherhood of God is clearly proclaimed. His steadfast love includes the men of Nineveh as well as his chosen people.

Jonathan Son of Saul the first king of Israel, and dear friend of David. Jonathan was a mighty warrior, swift as a gazelle, popular with the soldiers, brave in war against the Philistines, and totally unselfish in his devotion to David. The friendship between the two young men is proverbial: 'the soul of Jonathan was knit to the soul of David, and Jonathan loved him as his own soul'. Jonathan was killed in the disastrous battle with the Philistines at Mt. Gilboa. David's lament over Saul and Jonathan is one of the great poems of Hebrew literature. [*Refs.* 1 Samuel 14: 1-46; 18: 1-3; 31: 2. 2 Samuel 1: 17-27.]

Joppa A Mediterranean seaport on the southern coast of Palestine. In O.T. times Joppa was a poor and dangerous harbour with heavy surf, but it was the port for Jerusalem. The timber for the building of Solomon's Temple was taken down to the coast from the forests of Lebanon, floated in rafts to Joppa, and dragged through the hills to Jerusalem about forty miles away. The same method was used in the building of the second Temple. It was from Joppa that Jonah sailed on a ship going to Tarshish.

In the early days of the Church Peter visited Joppa and raised Dorcas from the dead. He stayed at the seaside home of Simon, a tanner, and on the rooftop had a vision of a sheet let down from heaven with all kinds of animals and reptiles and birds. [*Refs.* 2 Chronicles 2: 16. Ezra 3: 7. Jonah 1: 3. Acts 9: 36-43 10: 5-23.]

Jordan The largest and most famous river of Palestine, the Jordan rises near Caesarea Philippi at the foot of Mt. Hermon, flows through the Sea of Galilee and runs at last into the Dead Sea. Although the river appears on the map to cut the land of Palestine in two like a backbone, the Jordan in fact winds and twists like a snake through a jungle thicket, as modern aerial photographs show.

The Israelites thought of the Jordan as a boundary which marked off the promised land. The Jordan has its mention in a number of Bible events. Lot chose its well-watered valley in which to settle; Joshua led the children of Israel across Jordan dryshod; King David fled that way during Absalom's rebellion; Naaman washed in Jordan to be healed; John the Baptist preached on Jordan's bank, and there Jesus was baptized. [*Refs.* Genesis 13: 10. Joshua 3: 17. 2 Samuel 17: 22. 2 Kings 5: 10, 14. Jeremiah 12: 5. Matthew 3: 5, 13. Mark 1: 5, 9.]

Joseph (1) The son of Jacob and his beloved wife Rachel, born when Jacob was in the land of Haran. Joseph is chiefly famous for the series of stories which tell of him from shepherd boy in Canaan to minister of state in the land of Egypt. Joseph was the favourite son of his father who spoiled him. His dreams made his brothers jealous and they sold him to Ishmaelite traders who took him down to Egypt. Joseph became overseer in the house of Potiphar, an officer of Pharaoh, but he was put in prison because Potiphar's wife told lies about him. There, however, he interpreted the dreams of Pharaoh's butler and baker; and news of this gift came eventually to the Pharaoh, who was also troubled by dreams. Thus Joseph the Hebrew was brought to favour at the Egyptian court, made lord over the whole land of Egypt, and married a daughter of an Egyptian priest. He saved the country before and during the years of famine by building store cities full of grain. In course of time Jacob sent his other sons to Egypt to buy food. After various tests Joseph revealed himself to his brothers, declared his forgiveness, and sent for his father and the whole clan to join him in Egypt. The book of Genesis ends with the death of Joseph. The whole account contains a good deal of folklore drawn from different sources, but the background has authentic details both of shepherd life in Canaan and of the civilization of ancient Egypt. The theme of God's providence runs strongly through the tale.

In some later writings the name Joseph stands for the tribes who were his descendants or even for the whole people of Israel. [*Refs.* Genesis 30: 23-5; 37 to 50. Exodus 13: 19. Deuteronomy 33: 13, 16. Joshua 16: 1-4. Psalm 80: 1-2. Amos 6: 6.] (2) The husband of Mary the mother of Jesus, described in Matthew's Gospel as a 'son of David'. The same Gospel calls him a carpenter of Nazareth. Luke tells that: 'Joseph also went up from Galilee, from the city of Nazareth, to Judea, to the city of David, which is called Bethlehem, because he was of the house and lineage of David, to be enrolled with Mary, his betrothed, who was with child.' Joseph is mentioned as the father of Jesus in the story of the boy Jesus' visit to the Temple in Jerusalem. John's Gospel also directly calls Jesus of Nazareth 'the son of Joseph'. Nothing else is told of Joseph, though many pious legends have grown up about him. [*Refs.* Matthew 1: 16, 18-25; 2: 13, 19; 13: 55. *Luke* 2: 4, 16, 41, 48; 4: 22. John: 45; 6: 42.] (3) Joseph the brother of Jesus. In the A.V. the Greek form *Joses* is used. [*Ref.* Matthew 13: 55.] (4) Joseph of Arimathea is mentioned variously in all four Gospels as a rich man, a member of the Jewish Council, a good man, a disciple of Jesus, though secretly. After the Crucifixion Joseph asked Pilate for the body of Jesus, wrapped it in a linen shroud, laid it in his own new tomb hewn in the rock, and rolled a stone against the door of the tomb. John also speaks of it being in a garden. [*Refs.* Matthew 27: 57-60. Mark 15: 42-6. Luke 23: 50-3. John 19: 38-41.] (5) Joseph called Barsabbas was one of two followers of Jesus who had accompanied the other disciples during his ministry and was witness to his Resurrection. He is mentioned with Matthias as a candidate to take the place of the traitor Judas Iscariot in the number of the twelve. The choice, however, fell on Matthias. [*Ref.* Acts 1: 21-6.]

Joses The Greek form of the name Joseph. The name of a brother of Jesus. [*Refs.* Mark 6: 3; 15: 40, 47.]

Joshua The son of Nun, servant of Moses, leader in battle against the Amalekites, and eventually successor of Moses in the advance on Canaan. The book which is named after him tells of Joshua's divine commission to lead the people of Israel over the Jordan to possess the promised land. Joshua sent out spies who brought news that the inhabitants of the land were faint-hearted at the threat from Israel. He led his people over a miraculously dried-up Jordan, was inspired to cast down Jericho, and went on to the conquest and division of the land. To Joshua is attributed the speech at Shechem in which before his death he reminds them of their ancestry, their deliverance from Egypt, counsels them to put away the foreign gods which were among them, and to serve only the Lord, the God of Israel. The name *Jesus* is the Greek form of the Hebrew *Joshua*. [*Refs.* Exodus 17: 9-16; 33: 11. Numbers 13: 16*f*; 27: 18-23. Deuteronomy 1: 38; 31: 7, 14. Joshua 1: 1*f*.]

Joshua, The Book of The sixth book of the O.T. It is named after Moses' servant and successor, the hero of the invasion of Canaan by the tribes of Israel. The Book of Joshua comes at the beginning of the Jewish list of 'the former prophets', i.e. the books of Joshua, Judges, Samuel and Kings, which gather together the story of God's people from the crossing of the Jordan to the Exile. The narrative of the Book of Joshua takes up the story from the end of Deuteronomy and includes tribal traditions and lists of people and places connected with the conquest of the promised land. The material comes from several sources, some of it dating back to the time of Joshua, some much later. The final editing of the book took place in the days after the Exile and gives the impression that the Israelites swept in and overran the whole of Canaan in one swoop. Other accounts, as in the Book of Judges, suggest a much slower and less decisive conquest.

The first part of the book, chapters 1-12, continues the theme of Deuteronomy and comes from the same historians. The teaching here is 'as I was with Moses, so I will be with you'. Joshua 10: 12-13 contains a fragment of a Hebrew poem from the lost Book of Jashar, apparently a collection of ballads.

Joshua 24 stands by itself. It tells how Joshua reminded the assembled tribes of Israel of all that God had done for them from the days of Abraham through all the time of the Exodus and to the conquest of the land of promise. He called the Israelites to choose which God they would worship. The people responded by vowing solemnly to keep the Covenant with the Lord, the God who had brought them out of Egypt. Most scholars believe that this covenant at Shechem involved not merely the Jacob clans of the Exodus but united with them kindred tribes of Canaan who had never gone down into Egypt. It is a declaration that one and all they will serve the Lord.

Josiah A seventh-century B.C. king of Judah who came to the throne at the age of eight on the death by murder of his father, Amon. Josiah reigned thirty-one years in Jerusalem and he is praised by the writers of the O.T. as one who 'did what was right in the eyes of the Lord, and walked in all the way of David his father'. This approval was brought about by the fact that he instituted a wholesale reformation of religion in the Temple and throughout the land, following the discovery of the book of the law in the Temple while the building was being repaired. Josiah commanded all Baal images, vessels and symbols to be destroyed by fire, he deposed the idolatrous priests, restored the custom of the Passover, cast down all local altars and centralized worship in the Temple in Jerusalem. The words of the book of the Covenant were read in the hearing of priests, prophets and people of Jerusalem, and Josiah took an oath with his people to perform the words written in the book. Josiah perished in battle against Pharaoh Neco of Egypt at Megiddo in 609 B.C. [*Refs.* 2 Kings 22: 1-23: 30. 2 Chronicles 34-5. Jeremiah 1: 2.] *See also*: MEGIDDO

Jotham (1) The youngest son of Gideon. He stood on the top of Mt. Gerizim and told the men of Shechem the parable of the trees who 'once went forth to anoint a king over them' and chose the bramble to be their ruler. [*Ref.* Judges 9: 5-21.] (2) A king of Judah in eighth century B.C., son of Uzziah (Azariah), who reigned sixteen years in Jerusalem. According to the writers of 2 Chronicles, Jotham 'did what was right in the eyes of the Lord', and also built cities, forts and towers, as well as strengthening Jerusalem. [*Refs*. 2 Kings 15: 32-8. 2 Chronicles 27.]

Jubilee One of the few Hebrew words which has passed into the English language. It comes from the Hebrew *yobel* which means 'a ram' or, in this sense, 'a ram's horn blown as a trumpet'. The Jewish time of jubilee described in the priestly Book of Leviticus was to be kept after seven times seven years, that is, the fiftieth year. Its dawn was to be proclaimed throughout the land by the blowing of trumpets, and during a whole year no one was to sow his fields or reap a harvest or gather grapes from the vines. God himself would bless the land so that it brought forth its own fruit richly, without the toil of cultivation. In the same year Hebrew slaves were to be set free, and it was to be a time of general rejoicing. It is unlikely that this ideal situation ever happened. [*Ref.* Leviticus 25: 10*f*.]

Judah or **Judea** Judah was originally the name of one of the tribes of Israel, named after a son of Jacob from whom they were said to be descended. Later the name came to be applied not only to a people but also to the part of Canaan they occupied. After the split in the kingdom following the death of Solomon, Judah and Benjamin formed the southern kingdom in the hill country, centred on the religious and political capital, Jerusalem, and ruled over by descendants of the house of David. The Greek form of the name is *Judea* and it is therefore the form generally used in the N.T. Here it applies to the part of Palestine ruled over by Herod the Great, his son Archelaus, and eventually by Roman procurators such as Pilate. [*Refs*. 2 Samuel 2: 10-11. 1 Kings 12: 20. Matthew 2: 1, 22. Luke 3: 1.] *See also*: ISRAEL

Judas (1) Judas the son (or brother) of James, who is mentioned as one of the twelve chosen disciples of Jesus. [*Refs*. Luke 6: 16. John 14: 22. Acts 1: 13.] (2) A brother of Jesus. [*Refs*. Matthew 13: 55. Mark 6: 3.] (3) Judas Iscariot. Nothing is known of him except through the Gospel story of how he betrayed

Jesus, but it may be noted that his name always comes last in the lists of the twelve disciples. The meaning of Iscariot is not clear, but it may be that Judas belonged to a village called Kerioth. Judas went to the chief priests and offered to betray Jesus for money, the amount being stated as thirty pieces of silver. He led a crowd to Gethsemane, kissed Jesus as a sign, and thus delivered his Master into their hands. After Jesus was condemned to death, Judas repented of his act and brought back the money. He threw the pieces of silver down in the Temple and went and hanged himself. John's Gospel says that Judas was keeper of the disciples' money-bag and that he was a thief. [*Refs*. Matthew 10: 4; 26: 14, 25, 47. Mark 3: 19; 14: 10, 43. Luke 6: 16; 22: 3, 47, 48. John 6: 71; 12: 4-6; 13: 2, 26, 29; 18: 2, 3, 5. Acts 1: 16, 25.] (4) Judas the Galilean, a rebel mentioned by the Pharisee Garnaliel, teacher of the law. [*Ref.* Acts 5: 37.] (5) A Christian disciple in whose home at Damascus Saul of Tarsus stayed after his conversion on the Damascus road. [*Ref.* Acts 9: 11.] (6) Judas called Barsabbas who was sent with Silas to Antioch with a letter of greeting and instruction from the apostles and elders of the Church in Jerusalem regarding the duties Gentiles must observe in the fellowship of the Christian faith. [*Ref.* Acts 15: 22-7.]

Jude The opening words of the letter of Jude claim that he is a brother of James, and therefore, one must assume, of Jesus. But the content of the letter indicates a date near the beginning of the second century A.D., so this Jude cannot be identified in the Gospel story. [*Ref.* Jude 1: 1.]

Jude, The Letter of The opening words of this short letter claim that the writer is 'Jude, a servant of Jesus Christ and brother of James'. This seems to identify him with the Juda or Judas mentioned in Mark 6: 3 as a brother of Jesus and James. But the writer, in fact, goes on to speak of looking back on the age of the apostles (17) and the date of the letter is probably near the beginning of the second century A.D. It is a 'catholic' letter, that is, one addressed to the whole Church, not to one particular group. The writer's purpose is to appeal to his readers to 'contend for the faith which was once for all delivered to the saints'. He launches into a whole-hearted attack on false teachers—ungodly persons who defile the flesh, reject authority, revile whatever they do not understand, grumblers, malcontents, loud-mouthed boasters, scoffers, worldly people. Not only is their teaching false, but it leads to immoral living, and that is also roundly condemned.

The author makes no quiet appeal to reason. He calls down punishment on all who have perverted the grace of God. At the end, however, there is a quieter word directed to true members of the Church: 'but you, beloved, build yourselves up on your most holy faith; pray in the Holy Spirit; keep yourselves in the love of God'. And the letter closes with a noble doxology.

A point of particular interest is the reference at 12 to the 'love-feasts'—social meals shared by the early Christians as a sign of their fellowship in Christ.

Judea *See* JUDAH

Judges The seventh book of the O.T. and part of the Jewish collection called 'the former prophets'. It takes the narrative from the death of Joshua to the time of Saul, the first of the kings. The title 'Judges' is misleading. These men and women, such as Deborah, Gideon, Jephthah, Samson, were tribal leaders in time of warfare against their enemies or quarrels among themselves. The book tells of a period when there was no spiritual leader like Moses and not yet a king to rule over them. The repeated refrain is: 'In those days there was no king in Israel' with the rueful commentary: 'every man did what was right in his own eyes'.

These tales of the Israelite tribes have been carefully edited at a much later date to point a moral. The pattern is made clear time and again in Judges 2: 6 to 16: 31. The people forsook the Lord their God and served other gods; God was angry and allowed other nations to oppress them; they repented and cried to God for help; he gave them a hero-deliverer who rallied them against the enemy; at last the land had rest. Battles long ago make up the stories of Judges, but faithfulness to the God of their fathers is the theme of the book.

K

Kadesh Also called Kadesh-barnea, a desert oasis on the edge of the Negeb in southern Palestine. Kadesh is best known as the place where the Israelites spent most of their forty years in the wilderness on their journey from Egypt to the promised land. Moses' sister Miriam died there. It was at Kadesh that they were disciplined into a people. From Kadesh Moses sent out spies to view the hill-country of Canaan. [*Refs.* Numbers 13: 25-0; 20: 1. Deuteronomy 1: 2, 46.]

Kedar A wandering shepherd tribe of the desert to the east of ancient Damascus. They were said to be descended from Ishmael, the outcast son of Abraham and Hagar. The flocks of Kedar and their black Bedouin tents are often referred to in O.T. song and story. [*Refs.* Genesis 25: 13. Psalm 120: 5. Song of Solomon 1: 5. Isaiah 42: 11; 60: 7. Jeremiah 49: 28-9.]

Kenites A Midianite tribe of Bedouin coppersmiths or tinkers whose fortunes were intermingled with the Hebrews in the days of their desert wanderings and occupation of Canaan. Tradition connects them with the shepherd clan who befriended Moses when he fled from the anger of Pharaoh. Moses settled among the Kenites, married one of their daughters, and was himself for a time a shepherd among them. Kenites of a later age went into Canaan along with the invading Hebrew tribes. [*Refs.* Exodus 2: 16-22; 18: 1-12. Judges 1: 16; 5: 241. 1 Samuel 15: 6.]

Kidron A valley between Jerusalem and the Mt. of Olives, and the stream running through it. Kings of Judah in o.t. times used the valley as a place to burn heathen idols during times of reformation of religion.

King David crossed the Kidron when he had to flee before his rebellious son, Absalom. Jesus went that way on the road to Gethsemane. [*Refs.* 2 Samuel 15: 23. 1 Kings 15: 13. 2 Kings 23: 4-6. John 18: 1.]

Kings, 1 and 2 These books formed one complete work in the original Hebrew Scriptures, telling the story of the people of Israel from the last days of King David to the destruction of Jerusalem by Nebuchadrezzar. A brief outline of contents would be:

(a) 1 Kings 1-11: Last days and death of David and the reign of Solomon.

(b) 1 Kings 12 to 2 Kings 17: The division of the kingdoms into Israel and Judah and their various kings to the downfall of Israel, the northern kingdom.

(c) 2 Kings 18-25: The history of Judah, the southern kingdom, from the reign of King Hezekiah to the downfall of Jerusalem.

This account of the kingdoms of Israel and Judah set among the great powers, their battles, division, decline and fall, is made up from court and Temple records which were later edited and revised in the time of Exile. For example, 1 Kings 11: 41 mentions a lost 'book of the acts of Solomon' from which, no doubt, some of the details of his reign are drawn. An important source was 'the Book of the Chronicles of the Kings of Israel', mentioned in 1 Kings 14: 19, and 'the Book of the Chronicles of the Kings of Judah', in 1 Kings 14: 29. These books, mentioned more than thirty times, are not to be confused with the books of Chronicles in our present Bible.

The long, detailed account of the building of the Temple, its measurements and furnishings, was probably derived from Temple records which were carefully kept. Official 'recorders' or court secretaries are mentioned from the time of David onwards, e.g. in 2 Samuel 8: 16, 1 Kings 4: 3, 2 Kings 18: 18.

There is certainly a cold official look to the brief statistics of some of the kings. For instance, in 2 Kings we have again and again a short formula stating the name of a king, how long he reigned, the name of his mother, where he was buried, with a few words about contemporary events and a curt summing-up of the value of his reign, e.g. 2 Kings 15: 1-7.

The editor's hand is clearly seen in the way he makes moral comments on this ruler or that. Kings are not valued for their valour or political wisdom or length of reign or prosperity, but only according to whether or not they 'did what was right in the sight of God'. The editor's purpose is to show God at work in his people's history, so that those who read may learn the lesson of their nation's failure to trust in God.

1 and 2 Kings bring to an end that part of the o.t. which the Jews call 'the former prophets', i.e. our books Joshua to 2 Kings. They form a continuous narrative of God's dealings with his people Israel from the entry into the promised land to the downfall of Jerusalem and the Exile in Babylon.

Kishon A small, rushing river in the plain of Jezreel which flows into the Mediterranean near modern Haifa. It is mentioned dramatically in the story of Deborah, Barak and Sisera in the Book of Judges. For most of the year the Kishon is almost dry, but in the rainy season it becomes a raging torrent which floods the land on both banks. The chariots of Sisera's army were bogged down in the mud, and Barak and the men of Israel were able to attack and wipe out the fleeing, floundering charioteers. Deborah's savage battle-hymn of triumph is one of the oldest of Hebrew poems:

'The torrent Eishon swept them away,
the onrushing torrent, the torrent Kishon.'

It was by the side of Kishon also that Elijah slew the prophets of Baal after the encounter at Mt. Carmel in the days of King Ahab. [*Refs.* Judges 4: 4-9, 13-16; 5: 21. 1 Kings 18: 40.]

Kittim *See* CYPRUS

Kue *See* CILICIA

L

Laban A descendant of Nahor and wealthy shepherd of Mesopotamia. Rebekah, who married Isaac, was Laban's sister. In due course, when her son Jacob had to flee from the anger of Esau, she sent him to seek refuge with Laban. Jacob married Laban's two daughters, Leah and Rachel, and their children became the forefathers of the Israelite tribes. [*Refs.* Genesis 24; 27: 42-5; 29 to 31.]

Lachish An important double-walled fortress city in southern Judah about thirty miles from Jerusalem. It is mentioned as a town captured by Joshua and fortified by Rehoboam, but it comes to prominence in o.t. history in the days of King Hezekiah of Judah when Jerusalem was under attack from Assyria. Sennacherib, king of Assyria, took the fortified cities of Judah and made Lachish his military headquarters for his threat against Jerusalem. Hezekiah capitulated for the time being and paid tribute of gold and silver. A century later, when Nebuchadrezzar laid siege to and broke down Jerusalem, Lachish was one of two fortified cities that held out. An important archaeological discovery, a collection of clay fragments with writing on them (known as the Lachish letters), tells of the fighting and conditions during the Babylonian attack. [*Refs.* Joshua 10: 31. 2 Kings 14: 19; 18: 14-17. 2 Chronicles 11: 9; 32: 9. Isaiah 36: 2; 37: 8. Jeremiah 34: 7.]

Lamentations, The Book of This book, which is found among the Writings of Hebrew Scriptures, consists of five short poems lamenting the downfall of the city of Jerusalem in 587 B.C. It was not written by Jeremiah but belongs rather to the time of the Exile. No doubt the poems were attributed to Jeremiah because they echo his words of doom concerning the final anguish of Jerusalem.

The first four poems, in chapters 1-4, are in the form of acrostics on the Hebrew alphabet, a device which can be found in a number of the Psalms. Chapters 2 and 4 are vivid with all the horror of an eye-witness account of the destruction of the city. Infants and babes faint in the streets of Jerusalem, crying out for food; women boil and eat their own children; young men are unrecognizable, their skin blackened and shrivelled on their bones. The last poem, in chapter 5, is a prayer to God for mercy in the time of their complete defeat.

Laodicea A city of Asia Minor near Colossae. It was the home of one of the seven Churches of Asia mentioned in the Book of Revelation, the writer of which poured scorn on the self-centred satisfaction and luke-warmness of its members. The word *Laodicean* became a term of contempt for indecision and caution. [*Refs.* Colossians 2: 1; 4: 13. Revelation 3: 14-22.]

Lazarus (1) The brother of Mary and Martha. They lived at Bethany and were dear friends of Jesus. John's Gospel tells how Jesus raised Lazarus from the dead after his body had been in the tomb for four days. [*Ref.* John 11: 1-44.] (2) The name of the beggar in Jesus' parable about a rich man and a poor man. [*Ref.* Luke 16: 19-31.]

Leah The elder daughter of Laban the wealthy shepherd of Mesopotamia. Through her father's trickery Leah became the first wife of Jacob. [*Ref.* Genesis 29: 21-7.]

Lebanon The name means 'white mountain'. The Lebanon is a chain of mountains a hundred miles long, parallel to the coast of Palestine and forming the northern boundary of the 'promised land' in the eyes of the O.T. writers. The peaks rise to 10,000 feet and are always white with snow. The forests of Lebanon were famous for their mighty cedars in ancient times and supplied timber for the buildings and furniture of one civilization after another—Egypt, Assyria, Babylon. Their beauty and fragrance were praised in Hebrew poetry. Hiram, king of Tyre, supplied David and Solomon with the cedar and cypress of Lebanon for the building of their royal palaces and for the Temple in Jerusalem. [*Refs.* Deuteronomy 11: 24. 2 Kings 19: 23. Song of Solomon 5: 15. Jeremiah 18: 14. Ezekiel 27: 5.]

Lebbaeus *See* THADDEUS

Leprosy A loathsome contagious disease affecting the tissues and skin, found in many parts of the tropics and the east. Leprosy is frequently mentioned in the Bible, but the word was probably used of various skin troubles. There is a detailed description of the disease and the health laws about it in Leviticus 13-14. A leper was usually outcast from home and family unless he could show himself to be once again 'clean'. Naaman, commander of the army of the king of Syria, is perhaps the most famous leper in O.T. story, but he does not appear to have been cut off from his family or his daily work. King Uzziah (Azariah) of Judah died a leper, shut off from his people and from entering the Temple. The Gospels have a number of stories of Jesus healing lepers.

The word *leprosy* was sometimes applied in the O.T. to patches of mould or mildew in woollen and linen clothes and in the walls of houses. [*Refs.* Leviticus 13-14. 2 Kings 5. 2 Chronicles 26: 19-23. Matthew 8: 2-4. Mark 1: 40-5. Luke 5: 12-15; 17: 11-19.]

Levi (1) The name of the third son of Jacob and Leah, regarded as the ancestor of the Levites, the priesthood of Judaism. [*Ref.* Genesis 29: 34.] *See also*: LEVITES; PRIEST (2) According to Mark and Luke, Levi, the son of Alphaeus, was a tax collector called by Jesus to follow him. The name *Levi*, however, does not appear in the list of twelve disciples. In Matthew's Gospel the name Matthew appears at this point, as if Levi and Matthew were one and the same man. [*Refs.* Matthew 9: 9. Mark 2: 14. Luke 5: 27.]

Levites The tribe said to be descended from Levi, the son of Jacob. By ancient tradition, they were set apart to minister to the priests of the Tabernacle in the wilderness and later in the Temple in Jerusalem, and 'to have charge of all the furnishings of the tent of meeting, and attend to the duties for the people of Israel'. The Levites might be described generally as servants of the Temple. They are called priests in pre-exilic writings, but were subordinate to them in the work and worship of the Temple after the Exile, when they might not enter the holy place. One of the Levitical duties was to take charge of the instrumental music and singing of the Temple choirs, another was responsibility for the Temple treasuries. The Levites were given cities and land to live in and pasture lands for their cattle. A tithe of the offerings of the people of Israel was to go by right to the Levites for their support.

In the N.T. a Levite is mentioned in Jesus' parable of the Good Samaritan, and Joseph, called Barnabas in the early Church, was a Levite. [*Refs*. Numbers 1: 50; 3: 6-9; 18: 21*f*. Deuteronomy 18: 1-8. Joshua 21: 1-3. 1 Chronicles 24-6. Nehemiah 8: 7-9. Luke 10: 32 Acts 4: 36.]

Leviticus Leviticus is the third book of the Pentateuch or 'five books of Moses'. Unlike Genesis and Exodus where history, legend and tradition are mixed with law, the book of Leviticus is entirely made up of rules and regulations, the majority of which are religious. Examples are: laws concerning the proper offerings to be burned on the altar of sacrifice, the consecration of priests, clean and unclean beasts for food, leprosy and other diseases, hygiene, the annual festivals, the offering of tithes. Leviticus was probably composed by priests of Jerusalem after the return from Exile and they set the book in the time of Moses to show how important religious rules had been from earliest times for God's chosen people. In the years after the Exile the priestly writers who helped to shape the Pentateuch thought it their duty to ensure that all Jews kept themselves racially separate and pure. This was to be done by constant attention to the whole ritual of Jewish daily custom and worship and sacrifice. Thus Leviticus could be called the rule book of a nation dedicated to God. Within the chapters of ritual there is the Code of Holiness which is concerned with the proper behaviour of people who are covenanted to be 'a kingdom of priests and a holy nation' (Leviticus 17-26). Some of the teaching of the prophets in its finest form is enshrined in Leviticus 19 with its concern for the poor, the blind, the deaf, the old and the stranger. It is here that the words occur: 'You shall love your neighbour as yourself'

Libertines The word means 'freedmen', as it is translated in the R.S.V. and N.E.B. These were probably Jews descended from captives sent to Rome by Pompey and later liberated. They disputed with Stephen and accused him of blasphemy. [*Ref.* Acts 6: 9.]

Libya A country on the Mediterranean coast of north Africa, west of Egypt. [*Refs.* 2 Chronicles 12: 3. Nahum 3: 9. Acts 2: 10.]

Locust A winged insect of the grasshopper family which is carried by the wind in huge swarms and eats up all vegetation wherever it settles. Plagues of locusts were known in early Bible times and their destructive power is well described in Exodus 10. They still occur from time to time in Arabia and Egypt. Locusts were used as food by the Hebrews in the desert and John the Baptist ate them. [*Refs.* Exodus 10: 12-15. Leviticus 11: 22. Psalm 105: 34-5. Nahum 3: 15-17. Mark 1:6.]

Lord's Prayer The name given to the prayer taught by Jesus to his disciples. There are two versions in the Gospels, one in Matthew and one in Luke.

The form of the prayer in Matthew 6: 9-13 (R.S.V.) is:

'Our Father who art in heaven,
Hallowed be thy name.
Thy kingdom come,
Thy will be done,
On earth as it is in heaven.
Give us this day our daily bread;
And forgive us our debts,
As we also have forgiven our debtors;
And lead us not into temptation,
But deliver us from evil.'

This is the form of the Lord's Prayer which from early times has been used in the worship of the Church. Some ancient manuscripts add the doxology: 'For thine is the kingdom and the power and the glory, for ever, Amen', but this was probably not a part of the original prayer.

The version in Luke 11: 2-4 (R.S.V.) is shorter:

'Father, hallowed be thy name.
Thy kingdom come.
Give us each day our daily bread;
and forgive us our sins,
for we ourselves forgive every one who is indebted to us;
and lead us not into temptation.'

Additions or alterations to this form of the prayer in Luke are to make it more like the 'Church' version found in Matthew. Probably the original was shorter still. All the phrases of the Lord's Prayer can be found in devout Jewish teaching, but it was Jesus who made it universal.

The prayer deals first with the glory of God and secondly with the needs of Man. The most important word in the whole prayer is the first— 'Father'. Jesus used the Aramaic *Abba*, the everyday family word by which a Jewish child would address his own father. The phrase 'lead us not into temptation' is difficult. The N.E.B. translates it: 'do not bring us to the test'. It was used in Jewish prayer as a simple petition: 'lead us not into sin or iniquity or temptation', in other words, 'keep us from moral danger'. No doubt that meaning is present in the Lord's Prayer. We must also remember, however, the members of the early Church by whom this prayer was first repeated and who constantly faced the 'test' of suffering and persecution and martyrdom.

Lord's Supper The N.T. name for the Eucharist or Holy Communion, founded on the last meal Jesus shared with his disciples before his death. The Gospel writers, Mark, Matthew and Luke all mention the Last Supper and tell how Jesus took bread, blessed, broke and gave it to his disciples with the words: ' "Take; this is my body." Likewise he took a cup, and when he had given thanks he gave it to them, and they all drank of it. And he said to them, "This is my blood of the covenant, which is poured out for many." '

John makes no mention in his Gospel of the details of the Supper, but instead substitutes his account of Jesus washing his disciples' feet. Paul, on the other hand, whose account is the earliest of all, instructs the believers in Corinth in the solemn rite of commemoration which they are to follow in word and action by taking the bread and the cup in remembrance of the death of their Lord.

This commemoration has become the central sacrament of the Christian Church, whether it be known in different branches of the Church as the Lord's Supper, the Breaking of Bread, the Eucharist, or the Holy Communion. [*Refs.* Matthew 26: 26-8. Mark 14: 22-4. Luke 22: 14-20; 24: 35. John 13: 2*f*: Acts 2: 42; 20: 7. 1 Corinthians 11: 20-8.]

Lot Nephew of Abraham. Lot went with his uncle from Ur to Haran and then to the land of Canaan. Both grew rich in flocks and herds and tents so that there was no room in the land for them to live together and their herdsmen quarrelled. Abraham offered Lot his choice to go to the right or the left. Lot chose the well-watered Jordan valley, leaving the hills of Canaan to Abraham. But later he and his family had to flee from the fire and brimstone that fell on Sodom and Gomorrah. [*Refs.* Genesis 11: 31; 12: 4; 13: 1-13; 19: 24-9.] *See also*: HARAN

Luke Luke is mentioned by name three times in N.T. letters as 'beloved physician', 'fellow worker', and friend and companion of Paul the apostle. Ancient tradition declares him to be the author of the third Gospel and of the Acts of the Apostles. Luke was almost certainly a Gentile, and, if we accept that the 'we' sections of the Acts form part of a travel diary, he was with Paul some time during his second and third missionary journeys and sailed with him on the eventful voyage to Rome. [*Refs.* Colossians 4: 14. 2 Timothy 4: 2. Philemon 24.] *See also*: LUKE, THE GOSPEL OF; ACTS OF THE APOSTLES; PHILIPPI

Luke, The Gospel of The Gospel according to Luke and the Acts of the Apostles together make up a single work by one author, and Luke 1: 1-4 forms an introduction to the whole. Both books begin with a dedication to the same person, Theophilus, possibly a Roman official of high rank. The Gospel claims to be 'an orderly account' of all that Jesus began to do and teach, and Acts continues the story after the Resurrection of Christ, in the life and work of the apostles, from Jerusalem to Rome. Taken together, these two books make up a quarter of the N.T. This Gospel is not a brief handbook for Christian believers like the Gospel according to Mark. Luke, the Gentile, sets out his work like a history, to inform other non-Jews of the words and events on which the Christian faith is based, and to commend that faith to the authorities of the Roman Empire. It is the longest of the Gospels, the most detailed and memorable in its stories of Jesus, the most universal in its interest in all sorts and conditions of men and women. With good reason the Gospel according to Luke has been called 'the most beautiful book in the world'.

We know more about Luke the man than about any of the other Gospel writers. Paul refers to 'Luke, the beloved physician' (Colossians 4: 14) and he appears to have been with him in Rome (Philemon 24 and 2 Timothy 4: 11). More substantial evidence is to be found in the Acts of the Apostles where Luke is the companion of Paul on his missionary travels, possibly the 'man from Macedonia' who appeared in a vision to the apostle. At all events, the narrative in Acts 16: 11 suddenly breaks into the first person as if to indicate that the author is keeping a diary of his journey with Paul. This 'we' section of the book brings them eventually to Caesarea in Palestine (Acts 21: 8f). The following narrative would indicate that Luke was two years in Palestine while Paul was in prison there, before they sailed together under military escort for Rome (Acts 27: 1). It was probably during that time that Luke gleaned some of the material about Jesus which we find in his Gospel.

Luke is one of the Synoptic Gospels, a term applied to Mark, Luke and Matthew, because they can be set side by side and 'seen together' (which is the meaning of the Greek word *synopticos*). It should also be noted that Luke, like Matthew, copies a good deal of his material from Mark. The sources of Luke's Gospel can be set out thus: (1) The Gospel according to Mark from which he copies more than a third of his work. Unlike Matthew, however, Luke does not weave bits of Mark's Gospel into his own story. He simply sets down portions of Mark complete as he needs them, and then goes on to other material. For example, the account of Jesus' visit to Capernaum in Luke 4: 31-44 is copied directly from Mark 1: 21-39. (2) A collection of the 'sayings' of Jesus which the scholars call *Q*, from the first letter of the German word *Quelle* meaning 'source'. This source *Q* is also used by Matthew. For example, both Luke and Matthew have the teaching of Jesus which we call the 'beatitudes', though each of these writers sets them down in his own way. Compare Luke 6: 20-3 with Matthew 5: 2-12. *See also* Luke's version of the Lord's Prayer in Luke 11: 2-4 and Matthew's in Matthew 6: 9-13. Another example is the so-called 'golden rule': 'As you wish that men would do to you, do so to them' (Luke 6: 31), which is found in Matthew 7: 12 as: 'Whatever you wish that men would do to you, do so to them.' (3) Perhaps it was when he was two years in Palestine during Paul's imprisonment that Luke first came across the 'sayings' of Jesus (the source *Q*) in some written form. There, also, he had opportunity to meet people who had been friends and followers of Jesus. There were many disciples, both men and women, to be met in Caesarea and in Jerusalem. Thus we find a third and very important source in the shaping of Luke's Gospel, namely, the stories of Jesus which he alone tells. We call this source *L* because it belongs uniquely to Luke. This material is so extensive that we give it in full: Luke 3: 1 to 4: 30; 5: 1-11; 6: 12 to 8: 3; 9: 51 to 18: 14; 19: 1-28, 37-44, 47-8; 22: 14 to 24: 53. (It is possible that Luke gathered together this material with the 'sayings' of Jesus even before he had come across a copy of the Gospel of Mark.) This section not only includes a very full account of the Last Supper, arrest, trial, Crucifixion and Resurrection of Jesus, it also contains some of the best-known and best-loved stories and incidents in the life of Jesus: such parables as the good Samaritan, the lost sheep, the lost coin, the two sons, and the encounter with the ten lepers and with Zacchaeus. (4) Luke's history book properly begins at chapter 3: 1, where he mentions the leading rulers of the day. But by way of prologue to the history he sets down a series of poems centred on the announcement and the birth of Jesus. The writer was a Greek, but these are Jewish religious songs. They include the *Magnificat*, or song of Mary, the *Benedictus*, or song of Zechariah, the *Gloria in Excelsis*, or song of the angelic host at Bethlehem, and the *Nunc Dimittis*, or song of Simeon. They express in poetic form Luke's belief that Jesus is born to be Saviour of the world. Before ever he sets the scene of Jesus' life among the great and humble of the earth, he sings of the joy of high heaven that God has visited and redeemed his people.

To sum up the sources, we may say that Luke's Gospel is composed thus: $Q + L +$ parts of Mark $+$ Jewish poems.

A short outline of the Gospel of Luke is:

(a) Luke 1: 1-4: Dedication to Theophilus.

(b) Luke 1: 5 to 2: 52: The birth poems and stories of Jesus' childhood.

(c) Luke 3: 1 to 4: 13: The setting of the ministry, John the Baptist, the baptism of Jesus, the temptations.

(d) Luke 4: 14 to 9: 50: The ministry in Galilee, teaching and encounters, Peter's confession, the Transfiguration.

(e) Luke 9: 51 to 19: 44: The journey to Jerusalem, further teaching and encounters.

(f) Luke 19: 45 to 24: 53: Teaching and incidents in Jerusalem, the Last Supper, the arrest and trial of Jesus, the Crucifixion, Resurrection appearances.

The date of Luke's Gospel is difficult to fix accurately. The ending of the Acts of the Apostles suggests a limit of A.D. 63 for the events of his two-fold story. The Gospel may have been composed some time between A.D. 75 and 85.

The book is noticeably concerned to appeal to Gentile readers in the Roman world. More than once Luke mentions the emperor of the time, as well as other officials. He explains, for the benefit of his non-Jewish readers, the meaning of Hebrew words and terms, or tells that Capernaum was 'a city of Galilee' and that Arimathea was 'the Jewish town'. A striking feature of the Gospel is his courteous mention of women. The most notable feature of Luke's Gospel, however, is the way in which he portrays Jesus as the Son of God who has compassion and loving concern for Jews and Gentiles alike: Romans, Samaritans, poor people, outcasts of society, sinners in the sight of the religious law, 'tax-gatherers and other bad characters'. Here, truly, is the Saviour of the world, 'a light to lighten the Gentiles, and the glory of thy people Israel'.

Lydda A town in the plain of Sharon where Peter healed a paralysed man named Aeneas and where many 'turned to the Lord'. Lydda is by tradition the place where St. George slew the dragon. [*Ref.* Acts 9: 32-5.]

Lydia A rich woman who sold purple goods in the city of Philippi. She listened to Paul and was baptized, along with her household. Paul and Silas stayed with her. Lydia was the first known Christian convert in Europe. [*Refs.* Acts 16: 14-15, 40.]

Lysanias The name of the ruler said by Luke to have been tetrarch (governor) of Abilene in the time of Jesus. Abilene was a district in Lebanon, north and west of Damascus. [*Ref.* Luke 3: 1.]

Lystra A Roman colony in Asia Minor visited by Paul and Barnabas on their first missionary journey. Paul preached there and also healed a man who had been a cripple from birth. As a result the apostles were hailed as gods. Jewish visitors, however, stirred up the people against them, and Paul was stoned and left for dead. He was helped to recover by believers in the city. It was at Lystra, on one of his pastoral visits, that Paul met Timothy and took him with him as his helper. [*Refs.* Acts 14: 6-23; 16: 1.]

M

Macedonia Part of northern Greece which came into importance under Philip of Macedon and his son Alexander the
Great. In N.T. times Macedonia was a Roman province. Paul
came there after he had a vision at Troas of a 'man of Macedonia who stood and besought him, saying: 'Come over to Macedonia and help us'.' With Paul's arrival in Philippi the gospel came to Europe. Thereafter the apostle visited Thessalonica
and other towns of the province and established Churches.
He was later to praise their generosity to him and to the poor
Christians at Jerusalem. [*Refs.* Acts 16: 9 to 17: 13; 19: 21; 20:
1-3. Romans 15: 26. 1 Corinthians 16: 5. 2 Corinthians 8: 1-5.
1 Thessalonians 1: 7-8.]

Magog *See* GOG

Malachi, The Book of This is an anonymous work, for the name
Malachi simply means 'my messenger'. It appears among the
'Latter Prophets' of the Hebrew Scriptures and is the last of
the O.T. minor prophets. The book comes from about 460 B.C.
The Temple has been restored and is frequently mentioned,
but the religious reforms of Nehemiah and Ezra have not yet
taken place. The land is under the rule of a Persian governor.
The main theme of the work is to rebuke priests and worshippers for their casual indifference to religious matters. The half-
hearted priests offer on the altar animals which are blind, lame
and sick. ' "What a weariness this is," you say, and you sniff at
me, says the Lord of hosts' (1: 13). It would be better to shut

the doors of the Temple altogether than to behave like this. Their teaching and their life, too, are corrupt. In spite of their false worship, however, the Lord's messenger is soon to come among them. The day of the Lord is near and it will be a day of judgment. 'Who can endure the day of his coming, and who can stand when he appears?' (3: 2). The warning ends with a prophecy of the coming of Elijah as herald of the great and terrible day of the Lord. This belief remains in the prayers and customs of the Jewish people to the present day.

Malchus According to John's Gospel, Malchus was the name of the high priest's slave whose right ear Simon Peter cut off with his sword in the garden where Jesus was arrested. [*Ref.* John 18: 10.]

Mammon The word means 'riches'. In the N.T. Mammon is personified as if wealth were a god that men worship. Modern versions of the Bible translate *Mammon* simply as 'money'. [*Refs.* Matthew 6: 24. Luke 16: 9, 11, 13.]

Manasseh (1) The elder son of Joseph and therefore ancestor of one of the famous tribes of Israel. His mother was Asenath, daughter of a priest of Egypt. The tribe of Manasseh settled east and west of Jordan when they came to possess the promised land. Notable members of the tribe were Gideon and Jephthah. [*Ref.* Genesis 41: 51. Joshua 17. Judges 6: 15.] (2) Son of King Hezekiah and spoken of as the most wicked king in the story of Judah. His long reign (687-642 B.C.) was peaceful and prosperous, but Manasseh made himself a vassal of the empire of Assyria. In token of his appeasement he built pagan shrines in towns up and down Judah and encouraged heathen Baal worship, including the Assyrian cult of the sun, moon and stars. Manasseh also indulged in astrology and magic, and even human sacrifice. Thus the O.T. writers look on this period as the dark age of their history and on Manasseh as their most evil king. [*Ref.* 2 Kings 21: 1-18.]

Manna Manna is a sweet, sticky substance produced by insects which feed on the tamarisk bushes in the Arabian desert. The honeydew drops evaporate in the heat and lie on the ground like hoar frost. Manna can be gathered in the cool of the morning and eaten. The Israelites ate manna during their years of wandering in the desert and they regarded it then and for ever after as God's gift of 'bread from heaven'. [*Refs.* Exodus 16: 13-21, 31. Psalm 78: 24-5. John 6: 31.]

Manoah The father of Samson, to whose wife an angel of the Lord appeared to tell her she would bear a son who was to begin to deliver Israel from the Philistines. [*Ref.* Judges 13: 2*f*.]

Mark Sometimes known as Mark, sometimes John, sometimes 'John called Mark'. Mark (Latin *Marcus*) was a very common name in the Roman Empire, so we cannot positively say that only one Mark is referred to in the N.T. It is usually assumed, however, that John called Mark was the author of the Gospel that bears his name. If so, he was apparently a Jew of Jerusalem, kinsman of Barnabas, and had connections with Cyprus. John Mark went with Barnabas and Paul as their servant on their first missionary journey; but when they sailed from Cyprus to Asia Minor, he left them and returned to Jerusalem. Many years later he was with Paul in Rome. A popular literary tradition of the second century A.D. suggests that Mark was the interpreter of Peter and wrote down his reminiscences of Jesus. [*Refs.* Acts 12: 12, 25; 13: 5, 13; 15: 37-9. Colossians 4: 10. 2 Timothy 4: 2 Philemon 24. 1 Peter 5: 13.] *See also*: MARK, THE GOSPEL OF

Mark, The Gospel of The Gospel according to Mark is thought to be the earliest of the four Gospels although it stands second in order in our English N.T. Mark, Matthew and Luke are commonly called the Synoptic Gospels because they can be set side by side and 'seen together' (the meaning of the Greek word *synopticos*) with a common viewpoint of the life and work of Jesus. Mark's is the shortest of the Gospels. There is an old tradition that Mark wrote down the reminiscences of Peter. A second century bishop called Papias wrote: 'Mark, who was the interpreter of Peter, wrote down accurately, as far as he remembered them, the things said or done by the Lord, but not however in order.' This may or may not be strictly true, but at least it gives us a clue to the shape of the book. Mark certainly did not set out to write a straightforward life of Jesus. Instead of beginning, as Matthew and Luke do, with the birth of Jesus, Mark is concerned to concentrate on the supreme importance of the suffering and death of Christ. The earlier part of his work, beginning in Galilee, consists of a series of self-contained paragraphs or sections often about separate and isolated incidents. These stories about Jesus were used again and again in the preaching and teaching of the early Church. Examples are clearly shown in Mark 2-3. The Gospel, therefore, does not flow in an orderly story from Nazareth to Jerusalem. We find that we are not necessarily told the time and place of various encounters, merely 'immediately' (a favourite word of Mark's) or 'in the morning', or 'after some days', or 'when evening had come', and vague phrases such as 'a lonely place' or 'beside the sea' or 'the synagogue' or 'into the hills' must suffice for location.

Thus the first part of this Gospel is made up of teaching material about Jesus. Its purpose is clearly stated in the opening verse: 'The beginning of the gospel of Jesus Christ, the Son of God. Some stories possibly derive from the authentic memory of Peter the apostle. But they are selected with a teaching purpose, to instruct members of the Church about the words and work of God's Messiah. On the other hand, the close-knit Passion narrative which forms the latter part of Mark's Gospel is concerned with the question: 'If Jesus was the long-expected Messiah, why did he have to die on the cross as a criminal?'

We cannot be certain who the author was, but it is usual to identify Mark the Gospel writer with John Mark, the companion of Paul and friend of Peter mentioned several times in the N.T. If so, he appears to have been a Jew who lived in a large house in Jerusalem where the early disciples met for prayer and which may have been the scene of the Last Supper. This John Mark had connections with Cyrus. He went with his relative Barnabas and the apostle Paul as their servant on their first missionary journey, but left them and returned to Jerusalem. Mark was later with Paul in Rome. (*See* Acts 12: 12, 25; 15: 37-9. Philemon 24. Colossians 4: 10. 2 Timothy 4: 11.) Ancient tradition again suggests that Mark wrote his Gospel after Peter and Paul were put to death under the emperor Nero. This gives us a date for the book about A.D. 65. It may well have been written in the city of Rome itself, at the heart of the Empire, to encourage Gentile Christians enduring persecution, suffering and cruel death for their faith. It is rightly called 'a Gospel for martyrs'.

A brief outline of the Gospel is:

(a) Mark 1: 1-13: Prologue, the baptism and temptation of Jesus.
(b) Mark 1: 14 to 8: 26: Jesus' ministry of teaching and healing in Galilee.
(c) Mark 8: 27 to 10: 52: The journey to Jerusalem.
(d) Mark 11: 1 to 16: 8: The last days in Jerusalem, the Crucifixion and Resurrection.

The ending of Mark's Gospel presents a vexing problem. The original ending at Mark 16: 8 concludes with the words: 'and they said nothing to any one, for they were afraid'. We can only guess why the work comes abruptly to an end at this point, without any mention of an appearance of the risen Christ. Perhaps the scroll of the Gospel, written on papyrus, was damaged. Perhaps the writer was unable for one reason or another to finish his work. The verses Mark 16: 9-20, made up from other and later sources, were added probably as late as the second century.

This short, vivid book, simple in its telling, written not in the classical Greek of great literature but in the common tongue of ordinary people, is the basic handbook of the Christian faith, to teach believers about their Lord.

Mars Hill *See* AREOPAGUS

Martha The sister of Mary and Lazarus, friends of Jesus, who lived at Bethany. Martha welcomed Jesus to their home but complained that Mary was not helping her to prepare a meal. Jesus rebuked Martha for her over anxiety. It was Martha on another occasion who appealed to Jesus for help when her brother Lazarus had died, and to whom Jesus said: 'I am the resurrection and the life.' [*Refs*. Luke 10: 38-42. John 11; 12: 1-8.]

Mary (1) The wife of Joseph and mother of Jesus. There is not a great deal of information about her in the Gospels. The legendary birth stories in Matthew and Luke mention her, the latter Gospel calling her 'the virgin' and stating that she was kinswoman of Elizabeth, the mother of John the Baptist. It is Luke's Gospel also which includes the so called 'Song of Mary' or *Magnificat* and the story of Simeon's blessing of the child in the Temple, as well as the account of the visit to Jerusalem when Jesus was twelve years old. Matthew's Gospel calls Jesus the carpenter's son, names his mother Mary, and speaks of brothers and sisters of Jesus. Mark also mentions his mother and brothers and sisters. John's Gospel says that the mother of Jesus was present at the first of the miracles, the turning of water into wine at the marriage at Cana in Galilee, and states that Jesus went to Capernaum to stay with his mother and his brothers and his disciples. He tells, too, that she stood by the cross, though he nowhere names her. The book of the Acts notes that Mary was in the company of the disciples of Jesus in the upper room in Jerusalem after the Crucifixion. Thereafter the Bible record of Mary falls silent, and a vast literature of pious devotion, legend and dogma takes over. [*Refs*. Matthew 1: 16, 18, 20; 2: 11; 13: 55. Mark 6: 3. Luke 1: 27*f*; 2: 5, 22*f*, 41*f*. John 2: 1*f*, 12; 19: 26. Acts 1: 14.] (2) Mary of Magdala, a town on the Sea of Galilee. She was also known as Mary Magdalene. She is mentioned among the women 'who had followed Jesus from Galilee, ministering to him', who witnessed the Crucifixion, and who went early in the morning of the first day of the week to see the sepulchre where the body of Jesus had been laid. The longer ending to Mark's Gospel tells that the risen Jesus 'appeared first to Mary Magdalene, from whom he had cast out seven demons'. Luke also mentions this detail concerning her. John's Gospel brings her into greater prominence by stating that she was the first to see the risen Lord, mistaking him at first for the gardener.

[*Refs.* Matthew 27: 56, 61; 28: 1*f*. Mark 15: 40, 47; 16: 1, 9. Luke 8: 2; 24: 10. John 19: 25; 20: 10.] (3) Mary, the mother of James (the younger) and Joseph (Joses), the disciples of Jesus. She is also mentioned among the women 'who had followed Jesus from Galilee, ministering to him', who looked upon his Crucifixion from afar, and who went to the tomb early in the morning of the third day with the other women. [*Refs.* Matthew 27: 56, 61; 28: 1. Mark 15: 40, 47; 16: 1. Luke 24: 10.] (4) Mary, the wife of Clopas. Mentioned among the women at the cross of Jesus. She cannot be more closely identified, but may be the same as Mary (3) above, the mother of James and Joses. [*Ref.* John 19: 25.] (5) Mary of Bethany, the sister of Martha and of Lazarus. She is mentioned by Luke as sitting at Jesus' feet, listening to his teaching, while her sister was 'distracted with much serving'. Jesus praised Mary for her devotion to him. John's Gospel tells that she anointed the Lord with ointment and wiped his feet with her hair, and that her brother Lazarus was raised from the dead. [*Refs.* Luke 10: 39*f*. John 11: 11; 12: 3.] (6) Mary, the mother of John Mark, in whose house in Jerusalem the followers of Jesus met for prayer. Tradition suggests that it was the house in which Jesus and his disciples met for the Last Supper. [*Ref.* Acts 12: 12.] (7) Mary, mentioned by Paul in the letter to the Romans as one 'who worked hard among you'. [*Ref.* Romans 16: 6.]

Matthew The name *Matthew* appears in the lists of the twelve chosen disciples of Jesus in the three Synoptic Gospels. The Gospel according to Matthew may have been named after this disciple, but it was not written by him. It is that Gospel, however, which tells how Jesus 'saw a man called Matthew sitting at the tax office; and he said to him "Follow me". And he rose and followed him'. The parallel stories in Mark and Luke mention Levi, the son of Alphaeus, at this point. Apart from these few references nothing is known of Matthew. [*Refs.* Matthew 9: 9; 10: 3. Mark 2: 14*f*; 3: 18. Luke 5: 27-32; 6: 15. Acts 1: 13.] *See also*: MATTHEW, THE GOSPEL OF

Matthew, The Gospel of The Gospel according to Matthew is the first book in our English N.T., but it was not the first to be written. The letters of Paul the apostle came before any of the Gospels. Then came the Gospel according to Mark, and it is generally agreed that the author of Matthew's Gospel copied some of his material from Mark as well as adding some from elsewhere. The writer is unknown to us. He was not Matthew the disciple of Jesus, though the book may have been named after that Matthew to give it importance in the early Church. The first three books in our N.T. are called the Synoptic Gospels, the Greek word *synopticos* meaning literally 'seeing together'. In other words, Matthew, Mark and Luke can be put side by side and we see a common pattern in their telling of the story of Jesus. And, although they differ in many ways, it is plain that words, phrases, and even whole passages are at times practically identical in all three. It can also be shown that it was Matthew and Luke who copied from Mark.

Matthew's sources of material were: (1) The Gospel according to Mark from which he copies about half his book. For example, the account of Jesus' last days in Matthew 20: 17 to 28: 7 is based very largely on Mark. (2) A collection of the 'sayings' of Jesus which is also used by Luke. Scholars call this common source *Q*, from the first letter of the German word *Quelle*, meaning 'source'. These 'sayings' of Jesus form about a quarter of Matthew's Gospel. An example is the sermon on the mount, set down in one form in Matthew 51 and in another form in Luke 6: 20-49. (3) Some incidents and teaching found only in Matthew's Gospel and therefore described by scholars as the source *M*. For example, the visit of the wise men in Matthew 2: 1-12, and the parable of the sheep and the goats in Matthew 25: 31-46.

So, in summary form, we may say that Matthew's Gospel is composed thus: Part of Mark + *Q* + *M*.

We can also notice how Matthew arranged his material. He liked to have things in order, in threes and fives and sevens. Thus there are three temptations (4: 1-11), three commands— 'ask...seek...knock' (7: 7), three healings—the leper, the centurion's servant, Peter's mother-in-law (8: 1-15) and three denials by Peter (26: 69-75). In Matthew 5: 21-48 we read five times: 'You have heard that it was said...but I say to you.' And in Matthew 23: 13-36 there are seven 'Woes' spoken against the scribes and Pharisees.

A short outline of the Gospel is:

(a) Matthew 1-2: The genealogy and birth of Jesus.

(b) Matthew 3-7: The teacher in Galilee.

(c) Matthew 8: 1 to 11: 1: Calling, commission, and instruction of the disciples.

(d) Matthew 11: 2 to 13: 52: Teaching and parables about the kingdom of heaven.

(e) Matthew 13: 53 to 18: 35. Travelling, transfiguration and teaching that he must suffer.

(f) Matthew 19: 1 to 25: 46. The journey to Jerusalem and warnings of the last days.

(g) Matthew 26: 1 to 28: 18: The Crucifixion and Resurrection.

Within this framework we find five blocks of teaching material each of which ends with the words: 'And when Jesus finished these sayings, or parables.' These five passages remind us of the 'five books of Moses' in the O.T. Just as the old law of God was given by Moses, so the new law is taught by Jesus. The portions are:

(a) Matthew 5: 1 to 7: 28: The Sermon on the Mount.

(b) Matthew 10: 1 to 11: 1: The commission to the disciples.

(c) Matthew 13: 1-53: Parables of the kingdom of heaven.

(d) Matthew 18: 1 to 19: 1: Teaching for the Church.

(e) Matthew 23: 1 to 26: 1: Warnings about the last days.

This book, then, is clearly no haphazard bit of writing nor merely a collection of stories about Jesus. It is as carefully put together as a cathedral. Not only can we see how the writer arranges his material, we can also learn why.

One main purpose is to say that Jesus is the fulfilment of O.T. hopes and prophecies. Hence the table of Jesus' ancestry at the very beginning of the Gospel and the use, twelve times over, of the phrase: 'that what was spoken by the prophets might be fulfilled", followed by a 'proof text' from the O.T. Another Jewish influence on the writer is his concern to say that Jesus is 'Son of David', born in Bethlehem and hailed more than once by this Messianic title. Matthew's is also notably a teaching Gospel, and the theme of Jesus' teaching is the kingdom of heaven.

The author is also concerned with the orderly life and discipline of the Church. Indeed, this is the only Gospel in which the word 'Church' is to be found (16: 18 and 18: 17). Matthew deals not only with the charge to Peter as the foundation of Christ's Church, but also with such topics as divorce, alms giving, fasting and prayer.

To sum up, we may say that Matthew was concerned to root his Gospel in O.T. prophecy, to instruct the believers in their faith in Christ, and to give some guidance for the discipline of Church members. His book was written for a Church of Jewish-Christians possibly at Antioch in Syria, who thought of themselves as 'the new Israel of God'. It was composed after the age of the first apostles when the Church was recognizably taking shape in the great cities of the Roman Empire, possibly about the year A.D. 85.

Matthias The follower of Jesus who was chosen by lot to replace Judas Iscariot as the twelfth disciple and to be a witness of the Resurrection. Nothing else is known of him. [*Ref.* Acts 1: 26.]

Medes The land of Media lay to the north-east of Mesopotamia, between the Black Sea and the Caspian Sea. The Medes are mentioned in the old Testament when Assyria was on the war path. When the king of Assyria captured Samaria, he carried the Israelites away to Assyria and placed them 'in the cities of the Medes'. The Medes allied themselves with the Chaldeans to overthrow Assyria, and were themselves eventually overcome by the Persians under Cyrus. The books of Daniel and Esther both refer to 'the laws of the Medes and the Persians'. The prophet Nahum's vivid account of the downfall of Nineveh refers to the attack by the Medes and Chaldeans in 612 B.C. [*Refs*. 2 Kings 17: 6; 18: 2. Esther 1: 19. Isaiah 13: 17. Daniel 5: 28; 6: 8. Acts 2: 9.]

Megiddo A very ancient fortress city of great strategic importance in northern Palestine. Megiddo guarded the pass at the entrance to the plain of Jezreel through which ran the one military and trade highway from Egypt to Mesopotamia. All travellers in peace or war, merchants and conquerors alike, had to go that way. Because of its position Megiddo has been the scene of many critical battles in ancient and modern times.

Solomon established a 'chariot city' at Megiddo and stabled there hundreds of horses and chariots in stables, with courts, ramparts, massive walls, houses for horsemen and officials, and stores for war equipment. Over three hundred years later, King Josiah of Judah flung his army in the path of the Egyptian Pharaoh Neco who was marching north to the aid of Assyria. Josiah died in that battle in 609 B.C.

Its antiquity as a battlefield made Megiddo proverbial as a symbol of war. The N.T. Book of Revelation mentions Armageddon ('the hill of Megiddo') as a place where the final battle between good and evil will be fought. [*Refs*. Judges 5: 19. 1 Kings 9: 15. 2 Kings 23: 29. 2 Chronicles 1: 14-17; 9: 25. Revelation 16: 16.]

Melchizedek The priest-king of Salem encountered by Abraham during his wanderings. His name came to be a symbol of ideal priesthood and the idea was expanded in the N.T. letter to the Hebrews with reference to Christ. [*Refs*. Genesis 14: 18. Psalm 110: 4. Hebrews 6: 20 to 7: 17.]

Melita The island of Malta in the Mediterranean. Paul was shipwrecked there on his voyage to Rome, and was kindly treated by the people of Malta. [*Ref.* Acts 28: 1-10.]

Messiah The Hebrew word *Messiah* occurs at only one place in the A.V. of the Testament, at Daniel 9: 25-6, where the sense is not at all clear. The R.S.V. correctly translates the word as 'anointed one'. In John's Gospel the Greek form *Messias* appears twice in the Authorized Version, with Messiah in the Revised Standard Version. In both cases the title 'Christ' is added by way of explanation. *Christ* also means 'anointed one'. The custom of anointing with oil in ancient times marked out a king or priest. In later Jewish thought, the hope arose that God would send an anointed king of David's line who would save his people from their suffering and who would bring in God's kingdom. This hope is clearly set out in Psalm 72, as well as in some of the Jewish literature produced between the Testaments. Teaching about the hoped-for Messiah took many forms. He would be deliverer, saviour, victorious conqueror, judge and ruler. It is not possible to define exactly how Jewish Messianic hopes were to be interpreted in N.T. times, except, perhaps, that he would be 'great David's greater son'. It is clear, however, that some N.T. writers thought of Jesus as the Messiah and therefore they named him the Christ. [*Refs.* Psalm 72. Isaiah 9: 7; 11: 1-9; 45: 1. Daniel 9: 25-6. John 1: 41; 4: 25.] *See also*: CHRIST

Micah A prophet of the second half of eighth century B.C. Judah and a contemporary of Isaiah. Micah was a countryman who belonged to the fertile lowland of Judah. He spoke out against the oppression of the poor by the rich—those who covet and seize and oppress, 'who tear the skin from off my people, and their flesh from off their bones; who abhor justice and pervert all equity'. He proclaimed that Samaria and Jerusalem would be destroyed. We know nothing of Micah apart from what we learn from the book which bears his name. [*Refs.* Micah 1: 1; 2: 1*f*; 3: 2-3, 9-12.]

Micah, The Book of The Book of Micah forms one of the 'Latter Prophets' of the Hebrew Scriptures and is the sixth of the twelve minor prophets in our O.T. All we know of Micah is that he was a contemporary of Isaiah of Jerusalem, belonged to the same kingdom of Judah, and prophesied at about the same time, towards the end of the eighth century B.C. Micah, however, was a man of the country rather than the city. He knew the life of the poor peasant as well as that of the wealthy citizen. His oracles are concerned with the daily hardships of the small farmer. This short book may be divided thus: (a) Micah 1-3: Prophetic protests against social injustice both in Jerusalem of Judah and Samaria the capital of Israel. Like the other prophets of his age—Amos, Hosea, Isaiah—this spokesman for God proclaims a divine judgment on the chosen people. The rich prey on the poor: 'they covet fields and seize them; and houses, and take them away' (2: 2). Bribery and corruption destroy the kingdom of Judah: 'its heads give judgment for a bribe, its priests teach for hire, its prophets divine for money' (3: 11). Micah warns of disaster and exile: 'Zion shall be ploughed as a field; Jerusalem shall become a heap of ruins' (3: 12). These final words were remembered and repeated a hundred years later by Jeremiah in the last days of Jerusalem (Jeremiah 26: 18). (b) Micah 4-5: These passages, which deal with the restoration of Jerusalem, probably belong to a much later date, during the Exile. The picture of a peaceful Zion where 'they shall beat their swords into ploughshares, and their spears into pruning hooks' (4: 1-3) is paralleled in Isaiah 2: 2-4. In 5: 2 there occurs the famous prophecy which is taken up in the N.T., concerning Bethlehem as the birthplace of the coming Messianic ruler. (c) Micah 6-7: A collection of oracles, again concerned with the corrupt condition of Israel. The most famous is the short passage in 6: 6-8 about the moral demands of God which give shape to the religion: 'He has showed you, O man, what is good; and what does the Lord require of you but to do justice, and to love kindness and to walk humbly with your God?' A peak of O.T. prophetic teaching.

Michael A guardian angel mentioned in the Book of Daniel as protector of God's people against the power of Persia and Greece. He appears in the N.T. in the Book of Jude as the archangel, and in Revelation. [*Refs.* Daniel 10: 13, 21; 12: 1. Jude 9. Revelation 12: 7.]

Midianites The Midianites were nomadic clans who were to be found in the Arabian desert and who frequently raided Canaan in the days of the Israelite settlement. Their ancestor was said to be a son of Abraham, so the Bible writers claim them as kin, though they were often foes. Moses fled from the wrath of Pharaoh to the land of Midian and found shelter with 'a priest of Midian' whose daughter he married. But war against Midian is also mentioned in the days of the desert wanderings, and in the time of the Judges Gideon decisively defeated them. The name is sometimes confused with Ishmaelites in the O.T. They are usually mentioned as a Bedouin people who were the first to use camels as domestic animals and for desert raids. [*Refs.* Genesis 25: 2; 37: 28. Exodus 2: 15*f*; 3: 1. Numbers 31: 1-12. Judges 6-7; 8: 22-8.] *See also*: ISHMAELITES

Millo A platform or rampart at the north end of 'the city of David' which David strengthened and made part of his enlarged fortress city of Jerusalem. Solomon still further added to the strength of this part of his capital and so, later, did King Hezekiah in the days of Assyrian attack. [*Refs.* 2 Samuel 5: 9. 1 Kings 9: 15; 11: 27. 1 Chronicles 11: 8. 2 Chronicles 32: 5.]

Miracles A miracle, by definition, is an object of wonder. It is a marvellous event exceeding the known powers of Nature, and therefore supposed to be due to some special act of God. St. Augustine said that a miracle is an occurrence which is contrary to what is known of Nature. The Bible writers, however, do not speak of 'Nature' or of 'natural events' as if things could happen within or without the known world. Everything that happens is an act of God, whether it is a cause of wonder or not—seedtime, harvest, rain, drought, evil as well as good, the inexplicable as well as the everyday.

Miracles in the Old Testament

The 'miracle' events of the O.T. are more properly called 'signs'. The Hebrew word *oth*, meaning 'sign', is applied to the mighty acts of God to which men respond with terror, awe and wonder, such as storm and thunder, flames of fire and tempest, whirlwind and flood. For example:

'The voice of the Lord is upon the waters...
'The voice of the Lord breaks the cedars...
'The voice of the Lord flashes forth flames of fire...'

(Psalm 29: 3*f*)

'When the waters saw thee, O God,
when the waters saw thee, they were afraid,
yea, the deep trembled.
The clouds poured out water;
the skies gave forth thunder;
thy arrows flashed on every side...
Thy way was through the sea,
thy path through the great waters;
yet thy footprints were unseen.'

(Psalm 77: 16*f*)

It is true that writers and readers of an earlier age did not critically seek to 'explain away' everything that they could not understand. Nevertheless, these mighty acts are not set down haphazardly here and there through O.T. writings. The 'signs' are recorded to point solemnly and deliberately to the great basic events in Hebrew history and belief. The first of these is the fact of the deliverance from Egypt. Jewish literature, prayers, and religious observances proclaim the Exodus as no accident of history but a unique act of God: 'He made known his ways to Moses, his acts to the people of Israel' (Psalm 103: 7). Therefore the narrative of this great event is planted about with 'signs' to indicate that God is at work throughout, beginning with Moses' encounter with God on Mt. Horeb. 'The angel of the Lord appeared to him in a flame of fire out of the midst of a bush; and he looked, and lo, the bush was burning, yet it was not consumed' (Exodus 3: 2). Thereafter there are 'signs' in plenty to mark the way from Egypt to the Sea of Reeds and beyond, to the mountain of God. These include rods turned into serpents, the ten plagues, the crossing of the Sea, water from the rock and manna from heaven. They are recorded to declare the dramatic act of God which brought their people from Egypt and made them a chosen people.

'When he wrote his signs in Egypt
and his miracles in the fields of Zoan.'

(Psalm 78: 43; see also 105: 26*f*)

These 'signs' remind all faithful Jews of what God has done for them. In that faith this story has been read and recited in Jewish worship at home and in synagogue all down the years. They are to:

'remember the wonderful works that he has done,
his miracles, and the judgments he uttered,
O offspring of Abraham his servant,
sons of Jacob, his chosen ones!'

(Psalm 105: 5-6)

This remembrance is to sustain them in times of greatest fear and distress: 'Remember what the Lord your God did to Pharaoh and to all Egypt, the great trials which your eyes saw, the signs, the wonders, the mighty hand, and the outstretched arm, by which the Lord your God brought you out' (Deuteronomy 7: 18-19).

Not only are they to remember. They are to teach these events to their children: 'When your son asks you in time to come...then you shall say to your son, "We were Pharaoh's slaves in Egypt; and the Lord brought us out of Egypt with a mighty hand; and the Lord showed signs and wonders, great and grievous...and he brought us out from there" ' (Deuteronomy 6: 20*f*).

The Exodus 'signs and wonders' continue into the Joshua stories until Canaan is reached at last. So Israel, under Joshua, passes dryshod through the Jordan as they did through the Sea of Reeds under the leadership of Moses. Jericho falls before them at the sound of a trumpet. The sun stands still to allow them victory in battle. (This ancient poem in Joshua 10: 12-14 is probably a song which has become literalized into a wonderful event.) The 'signs' of the Joshua story are, as it were, a literary fulfilment of the promise: 'as I was with Moses, so I will be with you' (Joshua 1: 5). No one will ever know what actually happened long ago in Egypt, in the desert, and in Canaan. We have no filmed record or radio interviews to bring these age-old events sharply into focus. What we have is a story recited in pious remembrance from generation to generation, and that story is marked by 'signs' to declare that God is mightily at work. Thus must the 'miracles' of the O.T. be interpreted.

The other large group of 'miracle' stories in the O.T. gathers round the work of Elijah and Elisha, the two prophets who especially reminded their people that 'the Lord, he is God'. Thus we have such tales as:

The widow's curse (1 Kings 17: 8f)
The widow's son healed (1 Kings 17: 17f)
Fire at Mt. Carmel (1 Kings 18: 20f)
Fire from heaven (2 Kings 1: 9f)
The waters of Jordan part (2 Kings 2: 7-8)
A chariot of fire (2 Kings 2: 11)
The waters of Jordan part (2 Kings 2: 14)
The children and the bears (2 Kings 2: 24)
Water in a dry land (2 Kings 3: 19-20)
The widow's oil (2 Kings 4: 2-7)
The farmer's boy raised (2 Kings 4: 8f)
Death in the pot (2 Kings 4: 38f)
Feeding a hundred men (2 Kings 4: 42-4)
Naaman the leper (2 Kings 5: 1f)
An axe head floats (2 Kings 6: 5-7)
The Syrian army blinded (2 Kings 6: 18-20)
Raising a dead man (2 Kings 13: 21).

There are other 'miracle' tales in the O.T., but most of them are grouped as above, round the Exodus events and round the prophets Elijah and Elisha. Some of these stories no doubt show legendary additions, as in the much later accounts of mediaeval saints. It must be remembered that all these stories of people and happenings were composed and edited long after the events themselves. This is not straightforward history. It is history written with a religious purpose, to point to the mighty acts of God. In that context the 'miracles' are the signposts.

Miracles in the New Testament

The usual word for 'miracle' in the Synoptic Gospels is *dunamis* which is translated 'mighty work' (*cf. dynamo, dynamic*). The Gospel writers all declare that Jesus did certain things which were 'mighty works'. These were often closely connected with the fulfilment of O.T. prophetic hopes. Consider, for example, how many of the healing acts fulfil the words of Isaiah 35: 5-6:

'Then the eyes of the blind shall be opened,
and the ears of the deaf unstopped;
then shall the lame man leap like a hart,
and the tongue of the dumb sing for joy.'

Thus the 'mighty works' of the N.T. have meaning for those who have eyes to see and minds to understand.

The 'mighty works' of the Synoptic Gospels may be grouped thus for the purpose of study:

(a) *Exorcisms*: the casting out of evil spirits. For example: A man with an unclean spirit (Mark 1: 23*f*. Luke 4: 33*f*). At sundown (Mark 1: 32-4. Matthew 8: 16-17. Luke 4: 40-1). The man called Legion (Mark 5: 1-20. Matthew 8: 28-34. Luke 8: 26-39).

It may be noted that other people besides Jesus were exorcists (see Matthew 12: 27). The Gospels state that Jesus' work in casting out evil spirits was not sorcery or black magic, but the direct act of God to show that the kingdom of God has come (Matthew 12: 28).

(b) *The healing of physical diseases*: Simon's wife's mother (Mark 1: 29-31. Matthew 8: 14-15. Luke 4: 38-9). Healings in Capernaum (Mark 1: 32-4. Matthew 8: 16-17. Luke 4: 40-1). The leper (Mark 1: 40-5. Matthew 8: 2-4. Luke 5: 12-14). The paralytic (Mark 2: 1-12. Matthew 9: 2-8. Luke 5: 18-26). The man with the withered hand (Mark 3: 1-6. Matthew 12: 9-14. Luke 6: 6-11). The woman with the flow of blood (Mark 5: 25-34. Matthew 9: 20-2. Luke 8: 43-8). Healings in Gennesaret (Mark 6: 53-6. Matthew

14: 34-6). The Syrophoenician woman (Mark 7: 24-30. Matthew 15: 21-8). The deaf mute (Mark 7: 31-7. Matthew 15: 29-31). The blind man at Bethsaida (*Mark* 8: 22-6). The epileptic boy (Mark 9: 14-29. Matthew 17: 14-18. Luke 9: 37-43). Blind Bartimaeus (Mark 10: 46-52. Matthew 20: 29-34. Luke 18: 35-43). Two blind men (Matthew 9: 27-31). A dumb demoniac (Matthew 9: 32-4. Luke 11: 14-15). The crooked woman (Luke 13: 11-17). The man with dropsy (Luke 14: 1-6). The ten lepers (Luke 17: 11-19). The slave of the high priest (Luke 22: 50-1). The centurion's servant (Matthew 8: 5-10. Luke 7: 1-10). A blind and dumb demoniac (Matthew 12; 22).

(c) *Raising the dead*: Jairus's daughter (Mark 5: 21f. Matthew 9: 18f. Luke 8: 40f). The widow of Nain's son (Luke 7: 11-17).

(d) *Nature miracles*: The stilling of the storm (Mark 4: 35-41. Matthew 8: 231. Luke 8: 22-5). Feeding of the five thousand (Mark 6: 30f. Matthew 14: 13f Luke 9: 11f). Feeding of the four thousand (Mark 8: 1-9. Matthew 15: 32-8). Walking on the water (Mark 6: 45-52. Matthew 14: 22-33).

Nature of the Miracles

The writer of John's Gospel uses the word *semeion*, meaning sign for the miracles of Jesus. For him the mighty works are 'signs' pointing to who Jesus is, the holy one of God. Others may see merely the wonders; the believer reads the signs and understands the truth. It is as 'signs' that the following miracles recorded by John are to be understood:

Water into wine (John 2: 1f)

The nobleman's son (John 4: 46f)

The sick man at the pool (John 5: 2f)

Feeding the five thousand (John 6: 5-14)

A man blind from birth (John 9: 1f)

The raising of Lazarus (John 11: 1f).

The stories of the miracles of Jesus arouse question and comment. The following points may be mentioned:

(1) They were not noted down at the time. There is no guarantee that the account of any Gospel event comes directly from

an eye-witness, or that the eye-witness is reliable. These stories are a mixture of memory and meaning. They come down through at least thirty years of telling and re-telling, and that re-telling is for a teaching purpose: 'Now Jesus did many other signs in the presence of his disciples which are not written in this book; but these are written that you may believe that Jesus is the Christ, the Son of God, and that believing you may have life in his name' (John 20: 30-1).

(2) There is carelessness of detail, change of emphasis here and there, and some doublets in the miracle stories of the Gospels. For example, blind Bartimaeus in Mark's account becomes two blind men in Matthew's Gospel. Similarly the man of the tombs called Legion by Mark becomes two demoniacs in Matthew's story.

(3) It must be noted that Jesus himself rejected the temptation to work wonders such as casting himself from a pinnacle of the Temple to win the allegiance of the people (Matthew 4: 5f. Luke 4: 9f). He refused to give the Pharisees 'a sign from heaven' (Mark 8: 11). The miracles of the Gospels are not mere wonder-stories. For the Gospel writers and the early Church they attest God's supreme revelation of himself in the life, work, death of Jesus. That is not to say that the reader today must accept them uncritically. We may understand the meaning of many of the miracle stories even where we put a question mark against their actual happening. It is important to use the aid of scholarly research and one's own thoughtful mind to come to some understanding of the making and meaning of the miracle stories of the Gospels. Trust in Jesus as Lord is one thing; trust in the verbal details of the Gospel accounts may be another.

The Acts of the Apostles

The Acts of the Apostles, in which Luke records the continuation of 'all that Jesus began to do and teach', also includes various stories of miracles at the hands of the disciples of Jesus. For example:

A lame man healed (Acts 3: 1-10)
Many signs and wonders (Acts 5: 12)
Stephen's wonders and signs (Acts 6: 8)
Philip's signs and miracles (Acts 8: 13)
Aeneas healed (Acts 9: 32-5)
Tabitha raised to life (Acts 9: 36-42)
Paul and Barnabas do signs and wonders (Acts 14: 3)
A cripple at Lystra (Acts 14: 8ƒ)
A slave girl at Philippi (Acts 16: 16-18)
Paul's miracles at Ephesus (Acts 19: 11ƒ)
Paul's healing acts at Malta (Acts 28: 7ƒ).

Miriam The sister of Moses and Aaron. She appears first in the legendary tale of the baby Moses in the reeds by the river of Egypt when she watched over the child and summoned a nurse from amongst the Hebrew women. Much later she led the dance and song of the Hebrew women after they had crossed the Sea of Reeds on their way to the promised land. Miriam died at Kadesh. [*Refs*. Exodus 2: 4-8; 15: 20-1. Numbers 20: 1.]

Moab Part of Palestine lying east of the Dead Sea, well-watered and fertile. Legend linked the Moabites with the Hebrews through Lot, nephew of Abraham. It was from Mt. Nebo in the land of Moab that Moses viewed Canaan, and there he died. The Israelites had to circumvent Moab on their entry into the promised land. Later references to Moab include Ruth the Moabitess who was an ancestor of David. David defeated Moab and exacted tribute from the Moabites. A later bloody battle is recorded in the days of Jehoram, son of Ahab, king of Israel. The land of Moab was eventually overcome by Nebuchadrezzar. [*Refs*. Genesis 19: 36-7. Numbers 22. Deuteronomy 32: 49; 34: 1,5, 8. Judges 3: 12-14, 27-30; 11: 17-18. 2 Samuel 8: 2. 2 Kings 3: 4-27. Psalm 60: 8. Isaiah 15. Jeremiah 48.]

Molech The name Molech or Moloch is kin to the Hebrew word for 'king'. Molech was a pagan Semitic god whose worship involved child-sacrifice by fire. The O.T. writers condemned this practice and the Hebrew Law forbids it, on pain of death by stoning. But there is no doubt that the sacrifice of first-born children by burning them before the god went on for centuries in Canaanite custom and was copied by the Israelites. Probably the god Milcom, to whom Solomon set up an altar, was the same as Molech. [*Refs.* Leviticus 18: 21; 20: 2-5. 1 Kings 11: 7. 2 Kings 23: 10.]

Moses There are no records dating from the time of Moses to give us a detailed account of his life and work. We know him only by way of tradition, legend, and popular story, most of which was written down centuries after his own time. Moses is for ever associated in Hebrew memory and Jewish writing with the Exodus from Egypt, the giving of the Law, the making of a Covenant, and the shaping of a nation who were to enter into and possess Canaan as the land of promise. He is thus regarded as the greatest man of all Hebrew history. Israel may claim descent from Abraham and Jacob, but it was Moses who made them know that they were especially the chosen people of God.

The stories of Moses begin with the tale of his preservation as a child in the bulrushes by the river Nile, his upbringing at the court of Pharaoh, his anger at the oppression of the Hebrew people, his flight to the land of Midian, and there, as a shepherd, his call from God at the burning bush. His task was to go back to Egypt to bring about the deliverance of God's people, Israel. Many wonders accompany his message to Pharaoh: 'Let my people go.' The plagues, the crossing of the Sea of Reeds, the gifts of manna, quails and water in the desert are all set down as signs that God is leading his people. It is Moses who brings the Commandments from the fire and smoke of Mt. Sinai and to whom all subsequent laws are in some way attributed as the Torah or 'laws of Moses', the body of divine teaching which makes the Jew separate and unique. Moses is set down not only as leader of his people, but also as the man with whom the Lord used to speak 'face to face, as a man speaks to his friend'. It is recorded that he was allowed to see the promised land at last from a mountain top in the land of Moab and there, among the hills, he died, 'but no man knows the place of his burial to this day'. In all the long legendary account, the writer's final tribute is: 'There has not arisen a prophet since in Israel like Moses, whom the Lord knew face to face, none like him for all the signs and the wonders which the Lord sent him to do in the land of Egypt, to Pharaoh and to all his servants and to all his land, and for all the mighty power and all the great and terrible deeds which Moses wrought in the sight of all Israel.'

The name *Moses* is said to mean 'drawn out of the water', but most language scholars would reject that meaning. They would prefer to state that Moses is, in fact, part of an Egyptian name. The historical Moses may be impossible to find, but the Moses of tradition and sacred story is clearly set before us. One might say that if there had been no Moses it would have been necessary to invent him. The Moses we do meet in the pages of the Bible has more than enough reality to let us believe that he was real, not merely a hero of ancient song and story. He is known by what he did, even if some of the details are legendary, as befits so great a man. Undoubtedly he was the outstanding leader, lawgiver and man of God of O.T. times.

In the N.T. not only does Jesus quote Moses as the lawgiver of the Jews. It is told that on the mountain of the Transfiguration Moses and Elijah, the two great prophets of Israel. appeared with Jesus, the inference being that 'a greater than Moses is here'. The N.T. bears witness to the belief that just as the deliverer of God's people under the old covenant was Moses, so, in the new covenant, the saviour is Jesus Christ. 'For the law was given through Moses; grace and truth came through Jesus Christ.' [*Refs*. Throughout the books of Exodus, Leviticus, Numbers, Deuteronomy. Joshua 1: 1. Psalm 77: 20; 103: 7. Isaiah 63: 11. Matthew 17: 3*f*. Mark 12: 26. Luke 9: 30; 24: 27. John 1: 17, 45; 7: 19. Acts 7: 20*f*. Hebrews 11: 23*f*.] *See also*: KENITES, NEBO

Mount of Olives *See* OLIVES, MOUNT OF

N

Naaman The commander of the army of the king of Syria in the days of war with Israel. He was a mighty man of valour, but he was a leper. Naaman was advised by a captured Israelite slave-girl to seek the aid of the prophet Elisha. The man of God told Naaman to go and wash in the Jordan seven times. When he reluctantly did so, his flesh became like the flesh of a child, and he was clean. [*Ref.* 2 Kings 5.]

Naboth A man of Jezreel who had a fertile vineyard close to the palace of King Ahab of Israel. Ahab offered to buy the vineyard or to give a fair exchange of land, but Naboth would not give up his family property. Queen Jezebel plotted and brought about the death of Naboth and told Ahab to take possession of the vineyard. But the prophet Elijah confronted the king, condemned his act in the name of the God of Israel, and foretold the total destruction of the royal house. [*Ref.* 1 Kings 21.]

Nahum, The Book of The Book of Nahum is to be found among the 'Latter Prophets' of Hebrew Scriptures and is included in the minor prophets of our O.T. We know nothing of the man Nahum apart from this writing. It consists of prophetic oracles in poetic form against the imperial power of Assyria and Nineveh its capital city. The opening (1: 1 to 2: 2) is in the form of an acrostic poem. Thereafter (2: 3 to 3: 19) speaks of the coming destruction of Nineveh which was eventually captured and sacked by the joint armies of the Medes and the Chaldeans in 612 B.C.

These chapters contain the most vivid and savage description of a conquering army in the whole of the O.T.—soldiers in scarlet, chariots and prancing chargers, plunder of gold and silver, desolation and ruin. The whole book can be summed up in the lines: 'Woe to the bloody city, all full of lies and booty—no end to the plunder!' (3: 1.)

Nain A town in Galilee where Jesus brought a widow's son back to life. [*Ref.* Luke 7: 11-15.]

Naomi The mother-in-law of Ruth in the O.T. book of that name. When Naomi was widowed and her two sons died in the land of Midian she went back to her home town of Bethlehem. Ruth, her loving Midianite daughter-in-law, went with her. Naomi arranged a marriage for Ruth with a rich farmer called Boaz and she nursed their son Obed who was to be the grandfather of David. [*Ref.* The Book of Ruth.]

Naphtali The second son of Jacob and Bilhah, who was Rachel's maid. writings writings O.T. claim Naphtali as ancestor of one of the twelve tribes, and men of Naphtali are mentioned here and there in tribal stories from the Exodus to the time of David. [*Refs.* Genesis 30: 7-8; 35: 25; 49: 21. Exodus 1: 4. Deuteronomy 33:23. Joshua 19: 32*f*. Judges 5: 18.]

Nathan A prophet at the court of King David. When David sent Uriah the soldier to his death in battle in order that he might take Uriah's wife, Bathsheba, the prophet confronted the king with his crime. Nathan told the simple, dramatic tale of the theft of the poor man's one little ewe lamb, and said to David: 'You are the man.'

Nathan is said to have influenced David against his plan to build a Temple to house the Ark of the Covenant. He also took a hand in affairs of state when David was old and dying, and saw to it that Solomon rather than Adonijah became king after David. [*Refs.* 2 Samuel 7: 1-17; 12: 1-25. 1 Kings 1: 1-48.]

Nathanael *See* BARTHOLOMEW

Nazarene A native of Nazareth. In the N.T. the term is used especially of Jesus and his followers. [*Refs.* Matthew 2: 23. Acts 24: 5.]

Nazareth A small town in the hills of Galilee of no importance except for Jesus of Nazareth. It was the home town of Joseph and Mary and the place where Jesus was brought up. When Jesus later came to teach in the synagogue at Nazareth the people of the town took offence at him, and he said: 'A prophet is not without honour, except in his own country, and among his own kin, and in his own home.' There is no record that Jesus even went there again. [*Refs*. Matthew 21: 11. Mark 1: 9; 6: 1-6. Luke 1: 26; 2: 51; 4 16-30.]

Nazirites The name means 'separated ones'. These men considered themselves dedicated to God, and thus set apart from others. They drank no wine or any strong drink, indeed they did not even eat grapes, fresh or dried. Nor did they cut their hair. Their long hair was a sign of their vow of dedication. They were forbidden to touch or go near a dead body. Parents sometimes consecrated their sons to be Nazirites before ever they were born. Samson was such a one, so also was John the Baptist. [*Refs*. Numbers 6: 1-21. Judges 13: 5; 16: 17. 1 Samuel 1: 11. Luke 1: 15.]

Nebo A high mountain in the land of Moab, east of the Dead Sea and across the Jordan from Jericho, from which Moses viewed the promised land, and where, tradition tells, he died. [*Refs*. Deuteronomy 32: 49; 34 1, 5.]

Nebuchadrezzar or **Nebuchadnezzar** Nebuchadnezzar, more properly spelled *Nebuchadrezzar*, was emperor of Babylon 605 B.C. and the most famous ruler of his day. He defeated the army of Egypt in one of the world's great battles, at Carchemish on the Euphrates, and thus laid the whole of the Middle East under his power. Nebuchadrezzar conquered the kingdom of Judah and made it a vassal state with a puppet king the throne. But, because of Jewish rebellion, he attacked the fortress capital city of Jerusalem three times, looting the treasures of the Temple and carrying off many of the leading people to Exile. The final siege of Jerusalem was long, ruthless and thorough. When the city fell in 587 B.C. Nebuchadrezzar's army broke down the walls, burned the gates, razed the Temple and other buildings to the ground, plundered all that was of value, and carried off the remaining citizens to Exile in Babylon. The downfall of Jerusalem has been remembered by Jews as the darkest day in their history, and Nebuchadrezzar is set down in Jewish historical records as the ruler who brought about their defeat and banishment from the promised land. He also appears in the non-historical book of Daniel as a strange, legendary figure, a man of wild dreams, who ended up eating grass like an ox. [*Refs.* 2 Kings 24: 1, 10; 25: 1, 8-12. Ezra 2: 1. Jeremiah 52: 4. Daniel 1: 1; 4: 33.]

Neco or **Nechoh** The Pharaoh of Egypt who defeated and killed King Josiah of Judah at Megiddo. Neco himself was defeated by Nebuchadrezzar of Babylon at the battle of Carchemish in 605 B.C. [*Refs.* 2 Kings 23: 29. Jeremiah 46: 2.]

Negeb A word which is translated 'south land' in the Authorized Version. The Negeb lay to the south of Judah from Beersheba to the Arabian desert. The Hebrew word means 'dry' and it is an area of sparse rainfall. [*Refs.* Genesis 12: 9; 13: 1. Deuteronomy 1: 7. Joshua 10: 40; 11: 16. 1 Samuel 27: 10.]

Nehemiah A Jew of the Exile who was cupbearer to Artaxerxes I, king of Persia. He learned from men of Judah that the wall of Jerusalem was broken down and its gates destroyed by fire. The Book of Nehemiah, which is our source of information about him, tells that he asked King Artaxerxes for permission to go to Jerusalem to rebuild it. He was appointed governor of Judah, supplied with timber for repairs, and sent off with an escort of Persian officers and horsemen to carry out the work. The book of Nehemiah tells of the organizing, carrying out and completion of that task in spite of attack from enemies. The year of his return to Jerusalem was about 445 B.C., and he seems to have remained as governor after the walls were rebuilt to enforce strict religious reforms. [*Refs.* Nehemiah 1: 1*f.*] *See also:* TOBIAH

Nehemiah, The Book of The Book of Nehemiah is closely linked with Ezra in Hebrew Scriptures and forms part of a larger work which includes 1 and 2 Chronicles. The writer, known as 'the chronicler', sets down the story of the faithful Jews who returned from Exile and devoted themselves to the rebuilding of the holy city of Jerusalem with the Temple in the midst. Part of the narrative of Nehemiah is told in the first person, as if it were extracts from a personal diary kept during the arduous days of the rebuilding of the walls of Jerusalem. The contents are:

(a) Nehemiah 1-6: Nehemiah comes to Jerusalem and in spite of opposition rebuilds the walls.

(b) Nehemiah 7-12: A list of the exiles who returned, Ezra's reading of the Law, the religious rejoicing that marked the completion of the work.

(c) Nehemiah 13: A second visit by Nehemiah to Jerusalem, and further reforms.

Nicodemus A Pharisee, a member of the Sanhedrin or Council of the Jews, who sought Jesus secretly by night to hear him teach. According to John's Gospel Nicodemus helped Joseph of Arimathea to lay the body of Jesus in the tomb after the Crucifixion. [*Refs.* John 3: 1-10; 7: 50-1; 19: 39-42.]

Nile The longest river in Africa and the life-blood of Egypt. The fertility of the land of Egypt has always depended on the rich soil brought down and deposited annually by the flood waters of the Nile. This made Egypt the granary of the ancient Mediterranean world. The Nile was also a great trade route linking the countries of the Middle East with the wealth of the heart of Africa. The Nile, often referred to as 'the river', appears early in the O.T. story. Abraham knew it, and Goshen on the fringe of the delta was the home of the Hebrew shepherds in the time of Joseph. Moses was hidden in the reeds of the river when he was a baby, and later a plague of Egypt turned the waters of the Nile to blood. [*Refs.* Exodus 1:22; 2: 3; 7: 20. Isaiah 19: 5-8. Jeremiah 46: 7-8.]

Nimrod According to Genesis, Nimrod was the great-grandson of Noah and a legendary hunter and builder of kingdoms, including Babylon. The name has become proverbial for a mighty hunter. [*Refs.* Genesis 10: 8-12. Micah 5: 6.]

Nineveh A city on the banks of the Tigris, the mighty capital of Assyria in ancient times. In the days of Sennacherib (705-681 B.C.) its walls, towers and gates, its water supply and canals, and its library made Nineveh glorious, and its streets saw many parades of captives and booty from conquered lands. There was no more hated city in Bible times, a symbol of Assyrian oppression, as the savage prophecy of Nahum shows. It is mentioned both for its wickedness and for its splendour in the story of Jonah. Nineveh was destroyed by an alliance of the Medes, Babylonians and Scythians in 612 B.C. [*Refs*. 2 Kings 19: 36. Jonah 1: 2; 3: 2-3. Nahum 1: 1; 2: 8-10; 3: 1-7. Zephaniah 2: 13.]

Noah The hero of the story of the Flood in Genesis. Noah was told by God to build an ark of wood to save his family and every kind of animal, bird, and creeping thing from the Flood which would destroy life on the earth. The tale has many contradictions which reveal that it comes from more than one source. Some of the strands are derived from an ancient Babylonian story found in the Gilgamesh epic, but the whole thing has been adapted by devout Israelite writers to show their own belief in the omnipotence of God. [*Refs*. Genesis: 6-9. Luke 17: 26-7.]

Numbers Numbers is the fourth book of the Pentateuch or 'five books of Moses'. It contains various stories of the Israelites' desert journey from Egypt to the promised land, including the sending out of the spies, the water from the rock, Balaam and his ass, and battles against various hostile tribes on the way to the borders of Canaan. Some of the material is repeated from the book of Exodus. Numbers also contains some early Hebrew poems and war songs. But the larger part of the book is concerned with religious laws and is the work of priestly editors after the Exile. These writers, who had a hand in shaping part of the book of Exodus and the whole of Leviticus set down their religious statistics and instructions as if they belonged to the time of Moses. This very composite book is not history, but a work of piety of a much later age than the time it seems to record.

O

Obadiah, The Book of The shortest book in the o.t., containing only one chapter of twenty-one verses. It is found among the 'Latter Prophets' of Hebrew Scriptures and is one of the twelve minor prophets of our o.t. We have no information about the man Obadiah apart from the heading to this book, nor about the time when he lived. All we can tell is that it must have been written after the downfall of Jerusalem in 587 B.C.

The work consists of a collection of brief poetic oracles against Edom. The people of Edom were by tradition the descendants of Esau and ancient enemies of the children of Israel. The territory of Edom, to the south of the Dead Sea, had been conquered by David. But in the days of the siege of Jerusalem the men of Edom took their revenge, and when the city fell to the Babylonians the Edomites seized part of Judah. This poem savagely reproaches Edom for their misdeeds: 'you should not have gloated over the day of your brother in the day of his misfortune; you should not have rejoiced over the people of Judah in the day of their ruin' (12).

Verses 1-4 are found also in Jeremiah 49: 14-16, and the same note of rebuke for Edom is found in Psalm 137: 7, Isaiah 34: 5-6, Lamentations 4: 21 and Ezekiel 25: 12-14. The Jewish writers had a long memory for revenge.

Og *See* BASHAN

Olives, Mount of The Mt. of Olives, or Olivet, was a line of hills east of Jerusalem across the Kidron valley. The villages of Bethany and Bethphage were on its slopes in N.T. times, and Gethsemane lay at the foot of the hill. King David fled from his rebellious son Absalom by way of the Mt. of Olives. The Gospels mention the hill a number of times, especially in connection with the night in which Jesus was betrayed and arrested. [*Refs.* 2 Samuel 15: 30-2. Ezekiel 11: 23. Zechariah 14: 4. Matthew 21: 1; 24: 3; 26: 30. Mark 11: 1; 13: 3; 14: 26. Luke 19: 29, 37; 21: 37; 22: 39.]

Omega The last letter in the Greek alphabet. It is used along with Alpha, the first letter, to express the greatness and completeness of God. Also as a title of Christ: 'I am the Alpha and the Omega, the first and the last, the beginning and the end.' [*Refs.* Revelation 1: 8; 22: 13.]

Omri Omri was commander of the army of Israel at a time of intrigue and civil war in the ninth century B.C. Encouraged by his soldiers he seized power and made himself the sixth king of Israel, 876-869 B.C. Although he is mentioned only briefly in the o.t., Omri was a powerful king whose rule was long remembered and whose power was respected by all the kings of the near east. He established a new capital for Israel on a hilltop at Samaria, fortified the city with strong walls and defences, and made it a wealthy trading-centre. He also kept peace with Judah in the south and made an alliance with Phoenicia in the north to hold Syria in check. As a seal of the Phoenician pact he arranged the marriage of his eldest son and heir Ahab to Jezebel, daughter of the king of Tyre, a union which was to bring dire trouble to Israel. [*Ref.* 1 Kings 16: 16-28.]

Onesimus *See* PHILEMON, THE LETTER OF PAUL TO

Ophir A country on the south-west coast of Arabia, the modern Yemen. Ophir is mentioned in the o.t. as a romantic distant source of gold. Solomon sent his fleet there for gold to adorn his armour, his throne, the Temple, and to fashion vessels for his table. [*Refs.* 1 Kings 9: 26-8; 10: 11. 2 Chronicles 8: 18; 9: 10, 20. Psalm 45: 9. Isaiah 13: 12.]

P

Paphos A town on the west of the island of Cyprus which was the headquarters of Roman administration in N.T. times. Paul and Barnabas encountered Sergius Paulus the proconsul there and amazed him by their 'teaching of the Lord'. [*Ref.* Acts 13: 6-13.]

Parables A parable is a story with a meaning. It should not be confused with a proverb, fable, legend, myth or allegory. A parable is a comparison—literally something placed 'side by side'—so that we may learn a truth. It is a metaphor or true-to-life story which is told to make the hearer think and come to a judgment. 'At its simplest the parable is a metaphor or simile drawn from nature or common life, arresting the hearer by its vividness or strangeness, and leaving the mind in sufficient doubt about its precise application to tease it into active thought.' (C. H. Dodd: The Parables of the Kingdom, the best short book on the parables of Jesus.)

Parables are a traditional part of Jewish teaching and one or two are to be found in the O.T. Perhaps the best-known is Nathan's parable, told to King David, of the rich man and the poor man (2 Samuel 12: 1-4). But the most famous parables in all literature are to be found in the N.T., in the teaching of Jesus. It was part of his unique genius to convey truth in a tale. The recorded parables are to be found in the Synoptic Gospels, but there are no parables in the proper sense of the term in John's Gospel. One memorable feature of the parables of Jesus is that they picture forth the everyday life of the people of the land—the farmer, sower, fisherman, merchant, village judge, a woman sweeping a house, children playing in the market-place, a wounded man left to die by the roadside. Yet such is the skill of their telling, that, although they belong to long-ago Palestine, they keep their meaning today.

The following points may be noted about the parables of Jesus:

(1) Sometimes they are as brief as a single metaphor or simile: 'a city set on a hill cannot be hid' (Matthew 5: 14) or 'If a blind man leads a blind man, both will fall into a pit' (Matthew 15: 14).

(2) Sometimes details are added to fill out the picture: 'No one lighting a lamp put it in a cellar or under a bushel, but on a stand, that those who enter may see the light' (Luke 11: 33) or garment; It he does, the patch tears away from it, the new from the old, and a worse tear is made' (Mark 2: 21).

(3) Other parables form a full-length tale with the meaning more clearly unfolded, e.g. The two sons (Luke 15: 11-32) and the good Samaritan (Luke 10: 25-37).

(4) It is important to remember that the parables of Jesus were first spoken to real people in a real situation of his own times. They were not intended primarily for readers, but for hearers. Each of the parables has a living setting. To understand the parable we have to find out the historical setting in which it was spoken, note who his hearers were, join their company, and listen to his voice in that 'there and then' situation. Any interpretation of a parable of Jesus, then, will depend on our answers to these questions:

To whom did he speak this parable: to disciples, scribes, Pharisees, the crowd?

What was the occasion, the setting in real life: a crowd on the beach, his disciples in the house, at a Pharisee's dinner table, confronted by a critical lawyer, surrounded by a mixed company of tax collectors, sinners, Pharisees and scribes?

Why did he tell it: did someone ask a question, or make a criticism, or does the story make clear a truth?

(5) It is equally important to note that each parable has one main point or meaning. The details of the story are there merely to make the picture more vivid. We must not turn a parable into an allegory, where every detail has its own symbolic meaning. Still less are the parables of Jesus to be used for latter-day moralizing or ethical commonplaces of our own devising.

(6) It is the case, however, that the original setting, purpose and meaning of some of the parables of Jesus may have been lost. The sayings of Jesus were treasured and passed on by word of mouth, but their earliest context was sometimes forgotten as we move away from Galilee into a different company of tellers and hearers in the wider Mediterranean world of the written Gospels. The passing of time, the way the stories were set down in literary form or linked together for a teaching purpose, may have obscured their first meaning. For example, we have no clue to the setting or purpose of such a vivid phrase as: 'Do not throw your pearls before swine, lest they trample them underfoot and turn to attack you' (Matthew 7: 6). Sometimes the parables of Jesus may have been embellished by the early Church to enforce some belief or teaching. Some may even have been turned into allegories to make the most of an original brief, vivid saying or story. We note, for example, that Mark 4 contains not merely a parable of four different kinds of soil (3-8), but also an allegorical interpretation of the parable (14-19) where the seed becomes 'the word', the birds become 'Satan', thorns become 'the cares of the world, and the delight in riches', and so on What we have here, surely, is a sermon of the early Church on the original parable of Jesus.

(7) For further study, there follows a list of the main parables of Jesus, apart from metaphors and similies, arranged according to the Gospel sources:

Parables found in Mark only:
The physician (Mark 2: 17).
The seed growing secretly (Mark 4: 26)

Parables found in Matthew only:
The tares (Matthew 13: 24-30).
Treasure hid in a field (Matthew 13: 44).
The pearl of great price (Matthew 13: 45-6).
The drag-net (Matthew 13: 47-8).
The unforgiving servant (Matthew 18: 23-35).
The labourers in the vineyard (Matthew 20: 1-16).
The ten virgins (Matthew 25: 1-13).
The sheep and the goats (Matthew 25: 31-46).
The two sons (Matthew 21: 28-32).

Parables found in Luke only:
The two debtors (Luke 7: 41-3).
The good Samaritan (Luke 10: 25-37).
The friend at midnight (Luke 11: 5-8).
The rich fool (Luke 12: 16-21).
The barren fig tree (Luke 13: 6-9).
The marriage feast (Luke 14: 7-11).
The tower builder and the king going to war (Luke 14: 28-32).
The lost coin (Luke 15: 8-10).
The prodigal son (Luke 15: 11-32).
The unjust steward (Luke 16: 1-8).
The rich man and Lazarus (Luke 16: 19-31).
The dutiful servant (Luke 17: 7-10).
The judge and the widow (Luke 18: 1-8).
The Pharisee and the tax collector (Luke 18: 9-14).

Parables found in Mark and Luke:
The watchful servants (Mark 13: 33-7. Luke 12: 35-8).
Salt (Mark 9: 50. Luke 14: 34-5).
The strong man despoiled (Mark 3: 27. Luke 11: .21-2).

Parables found in Matthew and Luke:

Taken to court (Matthew 5: 25-6. Luke 12: 58-9).

Children in the market place (Matthew 11: 16-19. Luke 7: 31-5).

The leaven (Matthew 13: 33. Luke 13: 20-1).

The lost sheep (Matthew 18: 12-14. Luke 15: 4-7).

The great banquet (Matthew 22: 1-14. Luke 14: 16-24).

The thief at night (Matthew 24: 43-4. Luke 12: 39-40).

Faithful and unfaithful servants (Matthew 24: 45-51. Luke 12: 42-6).

The talents and the pounds (Matthew 25: 14-30. Luke 19: 12-27).

The body and the eagles (Matthew 24: 28. Luke 17: 37).

The two houses (Matthew 7: 24-7. Luke 6: 47-9).

Parables found in Mark, Matthew and Luke:

The sower (Mark 4: 3-8. Matthew 13 3-8. Luke 8: 5-8)

The mustard seed (Mark 4: 30-2. Matthew 13: 31-2. Luke 13: 18-19).

The wicked husbandmen (Mark 12: Luke 20: 9-18).

The fig tree (Mark 13: 28-30. Matthew 24: 32-3. Luke 21: 29-31)

The lamp and the bushel (Mark 4: 21. Matthew 5: 15. Luke 8: 16; 11: 33).

New cloth on an old garment (Mark 2: 21. Matthew 9: 16. Luke 5: 36).

New wine in old wineskins (Mark 2: 22. Matthew 9: 17. Luke 5: 37-9)

Passover The most important of the three great festivals of the Jewish religious year. It is celebrated in the month *Nisan* of the Jewish calendar, which falls in March-April. Historically, the name *Passover* commemorates the 'passing over' of the homes of the Hebrews when the Egyptians suffered the loss of their first-born. A lamb was killed in each household, its blood was splashed on lintel and doorposts, and the flesh was eaten as a sacramental meal. For seven days unleavened bread was eaten. Another name associated with this time of year is 'the feast of unleavened bread', although this was not originally the same thing. The origin of the festival is lost in ancient times. Probably the Passover rite was at first a religious custom observed by shepherds at the opening of the year. The Feast of Unleavened Bread, on the other hand, appears to have been an agricultural festival, perhaps occurring about the same time of the year. They were eventually combined in religious practice and for ever after associated in Hebrew thought with the deliverance from Egypt which we know as the Exodus. The ritual is described in Exodus 12: 3-28, where the items of food are specified: a male lamb without blemish, eaten roasted, with unleavened bread and bitter herbs According to the account of the reform brought about by King Josiah in 628 B.C., a general keeping of the Passover had lapsed from the time of the Judges. Josiah restored the national custom as it is described in Deuteronomy 16: 1-8, centring the Passover at the Temple in Jerusalem instead of the homes of the people.

In N.T. times the Passover was celebrated in Jerusalem, the lamb being ritually offered as sacrifice in the Temple and then eaten in family groups at home. Luke tells how Jesus went up to Jerusalem with his parents when he was twelve years old 'according to custom'. The three Synoptic Gospels suggest that the Last Supper which Jesus shared with his disciples was 'the Passover and the Feast of Unleavened Bread'. John's Gospel, however states that Jesus was crucified just before the Feast. Paul speaks of the significance of the death of Christ in Jewish terms: 'Christ, our paschal lamb, has been sacrificed. Let us, therefore, celebrate the festival, not with the old leaven, the leaven of malice and evil, but with the unleavened bread of sincerity and truth.' [*Refs.* Exodus 12: 1-27, 43-9. Numbers 9: 2-14. Deuteronomy 16: 1-8. 11 Kings 23: 21-3. Matthew 26: 2, 17-19. Mark 14: 1, 12-14. Luke 2: 41-2; 22: 1, 7-11. John 2: 13; 11: 55; 13: 1; 19: 14. 1 Corinthians 5: 7-8.]

Patmos A barren island in the Aegean Sea off the west coast of Asia Minor. John, the author of the book of Revelation, was banished there as a political prisoner in the days of Roman persecution, and there he had his visions of the last days of the world. [*Ref.* Revelation 1: 9.]

Patriarchs The name given to the early forefathers of the Hebrew people, especially Abraham, Isaac, Jacob and his twelve sons from whom the tribes of Israel claimed their descent. [*Ref.* Acts 7: 8.]

Paul The first great missionary apostle of the Church to both Jew and Gentile, whose journeys, sufferings, words and works are described in the Acts of the Apostles and here and there in the Letters which he wrote to various Churches. His Hebrew name was Saul, no doubt after the first king of Israel who belonged to the same tribe of Benjamin, but he is better known to us as Paul. He was a Pharisee and a son of Pharisees, strictly trained in the law and traditions of the Jewish faith, schooled in Jerusalem as a young man at the feet of the famous Pharisaic teacher, Gamaliel. Paul also mentions his home town with pride: 'I am a Jew, from Tarsus in Cilicia, a citizen of no mean city', and he claimed to be a free-born Roman citizen. The familiar Latin form of his name means 'small', but we have no personal description of him in the N.T. A later tradition says that he was 'a man of moderate stature, with curly hair and scanty, crooked legs, with blue eyes, and large-knit eyebrows, long nose, and he was full of the grace and pity of the Lord, sometimes having the appearance of a man, but sometimes looking like an angel'. What is made plain in the N.T. more than once is that Paul suffered from what he himself called 'a thorn in the flesh'. Various conjectures have suggested that this might have been epilepsy or eye-trouble or malaria. According to his own account people said of him: 'His letters are weighty and strong, but his bodily presence is weak, and his speech of no account.' Like many Pharisees of his time Paul was not only a scholar and teacher of the Hebrew law, but he also worked with his hands. His trade was tent-making, weaving and stitching goat's hair cloth, and thus he earned his bread as he travelled up and down the lands of the Mediterranean.

Paul first appears on the scene as a young man in the company of fanatical Jews at the stoning of Stephen. There is little doubt that this martyrdom powerfully affected him. Paul immediately threw himself into the task of persecution of the Church, dragging off men and women to prison. On the road to Damascus, however, a light from heaven flashed about him and he heard a voice: 'Saul, Saul, why do you persecute me?' That was the moment of his conversion, to be confirmed a few days later by his baptism into the Christian faith. Thereafter Paul was as zealous to prove publicly that Jesus was the Christ as he had formerly been opposed to the idea. It was a dramatic change in his whole way of life and thought, to which Paul was to refer again and again.

The latter half of the Acts of the Apostles is largely taken up with the missionary journeys of Paul. The first of these, with the faithful Barnabas, was from the Church at Antioch, by way of Cyprus and across to Asia Minor. It was as a result of this that Paul felt himself called to preach the Gospel not only in the synagogues of the Jews, but also to the Gentile world. The second missionary journey, in the company of Silas, took the apostle eventually to Europe, and introduces the 'we' passages of the Acts which suggest that Luke was also with Paul. We read of believers in the great centres of the Roman empire—Philippi, Athens, Corinth, Ephesus and of Paul's teaching and work there. The account of the third missionary journey tells how Paul retraced his steps 'strengthening all the disciples' throughout Asia Minor and Europe, and came at last back to Jerusalem. There he was welcomed by the Christians, but attacked by Jews from Asia who stirred up a riot in the Temple. Paul was arrested, bound with chains, brought before the Council of the Jews, and eventually sent under escort of Roman soldiers to Caesarea, the Roman headquarters on the coast. He was in prison there for at least two years, during which time he was interrogated by the governor Felix, by Festus his successor, and by Herod Agrippa the Jewish 'king'. At last, when there was danger that he would be sent back to Jerusalem for trial Paul appealed to Caesar. In company with other prisoners and two faithful friends, he sailed for Italy. The voyage brought shipwreck on the island of Malta, but Paul came at length to Rome, where he was put under guard. The Acts of the Apostles closes with the statement that 'he lived there two whole years at his own expense...teaching about the Lord Jesus Christ quite openly and unhindered'. We know nothing more about him for certain, except that Paul must have written some of his letters while he awaited trial in Rome. He may have made other journeys, to Spain, Crete, Greece, but we have no certain knowledge of them. Tradition suggests that Paul was put to death by execution under Nero about A.D. 64-5.

Paul's many adventures for his Lord are vividly hinted at in his own words: 'Five times have I received at the hands of the Jews the forty lashes less one. Three times I have been beaten with rods, once was I stoned. Three times I have been shipwrecked; a night and a day I have been adrift at sea; on frequent journeys, in danger from rivers, danger from robbers, danger from my own people, danger from Gentiles, danger in the city, danger in the wilderness, danger at sea, danger from false brethren; in toil and hardship, through many a sleepless night, in hunger and thirst, often without food, in cold and exposure.

Something of Paul's spirit is revealed in his words: 'For the sake of Christ I am content with weakness, insults, hardships, persecutions, and calamities; for when I am weak, then I am strong. [*Refs*. Acts 7: 58*f*; 9: 1-31; 12: 25*f*. 18: 3; 21: 39; 22: 3, 28; 23: 6. 2 Corinthians 11: 24-8; 12: 7, 10. Philippians 3: 5-6.]

Pentateuch The name given to the first five books of the O.T. grouped together, that is, Genesis, Exodus, Leviticus, Numbers, Deuteronomy. They are sometimes known as 'the five books of Moses', as tradition ascribes them to him. Together they form the Jewish Torah or Law.

Pentecost The Greek word *pentecostos* means 'fiftieth', and refers to the Jewish festival which was held on the fiftieth day ('a week of weeks', i.e. seven times seven days) after

Passover or the Feast of Unleavened Bread. The O.T. name was the Feast of Weeks, originally held at the end of the wheat harvest. It was probably an ancient Canaanite festival taken over by the Hebrews and later associated in their religious customs with memories of the Exodus. Thus it came to be regarded as the anniversary of the giving of the sacred Law at Mt. Sinai. This is the background of the events recorded by Luke in the Acts of the Apostles, chapter 2. The coming of the Spirit of God on the assembled believers in Jesus was the giving of the new law. The Christian Church celebrates Whitsun on this date, the seventh Sunday after Easter. [*Refs.* Leviticus 23: 15*f*. Numbers 28: 26*f*. Deuteronomy 16: 9*f*. Acts 2: 1*f*.]

Persia The name of a people and the land they occupied in the days of their imperial power from 550-334 B.C., that is, from the emperor Cyrus to the rise of Alexander the Great. At its mightiest the Persian empire extended from India to the Aegean Sea, and took in Mesopotamia, Palestine and Egypt.

Isaiah of Babylon hailed Cyrus the Persian as one 'whom victory meets at every step...so that he tramples kings under foot', and saw in him 'the Lord's anointed' who would set free the Jews to return from Exile to their own land. The edict of Cyrus reveals something of the emperor's magnificence: 'Thus says Cyrus king of Persia: The Lord, the God of heaven, has given me all the kingdoms of the earth, and he has charged me to build him a house at Jerusalem, which is in Judah. Whoever is among you of all his people, may the Lord his God be with him. Let him go up.' A later Persian king, Darius I, continued this enlightened policy, so that the Temple in Jerusalem was rebuilt and replenished. The book of Esther mentions another Persian monarch, 'the Ahasuerus who reigned from India to Ethiopia'. Yet another was King Artaxerxes who allowed Nehemiah the Jew to go to Jerusalem to rebuild the walls and restore the gates of the city. The Persian Empire fell at last to Alexander the Great.

The ancient laws of the Medes and Persians were proverbial.

[*Refs*. 2 Chronicles 36: 22*f*. Ezra I: 1-4; 6: 1; 7: 1. Nehemiah 2: 1*f*. Esther 1: 2 Isaiah 41: 2; 44: 28; 45: 1.]

Peter The name given by Jesus to Simon Bar-Jona the Galilean fisherman, first of the twelve chosen disciples. The Greek word *petra* means 'rock' and the Aramaic equivalent is *cephas*. Peter and Andrew his brother came from Bethsaida, a fishing village on the Sea of Galilee, but in the Synoptic Gospels he is usually associated with the town of Capernaum. Peter's wife and mother-in-law are mentioned in passing in the N.T. Mark's Gospel tells that Jesus called Simon and Andrew from their fishing nets by the Sea of Galilee. John, on the other hand, indicates that Andrew was a disciple of John the Baptist and that he brought his brother to Jesus. It is John, also who records that Jesus named him Peter. In the list of apostles in all the Synoptic Gospels 'Simon, who is called Peter' always stands first.

Simon Peter was not only the leader of the twelve. He was also in the 'inner circle'—Peter, James, John—mentioned as being continually with Jesus, for example, in Capernaum, at the house of Jairus the ruler of the synagogue, on the Mount of Transfiguration, on the road to Jerusalem, and at Gethsemane. It was Peter who hailed Jesus as the Christ at Caesarea Philippi but who denied his master three times in the courtyard of the high priest. There is some emphasis in three of the Gospels that the risen Christ appeared to Peter after the Resurrection. John's Gospel tells of Peter's threefold commission by Jesus to 'Feed my sheep'. His importance in the early Church is made clear in the opening chapters of the Acts of the Apostles, where Peter takes the lead in the upper room in Jerusalem, on the day of Pentecost, in the Temple, and before the Council of the Jewish priests and leaders. His stature is emphasized by the legendary comment—'they even carried out the sick into the streets, and laid them on beds and pallets, that as Peter came by at least his shadow might fall on some of them... and they were all healed'. He all but disappears from the story after the account of the persecution by Herod. In the important reference to the Council of Jerusalem in Acts 15, however, Peter declared himself on the side of those who believed that the Gospel should be proclaimed to the Gentiles as well as to the Jews. Later records suggest that Peter was eventually crucified in the Neronian persecution in Rome, probably about A.D. 64-5. St. Peter's in Rome still commemorates not only the apostle's connection with the capital city of the Roman Empire but also the tradition that Christ appointed him leader of the Church in the much disputed passage which says: 'I tell you, you are Peter and on this rock I will build my church, and the powers of death shall not prevail against it.' [*Refs.* Matthew 4: 18; 8: 14; 10: 2; 16: 16-19. Mark 5: 37; 8: 29; 14: 37, 66*f*.; 16: 7. Luke 24: 34. John 1: 40-2; 13: 6*f*.; 20: 2-9; 21: 2*f*. Acts 1: 15*f*.; 2: 14*f*.; 3: 1*f*.; 4: 8*f*.; 9: 32 to 12 17; 15: 7-11. Galatians 2: 11*f*.]

Peter, The First Letter of This Letter is usually called one of the 'Catholic Epistles', that is, addressed to the universal Church rather than to a particular group. Its opening, however, mentions 'the exiles of the Dispersion in Pontus, Galatia, Cappadocia, Asia, and Bithynia', from which we may take it that the destination of this particular letter was the Churches of Asia Minor. Scholars today do not agree about its author or date of writing, but it is unlikely to be by Simon Peter the apostle. For one thing, the Greek language and style are much too good for a Jewish-born Galilean fisherman. It may be, of course, that Silvanus (Silas) who is mentioned at 5: 12 wrote the Letter at Peter's dictation and is responsible for its literary quality. But we must also ask why Peter should be writing to Gentiles in Asia Minor, with whom, so far as we know, he had no dealings. The mention of persecution in the letter suggests a date towards the end of the first century A.D., more than a generation after Simon Peter's death.

The Letter falls into two parts. 1: 3 to 4: 11 appears to be part of a baptismal sermon or, more probably, the kind of instruction given to Gentile converts about to be baptized into the Christian faith. The second part, at 4: 12 to 5: 11 is written to encourage believers to be steadfast in the face of persecution.

An outline of the contents is:

(a) 1 Peter 1: 1-2: An introduction, apparently by the apostle Peter addressed to Christians in Asia Minor, and the blessing.

(b) 1 Peter 1: 3-12: Thanksgiving to God for the new life which comes to believers through the Resurrection of Jesus Christ from the dead. There is joy even in trials which prove the genuineness of their faith.

(c) 1 Peter 1: 13 to 2: 10: The call to holiness of conduct. They will be judged according to their deeds. They have been set free by the precious blood of Christ, therefore they are to love one another earnestly from the heart, and put away all evil. They are the true Church of God, foretold in Scripture: 'a chosen race, a royal priesthood, a holy nation, God's own people.'

(d) 1 Peter 2: 11 to 3: 12: They are to maintain good conduct in an alien world. The writer urges loyalty to the emperor and to governors. There follows a code of behaviour for slaves, who are to take the example of Christ; wives who are to be chaste in behaviour and in dress; husbands, who are to honour women as the weaker sex. All are to be united in sympathy, love of the brethren, a tender heart and a humble mind.

(e) 1 Peter 3: 13-22: How to live with a clear conscience. Baptism is the sign and seal of newness of life in Christ.

(f) 1 Peter 4: 1-11: Live no longer by human passions but by the will of God. The end of all things is near; therefore keep sane and sober for your prayers. Various Christian virtues are praised, unfailing love being supreme.

(g) 1 Peter 4: 12-19: Here begins the second part of the Letter. There is a threat of persecution—a fiery ordeal which will put them to the test. They are to rejoice in so far as they share Christ's sufferings. They can glorify God by suffering as Christians.

(h) 1 Peter 5: 1-11: The duties of elders who lead the flock of God. Final ethical instruction to those who endure; God will restore, establish and strengthen them.

(i) 1 Peter 5: 12-14: A closing greeting, mentioning Silvanus and Mark. The mysterious reference to Babylon means Rome, the capital of the empire. The writer is making sure that the reader associates the letter with the authority of the apostle Peter who was a friend of Mark and who was put to death in Rome. Finally, the blessing.

The whole letter is a clear statement of how the Christian is to live and suffer in a pagan, persecuting world. It is true not only to the first century of the faith, but to every age.

Peter, The Second Letter of The opening words of the Letter strongly suggest that it is by Simon Peter the apostle. At 3: 1 there is mention of a former Letter, as if it were 1 Peter, and at 3: 15 a reference to 'our beloved brother Paul'. In fact, however, Peter was not regarded as the author even in the early traditions of the Church. This letter is the last of all the writing of our N.T. and is dated about the first quarter of the second century A.D. Chapter 2: 1-18 is taken almost word for word from Jude 4-16.

An outline of the contents is:

(a) 2 Peter 1: 1-2: Opening greetings as if from Simon Peter addressed to the universal Church, followed by the customary blessing.

(b) 2 Peter 1: 3-11: The readers are told how they are to abound in the fruits of the knowledge of our Lord Jesus Christ: faith, virtue, knowledge, self-control, steadfastness, godliness, brotherly affection, love.

(c) 2 Peter 1: 12-21: The Christian faith is not founded on 'cleverly devised myths' (as heretics suggest). 'We were eye-witnesses of his majesty.' There is a reference here to the Transfiguration of Jesus (*Mark* 9: 2-8).

(d) 2 Peter 2: 1-22: Mostly copied from Jude 4-16. It is an attack on false teachers.

(e) 2 Peter 3: 1-16: A reminder that the last days will be full of scoffers heretics who ask: 'Where is the promise of his coming?' Christ's second coming is indeed delayed, but 'the day of the Lord will come like a thief.' Therefore those who await the end must live in holiness and godliness.

(f) 2 Peter 3: 17-18: A final warning to be stable, growing in the grace and knowledge of our Lord and Saviour Jesus Christ. At the end, a doxology.

Pharaoh The title of the king of Egypt in ancient times. One pharaoh or another is mentioned in the Bible from the time of Abraham onwards It was a pharaoh who made Joseph ruler over all the land of Egypt after the latter had interpreted the king's dreams. A later pharaoh oppressed the Hebrews in the time of Moses, and yet another was the pharaoh of the Exodus. Solomon's chief wife was daughter of a pharaoh of Egypt. The last one of note in the o.t. story was Pharaoh Neco who defeated and slew King Josiah of Judah at Megiddo. [*Refs.* Genesis 41: 37-57. Exodus 1: 8; 12: 29. 1 Kings 3: 1. 2 Kings 23: 29-35.]

Pharisees The word means 'separated'. The Pharisees were a Jewish sect noted for their strict keeping of the written and unwritten Law and their formal, outward show of piety. They appear in the Gospels especially in antagonism to Jesus.

Originally the Pharisees were the spiritual descendants of the zealous Jews who upheld their sacred Law and religious customs in the face of Greek tyranny in the Maccabaean wars. They wished to be thought 'holy' and 'separate' from the unclean pagan world, especially the Gentile influence of Greece and Rome. Their earnest ideal was to teach the Jewish Law in every letter to anyone who would listen to them. To this end they would 'traverse sea and land'. The Pharisaic text was: 'Be deliberate in judgement, train many pupils, and make a fence about the Law.' Thus their whole life was dedicated to the study and teaching of the Law. The Pharisees also exercised considerable political influence in Palestine during the century before Christ. In N.T. times they were respected and honoured by ordinary people as religious patriots. They observed the rules of ritual washing, of diet and of tithing with scrupulous care, and they were fanatical about the keeping of the Sabbath.

A great deal of the teaching of Jesus must have won the approval of the Pharisees. His classic summing up of the Law: 'You shall love the Lord your God with all your heart, and with all your soul, and with all your strength, and with all your mind, and your neighbour as yourself', was sound Pharisaic teaching. At the beginning of his ministry, too, Jesus was welcomed as a preacher in the synagogues of Galilee. He sided also with the Pharisees as against the Sadducees in their teaching regarding resurrection from the dead. There is evidence that Jesus had friends among them. Nicodemus, for example, was 'a man of the Pharisees'. It was not the men Jesus picked out for criticism, but narrow legalism and hypocrisy of behaviour, and there his words were harsh. They are 'whitewashed tombs...serpents, a brood of vipers'. They 'devour widows' houses and for a pretence make long prayers'. 'They preach, but do not practise...they do all their deeds to be seen by men, for they make their phylacteries broad and their fringes long, and they love the place of honour at feasts and the best seats in the synagogues, and salutations in the market places, and being called rabbi by men.' In a famous parable Jesus sums up the Pharisee at prayer as all self-opinionated righteousness.

In due course the Pharisees turned against Jesus. They complained that Jesus mixed freely with outcast tax collectors and sinners. They accused him of being in league with the devil, and of speaking blasphemies. They blamed him for breaking the law of the Sabbath. Finally, they took sides with the Sadducees and the Herodians to destroy him.

In the Acts of the Apostles the Pharisees are mentioned with some respect. One, named Gamaliel, was 'a teacher of the Law, held in honour by all the people'. He was Paul's early tutor. Some Pharisees became believers in Christ, though they sought to insist also on the law of Moses. Paul openly claimed to be 'a Pharisee, a son of Pharisees'.

Perhaps the supreme fault of the Pharisees was that they could not discern what was important and what was unimportant in matters of religion. Jesus did not defy the Law of his people, but he did set God's mercy and goodness far higher than legal jots and tittles. [*Refs.* Matthew 9: 11, 34; 12: 2, 14; 23: 1*f*. Mark 3: 6. Luke 5: 17, 21, 30; 18: 10-13. John 3: 1*f*. Acts 5: 34; 15: 5; 23: 6-9; 26: 5. Philippians 3: 5.]

Philemon The name of a Christian believer in the town of Colossae to whom Paul wrote the personal Letter which bears his name. There was a Church in his house, and one would guess that he was a well-to-do man. [*Ref.* Philemon 1: 1.]

Philemon, The Letter of Paul to This short, personal letter is closely linked with the Letter to the Colossians, and a number of people closely associated with Paul are mentioned in both. The Letter was probably written by Paul from prison in Rome and it is addressed to Philemon Apphia (who may have been his wife), Archippus and the Church of believers who met in Philemon's house

The reason for writing was this: Onesimus, a slave of Philemon, had run away from his master, had somehow found his way to Rome where he encountered Paul and became a Christian. He had proved very useful to the apostle—the Greek word *onesimos* means 'useful'—but Paul felt he had to send him back to Philemon. This letter begs forgiveness for Onesimus and acceptance no longer as a slave but as a beloved brother in the Lord. Paul also mentions that he hopes soon to visit Philemon and ends with greetings from his fellow-workers in prison, and the blessing.

This short writing is the only private Letter in our N.T. and it reveals Paul's sensitive concern for both master and slave. There is an ancient, not very reliable tradition that Onesimus eventually became bishop of Ephesus. [*Ref.* Colossians 4: 7-9.]

Philip (1) One of the twelve apostles, fellow-countryman of Andrew and Peter, whose home was at Bethsaida, a fishing village on the east side of the Sea of Galilee. Philip is mentioned in the Gospel lists of the disciples but especially in the Gospel of John, where it is said that Jesus chose him by name. [*Refs.* Matthew 10: 3. Mark 3: 18. Luke 6: 14. John 1: 43-8; 6: 5-7; 12: 21-2; 14: 8-9. Acts 1: 13.] (2) One of the 'seven men of good repute, full of the Spirit and of wisdom', appointed to care for the widows in the early Church in Jerusalem. When persecution broke out following the death of Stephen, Philip went down to Samaria as a preacher and healer. It was he who encountered the Ethiopian on the desert road and interpreted to him the scripture of Isaiah the prophet. Later in the account of the Acts, Paul and his companions stayed with Philip the evangelist at Caesarea on his journey to Jerusalem. [*Refs.* Acts 6: 5; 8: 5-40; 21: 8.] *See also*: HEROD

Philippi A city of Macedonia, and the first centre in Europe to which Paul brought the Gospel. Philippi was a Roman colony named after Philip of Macedon, the father of Alexander the Great. In N.T. times it was an important centre of trade and stood on the highway that ran between Rome and Asia. It was by the river there that Paul encountered a small company of Jewish worshippers, preached Christ to them, and found converts, including Lydia, a woman of some substance in the city. Lydia became the first baptized believer in Europe. In Philippi Paul and Silas were also put in prison for healing a slave girl. An earthquake shook the place during the night and the frightened jailer was converted and baptized with all his household. It was to the Christians in Philippi that Paul addressed his Letter to the Philippians. Tradition has suggested that Luke the Gospel writer, beloved physician and travelling companion of Paul, may have been a native of Philippi. [*Refs.* Acts 16: 12-40; 20: 2-6. Philippians 1: 1. 1 Thessalonians 2: 2.]

Philippians, The Letter of Paul to the The first Christian Church in Europe was founded by Paul at Philippi on his second missionary journey (Acts 16: 12-40). Philippi was 'a leading city' of Macedonia, as Luke points out, and a Roman colony. In Paul's Letter to the Christians there is one of the 'letters from prison', namely, Colossians, Philemon, Ephesians, Philippians, and it used to be thought that they were all written when Paul was in prison in Rome, towards the end of his life (Acts 28: 30-1). Recent scholarship, however, has suggested that this Letter may have been written from Ephesus (Acts 19: 1, 10, 22) on Paul's third missionary journey, although Acts does not mention any imprisonment there. Wherever it was, Paul certainly refers repeatedly to his confinement (Philippians 1: 7, 13, 16, 17; 2: 17). He has even faced the possibility of death (1: 20-1).

It is also possible that these four chapters contain more than one letter. For example, there seems to be an ending at 3: 1— 'Finally, my brethren, rejoice in the Lord.' Yet at 3: 2, the writer not only begins again, but on an entirely different theme: an attack on false teachers whom he calls 'dogs' and 'evil-workers'. At 4: 4, again, we return to the theme 'Rejoice in the Lord always', and there is another 'Finally' at 4: 8. Rather surprisingly at the very end, comes 4: 10-23, in which Paul thanks the Philippians for generous gifts they have sent him at the hand of Epaphroditus. One might have expected him to have said 'thank you' at the beginning of the letter rather than at the end. Indeed, it has been suggested that if we re-arrange the whole letter to the Philippians we make better sense of it. Thus an outline of the material might be:

(a) Philippians 4: 10-23: Paul sends his thanks for the gifts (probably of food and money) sent to him by the Philippians through Epaphroditus. In his greetings he mentions among the Christians 'those of Caesar's household', i.e. Roman soldiers, the emperor's personal bodyguard.

(b) Philippians 1: 1 to 3: 1, and 4: 4-7: Perhaps a different letter, linked by the repeated use of the word 'rejoice'. It is specifically addressed to the Christians at Philippi and speaks of Paul's joy in their love. He gives an account of his imprisonment and how it has encouraged others to speak the word of God. Whether he sees them again or not, he urges them to complete his joy by 'being in full accord and of one mind' (2: 2.) At 2: 6-11 there is probably an early Christian Hymn. (Paul hopes soon to send Timothy to them so that he may have good news to bring back. Their messenger, Epaphroditus, has been ill, near to death, but soon he will be well enough to go back to Philippi.) At 4: 4-7 there is another thanksgiving, and the blessing.

(c) Philippians 3: 2 to 4: 3: If this is yet another letter, it is in quite a different tone. It warns his readers to beware of false teachers, especially Jewish legalists who insist on circumcision as being a rite of first importance. Paul himself, a circumcised Hebrew by upbringing, and a Pharisee by training, can state: 'whatever gain I had, I counted as loss for the sake of Christ'. As vehemently as in his other letters he declares that nothing comes before faith in Christ. 4: 8-9 gives a list of virtue to be thought upon and practised.

Philistines A non-Semitic sea-going people from the Aegean who tried to invade Egypt in the twelfth century B.C., were driven back, and settled along the coastal plain of Canaan. Their five walled cities—Ashdod, Askelon, Ekron, Gath and Gaza—controlled the trade-routes and war-paths. From there the Philistines made their way up the valleys into the hill-country and set up garrisons to control the central highlands of Canaan. Thus they came into conflict with the Israelite tribes who were fighting for living-space about the same time. The Philistines were superior to the Israelites in their unity as a people, their use of chariots, and particularly in their knowledge of working iron, by which they supplied themselves with superior tools and weapons. There are stories of battles between Israelites and Philistines from the time of the 'Judges' onwards, particularly in the Samson saga. Israel suffered defeat near Shiloh and the sacred Ark of the Covenant fell into enemy hands. Saul was able to unite the tribes of his people against of the Philistines, but he and his sons and their army were utterly defeated at Mt. Gilboa. David appears in a legendary tale as the slayer of Goliath of Gath, the giant champion of the Philistines. Eventually they disappeared from history, leaving only the name Palestine as a reminder of the days when they held sway over almost the whole land. Very little is known of Philistine culture. They are depicted in ancient wall-paintings as a fierce, warlike people, wearing feathered head-dresses and short kilts armed with long lances, swords and round shields. [*Refs*. Genesis 21: 32, 34. Exodus 13: 17. Judges 10: 6; 13: 1 to 16: 30. 1 Samuel 4-6; 9: 16; 13: 3 to 14: 52; 17: 1 to 19: 8; 31: 1-10. 2 Samuel 1: 19-26; 5: 17-25; 23: 13*f*.]

Pilate Pontius Pilate was the Roman procurator, or governor, of Judea from A.D. 26-36. Jewish records reveal that he was tactless, corrupt and cruel in his dealings with the Jewish people and callous in his attitude to their religious feelings. Pilate normally lived in his palace at Caesarea on the coast, but came up to Jerusalem to keep order during important festivals such as Passover. The Gospel accounts tell that it was Pilate who sentenced Jesus to be crucified, but they seek to excuse him from the blame of Jesus' arrest and death. In part this was due to the Gospel writers' wish to commend the Christian ways to readers throughout the Roman empire. Pontius Pilate was eventually removed from office for his misdeeds. It is one of the ironies of history that this insignificant and unworthy man is still continually remembered in the credal phrase: 'crucified under Pontius Pilate'. [Refs Matthew 27: 2*f*. Mark 15: 1*f*. Luke 3: 1; 13: 1*f*. John 18: 29*f*. Acts 13: 28.]

Plagues Plagues and pestilence are frequently mentioned in the O.T., usually referring to the diseases and famine which were a continual feature of life in Palestine. They were usually thought of as calamites sent by God as a warning or a punishment to 'smite' his wayward people. Leprosy is especially mentioned as a plague.

The ten plagues of Egypt are specifically the disasters which are recorded in the Book of Exodus as being sent by God at the hands of Moses and Aaron to afflict Pharaoh and the Egyptians, to compel them to let the Hebrews go. They are:

The water of the Nile turns to blood, the fish die, and the river becomes foul (Exodus 7: 14-25).

The plague of frogs upon the land of Egypt (Exodus 8: 1-14)

The plague of gnats, or lice (Exodus 8: 16-19)

The plague of flies (Exodus 8: 20-32)

The plague on cattle, horses, asses, camels, herds and flocks (Exodus 9: 8-12)

The plague of boils breaking out in sores on man and beast (Exodus 9: 8-12)

The plague of hail (Exodus 9: 18-35)

The plague of locusts (Exodus 10: 4-20)

The plague of thick darkness (Exodus 10: 21-9)

The death of all the first-born in the land of Egypt (Exodus 11: 4-8; 12: 29-32)

These accounts of the plagues come from different literary sources. They are not intended to be an objective historical report. It is true to say that nine out of the calamities can be described as 'natural' events, but the way in which they are set down reveals that the writers are more concerned with the teaching purpose—to declare them as 'mighty acts of God'. In the various stories the plagues are described as 'signs and wonders' which compel Pharaoh to let the Hebrews return to Israel. Like the other events and wonders of the outgoing from Egypt the plagues are remembered in later Jewish literature and religious custom as part of the 'tradition' of the Exodus and the making of a nation. [*Refs*. Deuteronomy 28: 60. Joshua 24: 5. 1 Samuel 4: 8. Psalm 78: 43-51; 105: 26-36; 135: 8.]

Pontus A region in the north of Asia Minor, on the shores of the Black Sea. In N.T. times it was a province of the Roman Empire and Jews from Pontus were in Jerusalem at the time of Pentecost. The First Epistle of Peter was written to the Christians in Pontus and other parts of Asia Minor who were under threat of persecution. [*Refs*. Acts 2: 9. 1 Peter 1: 1.]

Priest In the Biblical sense a priest was a man specially set apart for the duties of animal sacrifice and other religious rites in the tabernacle or local shrine and later in the Temple of Jerusalem. He was a link between the ordinary worshipper and his God. No doubt in early days of the Hebrew tribes the priestly office was not clearly defined or safeguarded by caste and custom. The patriarch Abraham, for example, is said to have offered a ram as a burnt- offering in place of his son Isaac. Priests are mentioned as custodians of the Ark and servants of the Tabernacles in the stories of the wilderness wanderings under Moses and the invasion of the promised land with Joshua as leader. It is impossible now to say how far the descriptions of their functions are the pious embellishments of a later age. Samuel as a youth was employed in priestly tasks in the shrine at Shiloh and later blessed the sacrifice offered at the 'high place' where his people worshipped. In rural days Canaan there were priests attached to local sanctuaries whose service it was to teach the people their duties to God and to each other, decide disputes, and make sacrifices at the festivals of the farming and pastoral year. Even David and Solomon performed ritual sacrifice, and in fact the Temple was the king's sanctuary where the priests were his servants. With the house of David, professional priests appear by name in the records. Zadok and Abiathar were important religious figures, though they held their position by favour of the monarch. Even as late as the time of Josiah, the Temple was purged, false priests deposed, and religion reformed, all at the command of the King. The abolition of local shrines and centralization of worship in Jerusalem, however, put autocratic power in the hands of the organized priesthood of the Temple.

After the return from Exile the priesthood was completely professional, devoted to the elaborate rules and ritual of the Temple, their caste and cult formally declared in Jewish religious literature. According to tradition all priests were supposed to be members of the Tribe of Levi, descended from

Levi, son of Jacob. it was also set down that all proper priests should be of the line of Aaron, brother of Moses. It is unlikely that this ancestry was in all cases rigorously observed, but the written insistence on it shows the power of a professional guild ensuring discipline among members and control over all priestly duties. Since the writers and eventual editors of a good deal of the O.T. belonged to the Jewish priesthood, it is not surprising that they laid great stress on the importance of their office. Nothing in the Bible is set down in greater detail than the order for the consecration of priests, their duties, their clothing for the rites of the sanctuary, their food and drink, as we find them in books of Exodus and Leviticus. Priestly writing forms a large part of the 'history' and tradition of God's chosen people from the creation to the settlement in Canaan, and records of later days were rewritten, combined and edited to present the priestly point of view. The O.T., in other words, is interpreted history, and the inspiration of the editors is that their people should be a 'a kingdom of priests and a holy nation'. Yet, running through the long, involved account of God's dealings with their people, there is also the constant prophetic warning. Where there is no moral concern for 'the alien, the fatherless or the widow', no ritual of the Temple will save them. The prophets constantly criticized the priests for the hypocrisy of mere outward show. To do justice and to love kindness is of greater value than all smoke of animal sacrifice and ritual obeisance. [*Refs.* Genesis 22: 16. Exodus 19: 6. Leviticus 3: 6*f*. 1 Samuel 2: 11; 9: 13. 2 Samuel 8: 17. 1 Kings 4: 2. 2 Kings 23: 4*f*. Ezra 1: 5. Hosea 4: 8-9. Micah 3: 11; 6: 6-8. Malachi 2: 7. Matthew 26: 3. Mark 14: 53. Luke 3: 2. Acts 4: 6; 5: 17.]

Priscilla Prisca or Priscilla was the wife of Aquila and a leader of the early Church. She and her husband were tent-makers, weavers of goat's hair, and Paul, who followed the same trade, stayed with them and worked with them in Corinth. At that time they were Jewish refugees from Rome. Priscilla and

Aquila went with Paul to Ephesus and their home there also became a centre of Christian worship and teaching. [*Refs.* Acts 18: 1-3, 18-19, 24-8. Romans 16: 3. 1 Corinthians 16: 19.] *See also*: AQUILA

Prophet The Greek word *prophetes* means 'one who speaks for, or on behalf of'. The Biblical prophets were thought to speak for God, being inspired to declare his will, hence the phrase 'Thus says the Lord'. The prophet usually addressed himself directly to a particular situation of his own times, in the acts of a king or of a nation. Thus Nathan rebuked David for his sin with Bathsheba, and Elijah confronted Ahab in the vineyard of Naboth. On other occasions the prophets could look beyond the immediate horizon and tell of the downfall of empires at the hand of the Almighty. They were often regarded as 'troublers of Israel', their message was disregarded, and many of these lonely spokesmen for God suffered greatly. Jeremiah was not alone in cursing the day he was born.

The prophet is sometimes confused with the seer in early O.T. writings, but the seer was rather one who interpreted signs and discerned meanings hidden to ordinary mortals, or explained the significance of disturbing dreams. In some narratives the prophets are found in ecstatic groups, seized by supernatural powers and working themselves into a frenzy of physical activity, sometimes to the accompaniment of music. There were also apparently schools of prophets, with master and disciples. The great Biblical prophets, however, are clearly marked out by their message. They were not popular foretellers or soothsayers. Rather, they spoke the word of God concerning men and nations, giving warning of cause and effect in moral terms. Thus men like Amos, Hosea, Isaiah, Jeremiah, declared that a divine necessity was laid on them. They could not contain the word of the Lord.

'The Lord God has spoken; who can but prophesy?'

(Amos 3: 8).

'The Lord took me from following the flock, and the Lord said to me, 'Go, prophesy to my people Israel'"

(Amos 7: 15).

'The word of the Lord that came to Hosea ... in the days of kings of Judah'

(Hosea 1: 1).

'Go, and say to this people ...'

(Isaiah 6: 9).

'The Lord said to me... "to all to whom I send you you shall go, and whatever I command you you shall speak" '

(Jeremiah 1: 7).

Prophecy, then, was a unique gift of God, an outpouring of the divine spirit, so that the chosen spokesmen might warn, exhort, encourage and declare God's will in the events of the nations of mankind and in particular in the acts of his chosen people, Israel.

The Bible writers recognized that other gods had their prophets—there were many prophets of Baal, for example, in the days of Elijah. There were also false prophets in plenty, men who claimed to speak a word from the Lord in time of peril to lull their people into false security. Jeremiah's counsel concerning them was to wait and see what happened: 'As for the prophet who prophesies peace, when the word of that prophet comes to pass, then it will be known that the Lord has truly sent that prophet' (Jeremiah 28: 9. *See also* Deuteronomy 18: 22). The true prophet, however stood sure in his conviction that he was the mouthpiece of God: 'Surely the Lord God does nothing, without revealing his secret to his servants the prophets' (Amos 3: 7). It is a conviction, not a question.

The prophets are by far the most significant men of Jewish history, as O.T. literature reveals. They are also Judaism's unique contribution to the insights of humanity. The utterances of the great Hebrew prophets are not merely of doom and disaster in the affairs of the nations, or even wisdom and counsel concerning human relationships. They are primarily ethical. Their keywords are righteousness and justice. God's prophets are concerned with right and wrong, true religion as against false, social justice, a cry against the oppression of the poor by the rich, fearless condemnation of the cruelty and pride of great nations. They speak of the eternal Yea and Nay, of well-doing and of evil-doing, and they declare without fear or favour which side God is on. In the darkest days, particularly during the Exile and after, they gave their people a promise of a future and a hope, grounding their trust in the goodness and steadfast love of God.

In the N.T., both John the Baptist and Jesus are named as prophets. In the early Church the word was used along with apostles, teachers, healers, helpers, workers of miracles, pastors, evangelists. Apparently the prophet's particular task in those days was to 'edify' or instruct the Church.

The literature of the O.T. bears witness to the place given to the prophets in Hebrew tradition. The prophets come next only to the sacred Law in importance and include writings which we might call history. Jewish Scriptures include the Former Prophets—Joshua, Judges, 1 and 2 Samuel, 1 and 2 Kings—and the Latter Prophets—Isaiah, Jeremiah, Ezekiel—and the Twelve—Hosea, Joel, Amos, Obadiah, Jonah, Micah, Nahum, Habakkuk, Zephaniah, Haggai, Zechariah, Malachi. The customary division in our own English Bibles has been:

Major Prophets: Isaiah, Jeremiah, Ezekiel.

Minor Prophets: Hosea, Joel, Amos, Obadiah, Jonah, Micah, Nahum, Habakkuk, Zephaniah, Haggai, Zechariah, Malachi.

The terms 'Major' and 'Minor', however, refer to the length or brevity of the writings, not to their importance. [*Refs*. Numbers 11: 25. Deuteronomy 13: 11; 34: 10. 1 Samuel 3: 20; 19: 20, 24. 2 Samuel 12: 15. 1 Kings 18: 20*f*. Jeremiah 1: 5. Ezekiel 2: 5. Amos 7: 14. Malachi 4: 5. Matthew 5: 12; 7:

15; 11: 9; 14: 5; 16: 14; 21: 11. Luke 24: 19. Acts 7: 52; 11: 27; 13: 1. 1 Corinthians 12: 28.]

Proselyte One who has become a convert from one religion to another. In the Bible it means a Gentile who has turned to the Jewish faith. He would have to be circumcised and then keep the Jewish Law. In N.T. times many Gentiles were attracted to the Jewish faith, and some Jewish proselytes in turn became Christians. [*Refs.* Matthew 23: 15. Acts 2: 10; 6: 5; 13: 43.]

Proverbs The Book of Proverbs is a collection of wise sayings, forming, with Job and Ecclesiastes, the Wisdom literature of Hebrew Scriptures. These maxims are mainly concerned with the moral education of the young, whose training has always been an important part of Jewish life. The 'proverbs' aim to show how a man should deal with all the affairs of life which confront him on this earth. A great deal of the advice is shrewd, practical, worldly-wise, and commends conduct which will make a young man prosper in wealth and health and bring him a good name in the community. There is a 'know-how' in social behaviour, a right and wrong way of doing things, and these brief, common-sense sayings are like a bunch of keys in the hand to fit all the possible situations of daily life.

The book was probably made up after the Exile from a number of earlier sources. Solomon was famous for his wise sayings, so the whole work is named after him. But it would be impossible to pin down proverbial sayings to one time or man, and though some may come from Solomon, others can be traced to an Egyptian source.

The Book of Proverbs may be divided thus:

(a) Proverbs 1-9: Advice to a young man in praise of wisdom.

(b) Proverbs 10: 1 to 22: 16: Proverbs about life and conduct attributed to Solomon, probably the oldest part of the book. Contrast between the behaviour of the upright and the wicked.

(c) Proverbs 22: 17 to 24: 22: 'The words of the wise'—

general precepts and warnings which have come from an Egyptian collection of instruction given to a pupil.

(d) Proverbs 24: 23-34: More 'sayings of the wise'.

(e) Proverbs 25: 1 to 29: 27: Proverbs of Solomon which the men of King Hezekiah of Judah copied. These are comparisons and moral lessons forming instruction to young men in training for service at the king's court.

(f) Proverbs 30: 1-33: The words of Agur, son of Jakeh of Massa. These are general observations, often drawing moral lessons from the world of Nature.

(g) Proverbs 31: 1-9: The words of Lemuel, king of Massa, which his mother taught him. Again note that this is instruction of the young.

(h) Proverbs 31: 10-31: Praise of a good and capable wife, the prize, as it were, of a wise young ma's search.

Psalms The Book of Psalms forms part of the Writings of the Hebrew Scriptures. They are often called 'the Psalms of David', partly because David was a skilled player on the lyre and known as 'the sweet psalmist of Israel', partly because he was regarded by the Jews as the real founder of the Temple where these sacred songs were collected and sung. It is true also that David's name stands at the head of a good many of them, though that does not necessarily mean that he was the author. See, for example, psalms 3, 5, 8, 23, etc. Other names at the head of individual psalms are: Moses (psalm 90) Solomon (psalms 72 and 127), Heman the Ezrahite (psalm 88), Ethan the Ezrahite (psalm 89), Asaph (psalms 50 and 73-83).

The collection of one hundred and fifty psalms in the Bible is divided into five books, each group closing with a doxology. The groups are: 1-41; 42-72; 73-89; 90-106; 107-150. Probably this division was to conform to the Pentateuch or 'five-fifths of the Law', but it has nothing to do with the date of the psalms or with particular themes.

The psalms were composed over a long period of time, covering most of the triumphs and disasters of Hebrew history. They take many forms and have different purposes in the circle of the year's worship in the Temple at Jerusalem. There are psalms to be chanted on public and national occasions, psalms to be sung by the Temple choirs, psalms for pilgrims to the holy city, psalms to accompany animal sacrifice in the sanctuary, songs of seed-time and harvest and other days of festival as well as prayers for private devotion. Here are some examples of different themes:

(a) Psalms which remind the worshipper of Zion, the hill in Jerusalem which symbolizes the very heart of the promised land, 'the holy habitation of the Most High' (46, 48, 76, 87).

(b) 'Songs of Ascent' or pilgrim psalms which recall the feelings of worshippers who have travelled from afar to stand in the Temple courts, especially at the time of annual festivals (84, 120-134).

(c) Psalms to remind us that God is enthroned over his people, Israel (47, 93, 96-9).

(d) Royal psalms which tell of the joyful days of a king's enthronement, wedding, anniversary, or victory over his enemies (2, 18, 20, 21, 45, 72, 101, 110, 132, 144).

(e) Thanksgiving for a good harvest (67).

(f) Lamentations in which the worshippers cry to God for deliverance from their foes (44, 74, 79).

(g) The *Hallel* psalms were always sung at the great festivals of Passover, Pentecost, and Tabernacles as a particular reminder of the deliverance of Israel from bondage in Egypt, which is what they are about. They were later used in the synagogues and Jewish homes after the final destruction of the Temple, and it was the custom for the worshipper to repeat the word 'Hallelujah' ('praise ye the Lord') again and again while these psalms were recited. This group of psalms is mentioned at the time of the Last Supper when Jesus and his disciples sang a hymn together before they went out to the Mount of Olives (113-18).

(h) The longest psalm (119) is in the form of an acrostic in which each section of eight verses begins with a letter of the Hebrew alphabet. Every verse has a reference to the

'law' or a synonym such as 'testimony', 'precepts', 'stat-
utes', 'commandment', 'ordinance', 'word', 'promise',
'way'. This seemingly artificial style of composition did
at least help one to memorize the words, as well as paying
pious tribute to the supremacy of the Law in Jewish belief. There are a number of other acrostic examples in the
Psalms (9, 10, 25, 34, 37, 111, 112, 145).

(i) There are also private prayers of the individual, proclaiming personal trust in God, as well as psalms of thanksgiving, particularly for healing, help, or deliverance from
some evil (4, 16, 23, 30, 32, 138).

(j) In addition, there are a number of wisdom psalms, full of
comforting phrases not unlike proverbs, reflecting daily
experiences of life, good and bad (1, 37, 73).

These are examples of different types of psalms, but there
are still others where it is not always possible to decide what
each one was originally used for, or to which group it should
belong. We have little information about the form of Temple
worship so long ago, except that annual festivals were held
there and the daily sacrifice of animals with appropriate
prayer and praise. All good Jews were taught to regard the
Temple as the house of God and the psalms express all the
proper emotions of worship, penitence, trust, adoration and
praise. The psalter covers all the experiences of national and
personal life, glad and sad alike, and all, as it were, 'in the
shadow of the Almighty'.

A number of musical instruments are mentioned here and
there in the psalms, particularly in psalm 150, and used, no
doubt, to accompany the Temple choirs. They are: trumpet,
pipe, harp and lyre, drums and cymbals. Finally, one notes a
mysterious Hebrew word Selah which occurs here and there
more than seventy times in the Book of Psalms. No one is
quite clear what it meant, except that it probably indicated
some kind of signal to the musicians, choirs or worshippers.
It may signify a pause or a musical interlude, or perhaps a
moment at which everyone is to bow reverently to the ground.

Publicans *Publicani* was the Latin name for tax-gatherers or collectors of 'public' taxes, and 'publicans' is the unfortunate A.V. translation of the word. In the Gospels publicans or tax-gatherers were outcast Jews despised and hated by their countrymen because they worked for the heathen Romans and because they unjustly demanded more than their due and pocketed the profit. They are mentioned along with 'sinners' and 'harlots'. Jesus showed himself a friend of publicans and was criticized for visiting their homes and eating with them. Levi (Matthew), the tax-gatherer of Capernaum, was called to be one of the twelve apostles, and Jesus visited the home of Zacchaeus 'chief of the publicans' in Jericho. Jesus also mentioned a publican compassionately in his parable of the Pharisee and the publican. [*Refs.* Matthew 9: 9-11. Mark 2: 14-16. Luke 5: 27; 7: 34; 18: 10-13; 19: 2.]

Q

Quail A small bird of the partridge family. Migrating quails fly with the wind and sometimes fall to the ground exhausted when the wind dies down. Thus quails were to be found in great numbers round the camp of the Hebrews in the desert and provided them with food. Manna and quails were for ever remembered as food sent by God to feed his chosen people. [*Refs*. Exodus 16: 13. Numbers 11: 31-2. Psalm 105: 40.]

R

Raamses or **Ramases** A store city in the Nile delta built by the Hebrews when they were set to work as slaves by the Pharaoh of Egypt. It was from Rameses that the Hebrews set out on the day of liberation. [*Refs.* Exodus 1: 11; 12: 37. Numbers 33: 3, 5.]

Rabbi A Hebrew word meaning 'master' or 'teacher', a title of respect among Jews. The rabbis taught the words and meaning of the Law which they knew in great detail. So far as we know, Jesus was not a trained scholar of the Law as most rabbis were, but his teaching was so memorable that many people called him 'rabbi'. [*Refs.* Matthew 23:8; 26: 49. Mark 9: 5; 10: 51. John 1: 38, 49; 4: 31; 9: 2, 11: 8.]

Rachel The younger daughter of Laban and the beloved wife of Jacob. She became Jacob's wife after he had served Laban seven years for Leah (her elder sister) and then another seven for her. Rachel was the mother of Joseph and Benjamin. [*Refs.* Genesis 29: 17-20; 30: 22-4; 35: 16, 20.]

Rahab A harlot in Jericho who hid the two spies sent there by Joshua and secretly let them down by a rope through the window because her house was built into the city wall. When Jericho fell to the invading Israelites, the only persons spared were Rahab and all who were in her house. Her name lingered in Jewish traditions of their early days in Canaan. [*Refs.* Joshua 2: 1*f.*; 6: 17, 23, 25. Hebrews 11: 31.]

Ramah Ramah means 'height' or 'hill town' and it was a common place name in O.T. times. One such Ramah was the home town of the prophet Samuel. It is the same place as Arimathea in the N.T. [*Refs.* 1 Samuel 1: 19; 7: 17; 19: 18. Matthew 27: 57. John 19: 38.]

Rebekah The sister of Laban, who became the wife of Isaac and mother of Esau and Jacob. Abraham did not wish his son to marry a woman of Canaan, so he sent his trusted servant to the ancestral homeland of Mesopotamia to find a wife for Isaac. The man came to the home of Laban at Haran and in due course Rebekah went with him to be the wife of Isaac in the land of Canaan. [*Refs.* Genesis 24; 25: 20-6, 28.]

Rechabites The Rechabites claimed their descent from a man named Rechab and his son Jehonadab. The latter aided Jehu in his revolt against the house of Ahab, and the destruction of the worshippers of Baal. The Rechabites were chiefly noted, however, for the fact that they drank no wine, did not culti-vate the land, and that they continued to live in tents long after other tribes had settled in towns and villages. Their way of life was a protest against a settled, farming civilization with its heathen gods, and an idealizing of the austere desert tradi-tions of their nomadic ancestors. [*Refs.* 2 Kings 10: 15, 23. Jeremiah 35: 2-10, 14, 18-19.]

Rehoboam Son and successor of King Solomon. At a corona-tion assembly at Shechem he had immediately to face a revolt led by Jeroboam caused by his father's policy of taxation and slave labour. Rehoboam asked the advice of the old men of the court, his father's counsellors, and they told him to 'speak good words to them when you answer them, then they will be your servants for ever'. The new king turned away to take counsel with the young men who had grown up with him and they said he should answer: 'My father chastised you with whips, but I will chastise you with scorpions.' He took this advice, and the outcome was the break-up of the kingdom. The northern tribes rallied to Jeroboam who became king over Israel. Rehoboam fled to the safety of Jerusalem and reigned as king of Judah. The historian of these times sets down

Rehoboam as a bad king because he encouraged heathen customs throughout the land. During his reign Jerusalem was attacked by Shishak, king of Egypt, who sacked Temple and palace and looted the treasures Solomon had accumulated. [*Refs*. 1 Kings 11: 43 to 12: 24; 14: 21-31. 2 Chronicles 10: 1-19.]

Resurrection Various accounts of the Resurrection appearances of Jesus are recorded in the N.T. The earliest is in Paul's first Letter to the Corinthians, where the apostle sets down the teaching of the early Church: 'that Christ died for our sins in accordance with the scriptures, that he was buried, that he was raised on the third day in accordance with the scriptures, and that he appeared to Cephas, then to the twelve. Then he appeared to more than five hundred brethren at one time ... then he appeared to James, then to all the apostles. Last of all ... he appeared also to me.' Paul goes on to base the Christian faith firmly on the fact of the Resurrection of Christ. He discusses the nature of the Resurrection body, spiritual, not physical: 'flesh and blood cannot inherit the kingdom of God nor does the perishable inherit the imperishable'.

Mark's Gospel, which is the first of the four, does not mention the Resurrection of Jesus directly at all. The Gospel ends with the visit of the women to the tomb where a young man said to them: 'Do not be amazed; you seek Jesus of Nazareth, who was crucified. He has risen, he is not here; see the place where they laid him.' The final words of the Gospel are: 'they said nothing to any one, for they were afraid'. An appendix at Mark 16: 9-20, written in the second century A.D., mentions a Resurrection appearance of Jesus to Mary Magdalene, and 'in another form' to two of them as they were walking in the country, afterwards to the eleven disciples as they sat at table.

The other Gospels are more detailed in their accounts of the Resurrection, and more materialistic. Matthew tells how Jesus met Mary Magdalene and the other Mary as they ran from the empty tomb, and that they took hold of his feet and worshipped him. He also records that the eleven disciples met Jesus on a mountain in Galilee—'but some doubted'. Luke's Gospel has an account of two of the disciples meeting Jesus on the road to Emmaus, but at first 'their eyes were kept from recognizing him'. There is a passing reference to an appearance to Simon (Peter) and finally the story of Jesus standing among his disciples in a room in Jerusalem. John's Gospel tells that Jesus spoke to Mary Magdalene outside the tomb, 'but she did not know that it was Jesus'. On the evening of that first day of the week Jesus stood among his disciples and showed them his hands and side. Thomas was not with them when Jesus came, and he would not believe. Eight days later, in the same place, Jesus appeared again to his disciples, the doors being shut. This time Thomas was with them and declared his faith in the risen Lord. After this John records an appearance of Jesus to some of his disciples on the beach by the Sea of Tiberias. The opening chapter of the Acts of the Apostles also records that Jesus appeared to the apostles whom he had chosen: 'To them he presented himself alive after his passion by many proofs, appearing to them during forty days, and speaking of the kingdom of God.'

Every book of the N.T. mentions or assumes the Resurrection of Jesus. It is the Gospels which record the empty tomb, angelic messengers, and that the event took place 'on the third day'. It must be remembered that none of these accounts was written for at least thirty-five years after the Resurrection. It is not surprising that there is diversity among them. There is some insistence in the early Church that an apostle must be 'a witness to his Resurrection'; 'This Jesus God raised up, and of that we all are witnesses.' It is necessary to make a careful examination of where the Gospels agree and where they differ, as well as what they really say. The thoughtful reader today is bound to ask questions about the manner of the appearances: a body of flesh and blood or a spirit; the well-known form of Jesus of Nazareth or 'another form'; a familiar friend who could be instantly identified or someone even Mary Magdalene or the two travellers on the way to

Emmaus did not recognize? Did he appear among his disciples with a material body which could take and eat boiled fish, or was it a manifestation which could pass through closed doors and instantly vanish from sight? Did the Resurrection appearances take place in Jerusalem or Galilee, or both? One thing is made plain. The risen Lord appeared only to those who were his friends and followers, not to strangers or foes.

Whatever the historical truth of the Resurrection, it is Paul, the earliest of the writers, who ponders its meaning and significance most deeply. None of the N.T. writers has any doubt that God raised Jesus from the dead and that this was a fulfilment of divine purpose. It is not the Jesus of history they remember and record, although the records of the Gospels linger over stories of the bodily resurrection. The Church worships a living Lord. Their witness does not rest in details of Christ's appearances here or there. It is centred in proclaiming the risen Christ and in sharing his living fellowship in 'the breaking of bread'. The proclamation in the N.T. is not primarily concerned with the mode of the Lord's rising from the dead, but with the fact of it. The modern mind is greatly concerned with the manner of the event; the Christian has always put his trust in the meaning of it. [*Refs.* Matthew 28. Mark 16. Luke 24. John 20-1. Acts 1: 1-10, 22; 2: 24, 32; 4: 2. Romans 6: 4. 1 Corinthians 15: 11*f.* Hebrews 13: 20.]

Reuben The eldest son of Jacob and Leah, and forefather of one of the twelve tribes of Israel. [*Refs.* Genesis 29: 32; 37: 22, 29.]

Revelation to John, The Five books of the N.T. bear the name of John: a Gospel, three Letters, and this book called The Revelation. The name John appears here at 1: 1, 4, 9 and at 22: 8, but there is no other evidence of identification except that the writer was apparently a prisoner on the lonely island of Patmos in the Aegean Sea (1: 9). It is unlikely that he was John the fisherman of Galilee, the apostle of Jesus. For one thing, he writes reverently and objectively about the apostles as from a viewpoint outside them and later than their day (18: 20 to 22: 14). For another, he makes no claim to be one of the select inner circle of the companions of Jesus. He is not, in fact, an 'eye-witness' as the first disciples were proud to claim. Nor is he closely connected with the fourth Gospel or the three Letters of John. The language and ideas are not alike. Finally, the date of the Book of the Revelation would appear to be very late in the first century A.D., if we are to take account of the Roman persecutions portrayed in its pages. This John, whoever he was, appears to have been a well-known leader writing from Ephesus, a stronghold of the Christian faith in the early days of the Church.

The literary form of the book is apocalyptic, and Revelation is sometimes known as The Apocalypse. This kind of writing was distinctively Jewish during the last two centuries B.C. and the first century A.D., after prophecy had disappeared from the scene. The Book of Daniel in the O.T. and Revelation in the New are our prime examples, but apocalyptic passages are to be found here and there throughout the N.T. (in Mark 13, for instance). The style belongs to a time of severe persecution, and its purpose is to maintain faith among the 'chosen people' as the Jews and later the Jewish-Christians believed themselves to be. Apocalyptic writing contrasts the present evil age with the glory of the new age which is to come when God finally overthrows the powers of evil and takes control. The present age will come to an end in cosmic conflict between God and Satan before the new age dawns. Believers are to be faithful through every possible terror and they will triumph in the new heaven and earth that is to be. Since the writer lived in a time of oppression, the writing is mysterious, full of imagery, symbols, hidden meanings. Only the faithful Christian will understand the truth of his message cloaked in the symbols of heads, horns, mythical beasts, dragons, horses, eagles, vultures etc. That is what the Greek word *apocalypsis* means—'a revelation or disclosure'.

The contents of the Book of the Revelation are strange to our minds today, and the meaning is often obscure. It must be remembered, however, that John was writing for his own day and for a particular situation. He was not merely dreaming about the future. He and his fellow-Christians did endure persecution, suffering, martyrdom. They believed that the worst evils of the present age had come upon them, therefore the new age of God's rule must be very near. This is a book for a time of crisis in the Churches of the first century. It was never intended to foretell later events in history or to provide a happy hunting-ground for lunatics to spell out contemporary meanings in the twenty-first century A.D.

The book falls into two parts. Chapters 1-3 are taken up with a message to the seven Churches of Asia Minor. Chapters 4-22 contain a series of apocalyptic visions in which the writer quotes a great deal from the O.T. To be noted is the continual use of the sacred number seven.

An outline of the contents is:

(a) Revelation 1: 1-8: Prologue to the whole work from John 'who bore witness to the word of God and to the testimony of Jesus Christ, even to all that he saw'.

(b) Revelation 1: 9 to 3: 22: The first vision: seven golden lampstands and in the midst one like a son of man. John is to write his vision to the seven Churches, namely, Ephesus, Smyrna, Pergamum, Thyatira, Sardis, Philadelphia, Laodicea. Each Church is personally addressed and it is plain that the writer is concerned not with general, pious exhortation, but in putting his finger on the weaknesses and the needs of each group of Christians. Thus, the Church at Ephesus has shown patient endurance, yet they have abandoned the love they had at first. The Church in Thyatira is tolerating a woman prophetess who is teaching false things and beguiling the members to immorality. The members in Laodicea are blamed for being lukewarm, neither cold nor hot.

(c) Revelation 4: 1 to 5: 14: A vision of the heavenly throne with living creatures surrounding it. Among the living creatures and the elders there was a Lamb standing, as though it had been slain. It is the Lamb who will bring about God's triumph over all things, until 'every creature in heaven and on earth and under the earth and in the sea, and all therein' shall bow before him and offer 'blessing and honour and glory and might for ever and ever!'

(d) Revelation 6: 1 to 7: 17: The Lamb opens the seven seals of a scroll and there is a vision of a white horse, a red horse, a black horse and a pale horse, which in turn symbolize war, killing, famine and plague spreading across the earth. Then there appear the souls of martyr saints and a cataclysmic disaster which occurs in heaven and on earth. Thereafter the servants of God—from all the tribes and peoples and tongues—are brought before the Lamb and cry aloud: 'Salvation belongs to our God who sits upon the throne, and to the Lamb.'

(e) Revelation 8: 1 to 11: 14: The opening of the seventh seal. A vision of seven angels with seven trumpets and the cosmic disasters which befall when the trumpets are sounded.

(f) Revelation 11: 15 to 13: 18: The seventh angel sounds his trumpet and victory is proclaimed: 'The kingdom of the world has become the kingdom of our Lord and of his Christ, and he shall reign for ever and ever.' A vision of a woman (the Church), a great red dragon (the power of Rome), a beast with ten horns and seven heads (the emperor), a second beast with the number 666 (probably a cryptic reference to Nero).

(g) Revelation 14: 1-20: The vision of the Lamb surrounded by the redeemed, singing a new song before the throne. This is the Last Judgment.

(h) Revelation 15: 1 to 16: 21: The wrath of God is spilled on the earth from seven golden bowls filled with terrible plagues.

(i) Revelation 17: 1 to 19: 10: A vision of the downfall of Rome ('the great harlot') under the symbolic name 'Babylon the great'.

(j) Revelation 19: 11 to 21: 5: Visions of the triumph of the new age. Christ the conqueror comes on a white horse followed by the armies of heaven on white horses, and all his enemies are destroyed. The dragon, who is the Devil and Satan, is seized and bound. Then the souls of the faithful martyrs come to life and reign with Christ. Finally, all the dead, great and small, stand before the throne for judgement, and the new heaven and the new earth appear with the new Jerusalem in the midst.

(k) Revelation 21: 6 to 22: 7: A vision of the new Jerusalem with the glory of God as its light, and the river of the water of life flowing through the midst.

(l) Revelation 22: 8-21: The end of the visions, a final warning that the end is near, and a last appeal to the Christians to be faithful. A warrant for all John has written: 'He who testifies to these things says "Surely I am coming soon." Amen. Come, Lord Jesus!'

Rhoda The name of a young girl in the Jerusalem house of Mary, the mother of John Mark. Rhoda is mentioned only in connection with Peter's miraculous escape from prison and his arrival at the house of Mary. The Greek word *rhoda* means 'roses'. [*Ref.* Acts 12: 13-15.]

Romans, The Letter of Paul to the This Letter is always held to be the most authentic of the writings of Paul, the one which most clearly sets forth his faith and teaching. It was probably written from Corinth, where Paul spent some time during his third missionary journey, before his last voyage to Jerusalem (Acts 20: 1-3). The Letter was addressed to a Church which Paul had not founded nor even visited—'all God's beloved in Rome'. Its object was two-fold, to announce that he is about to visit them, and to detail the Gospel he preaches. Apparently it was Paul's intention to stay a little time in Rome and then go to Spain, and thus carry the Gospel of Christ from the furthest east to the furthest west of the Mediterranean (Romans 15: 24).

The Letter to the Romans appears to end at three different places, namely: at 15: 13, where Paul's exposition of his faith comes to a close with a benediction; at 15: 33, which includes mainly personal comments about himself and his travel plans; and at 16: 20, which takes in a large number of greetings by name to fellow-Christians and concludes with a doxology. The three endings would appear to represent three different copies of the Letter. Chapter 16, which is quite different from the rest of the work, is usually thought to be a separate Letter to the Church in Ephesus where Paul had many friends. Perhaps a copy of the whole important Letter was sent to Ephesus with chapter 16 as a postscript of personal greetings.

A brief outline of the contents is:

(a) Romans 1: 1-7: Greetings to the 'saints' in Rome.

(b) Romans 1: 8-17: Paul's explanation of why he is writing to them: 'I am eager to preach the gospel to you also who are in Rome.'

(c) Romans 1: 18 to 3: 20: The power of sin in Gentile and Jew: 'none is righteous, no not one'.

(d) Romans 3: 21 to 4: 25: 'righteousness through faith in Jesus Christ for all who believe.'

(e) Romans 5: 1 to 8: 39: 'Peace with God through our Lord Jesus Christ ... for the wages of sin is death, but the free gift of God is eternal life in Christ Jesus our Lord.'

(f) Romans 9: 1 to 11: 36: The old Israel and the new—'For there is no distinction between Jew and Greek ... everyone who calls upon the name of the Lord will be saved.'

(g) Romans 12: 1 to 13: 14: The moral behaviour of the Christian believer, towards other people, and under the State: 'love is the fulfilling of the law'.

(h) Romans 14: 1 to 15: 13: The strong and the weak: 'we who are strong ought to bear with the failings of the weak, and not to please ourselves'.

(i) Romans 15: 14-33: Paul plans for the future: 'I hope to see you in passing as I go to Spain.'

(j) Romans 16: 1-23: Greetings to various friends, probably in the Church at Ephesus.

(k) Romans 16: 25-7: A concluding doxology, probably added later by another writer.

One fact which makes the letter to the Romans the most important of all Paul's writings is that it is not merely addressed to Christians in Rome, but to the wide world of Jew and Gentile alike. 'All have sinned and fall short of the glory of God'...all alike are justified by faith. This is indeed the manifesto of Paul's faith, and it lit a true understanding of the meaning of the Christian Gospel in others, notably St. Augustine, Luther, Wesley, Karl Barth. The Letter of Paul to the Romans is thus the most important piece of theological writing in all Christian literature.

Ruler of the Synagogue A Jewish elder who was responsible for the day-to-day administration of the worship and work of the synagogue. It was his duty to arrange for the services, to lead the worship in turn with others, and to invite adult male Jews to take some part in the service, for instance, to say prayers or to read the Scripture lessons. [*Refs.* Mark 5: 22, 35*f.* Luke 8: 41; 13: 14. Acts 13: 15; 18: 8, 17.]

Ruth, The Book of The eighth book of the O.T. is a short romantic tale which is apparently set 'in the days when the judges ruled'. It was in fact written after the Exile and is a story with a moral. It tells how Ruth, a foreigner, comes with her widowed mother-in-law Naomi to Bethlehem and is befriended by Boaz, a wealthy farmer who eventually marries her. There are two reasons for the telling of the story of Ruth. First, to mention that Ruth was great-grandmother of David, Israel's greatest king. Second, to make a plea for religious tolerance in post-exilic times when Ezra had forbidden his fellow-Jews to enter into mixed marriages. The lovely and loving Ruth was a foreigner not a Jew, but she fulfilled the law of God.

S

Sabbath According to ancient Hebrew tradition, the sabbath is a day of complete rest from the normal work and business of the week. It is especially associated in Jewish thought with 'joy' and 'peace' and 'light' as well as with rest from labour for the families of the chosen people, their domestic and farm animals, and even for slaves and strangers. The idea of the sabbath is basic in Jewish religion. It is the most holy of all their religious observances, the only one mentioned in the Ten Commandments as well as in their mythological account of the origin of all things in heaven and earth. The sabbath is there set down as a special day of God's own appointing from the beginning of the world. It marked the finishing of his work of creation: 'God blessed the sabbath day and hallowed it, because in it God rested from all his work which he had done in creation.'

Because their sacred writings spoke thus of the sabbath as a day of God's instituting, it was a sin to break the law of the sabbath. The prophets continually reminded their people to keep the sabbath as a delight. After the Exile, however, sabbath observance became more rigidly the very mark of Judaism. Eventually the legalists among Jewish teachers proclaimed what might or might not be done on that holy day. Thus, in the N.T. we find that the Pharisees watched Jesus continually to see what he would do on the sabbath, so that they might accuse him, particularly in his acts of healing.

Jesus, in reply, stated: 'The sabbath was made for man, not man for the sabbath.'

The Jewish sabbath today, as in age-old custom, begins with the kindling of the lights at sundown on Friday and lasts until sundown on Saturday. It is kept with rejoicing in the Jewish home, the gathering of the family together, the sharing of a meal, and special prayers over the food and wine. For the devout Jew the sabbath includes worship in the synagogue. [*Refs*. Genesis 2: 3. Exodus 20: 8-11; 31: 12-17. Numbers 15: 32-6. Deuteronomy 5: 12-15. Nehemiah 10: 31; 13: 15. Isaiah 56: 2, 6; 58: 13. Jeremiah 17: 21-7. Ezekiel 20: 12-21. Matthew 12: 1-14. Mark 1: 21*f*; 2: 23 to 3: 6. Luke 13: 10-17; 14: 1-6. John 5: 1*f*.; 9: 14*f*.]

Sabean *See* SHEBA

Sacrifice *See* FIRST-BORN

Sadducees A party of the Jews in N.T. times, made up of priests of the Temple and wealthy aristocratic families in Jerusalem. They were conservative in politics and in religion and resisted any change which might weaken their control over the ritual organization of the Temple. Within the Temple courts the Romans allowed them almost complete authority. The Sadducees held the written Torah, or Law of Moses, to be sacred and they rejected any teaching or interpretation of the Pharisees which went beyond the written letter of the Law. Thus they rejected belief in angels, demons, spirits and resurrection from the dead because such doctrine is not to be found in the five books of Moses. Jesus antagonized the party of the Sadducees in his teaching and by his action in driving out those who sold and those who bought in the Temple and overturning the tables of the money-changers. Notable Sadducees who appear in the Gospels and Acts are Annas and Caiaphas, the high priests. The Sadducees disappeared from Jewish history with the downfall of the Temple in A.D. 70. [*Refs*. Matthew 3: 7; 16: 1, 6; 22: 23, 34. Mark 12: 18. Luke 20: 27. Acts 4: 1; 5: 17; 23: 6-8.]

Salome (1) The daughter of Herodias who danced before the company on the birthday of Herod Antipas and so pleased the tetrarch that he promised to give her whatever she might ask. Prompted by her mother, Salome asked for the head of John the Baptist on a platter. The girl's name is not mentioned in the Gospels. [*Refs.* Matthew 14: 3-11. Mark 6: 17-29.] (2) The name of a woman who witnessed the Crucifixion in company with other women from Galilee and who went with them to the tomb early on the first day of the week, the Resurrection morning. [*Refs.* Mark 15: 40; 16: 1*f.*]

Salt Sea *See* DEAD SEA

Samaria, Samaritans Samaria was the name of the capital city of the northern kingdom of Israel. It was bought and fortified by King Omri and named, apparently, after the original owner, Shemer. The prophet Amos knew Samaria in the days of its prosperity and denounced its citizens for their oppression of the poor. Samaria fell in 721 B.C. to the Assyrians. Sargon, the conqueror, deported 27,290 Israelites and filled their land with a mixed population of other people from Babylonia and elsewhere in his territories. They intermarried with the poorest Israelites left in the land and their descendants were known as Samaritans. Thus we find that after the Exile the name Samaria was applied to an area of Palestine inhabited by settlers of mixed blood. These Samaritans tried to stop the rebuilding of the walls of Jerusalem in the time of Nehemia. The post-exilic Jews, fanatically devoted to purity of race and cult, rejected the Samaritans completely, and an age-long hostility set in. The Samaritans set up their own temple at Mt. Gerizim in opposition, as it were, to the Temple in Jerusalem.

In N.T.times the city of Samaria was rebuilt by Herod the Great and renamed Sebaste. The enmity between Jews and Samaritans is mentioned a number of times in the Gospels. Jesus, however, immortalized the Good Samaritan in one of the most memorable of his parables, and the Gospel was preached in the towns and villages of Samaria in the early days of the Church. [*Refs.* 1 Kings 16: 24. 1 Kings 17: 6, 24.

Amos 3: 12; 6: 1. Micah 1: 6. Ezra 4: 1-3. Nehemiah 4: 2.
Luke 9: 52; 10: 33*f*.; 17: 16-17. John 4: 4*f*. Acts 1: 8; 8: 5*f*.]

Samson The last of the Israelites' leaders mentioned in the Book
of Judges, and the first to do battle against the alien and
invading Philistines. The Samson cycle of stories is largely
legendary, portraying as they do a popular hero who put his
enormous physical strength to the discomfiture of the
Philistines but was himself betrayed by a woman. At the
beginning of the Samson saga an angel of the Lord tells how
the child who is to be born 'shall begin to deliver Israel from
the hand of the Philistines'. In manhood his exploits included
tearing a lion apart with his bare hands, killing a company of
the men of Ashdod, setting fire to their fields and orchards,
and slaughtering a thousand men with the jawbone of an ass.
Finally the secret of his strength was revealed to the Philistines
by Delilah. The Philistines took him, cut off his hair, gouged
out his eyes, bound him with strong fetters, and set him to
grind at the mill in the prison. But Samson's hair, in which
was the secret of his strength, began to grow again. The day
came when the Philistine lords at heathen sacrifice sent for
the blind Samson to laugh at him. Samson felt for the pillars
on which the house rested, pulled them down, and thus died
in the midst of a great company of Philistines. Samson is one
of the great folklore heroes of all time. He is a poor example in
a religious setting, but his story has inspired artists, poets and
musicians in later ages to retell the tale. [*Refs*. Judges 13: 2 to
16: 31.] *See also*: MANOAEI, NAZIRITES

Samuel Samuel was the son of Elkanah of Ephraim and his wife
Hannah. His home town, Ramathaim-zophim (later Ramah)
was in the highlands of central Palestine. Samuel is usually
known as the last of the Judges and the first of the prophets.
His name often ranks with that of Moses in Hebrew tradition.
Samuel appeared at a critical time for the tribes of Israel. According to the first of the books which bears his name, his
mother dedicated him to the Lord as a child, and a charming
tale tells how young Samuel, servant of Eli, 'was ministering

before the Lord, a boy girded with a linen ephod' and how, at the shrine in Shiloh, he heard the voice of the Lord speak to him. As a man Samuel played an important part in uniting the tribes against the growing threat of the Philistines. He was known as a 'judge', a 'seer' and a 'priest' who went on a circuit year by year to the sacred shrines 'and he judged Israel in all these places'.

It was Samuel the kingmaker who anointed Saul to 'reign over the people of the Lord' and to save them from the hand of their enemies round about. Later, following Saul's disobedience, Samuel went to Bethlehem to seek and anoint David as the future king of Israel. Thereafter Samuel disappears from the story. He died and was buried in his house at Ramah and remained for ever a legendary man of God in the history of the chosen people. The books which bear his name are made up of various traditions from a number of sources, including material from long after the time of Samuel. They pay tribute to the memory of one of the great spiritual leaders of Israel. [*Refs.* 1 Samuel. Jeremiah 15: 1. Hebrews 11: 32.] *See also*: HANNAH

Samuel, 1 and 2 Originally one book, named after Samuel, the seer and judge, priest, prophet and kingmaker. These writings tell of the beginning of kingship in Israel, and the chief characters in the history are Samuel, Saul and David. As in other 'historical' books of the O.T., there are at least two strands in the account of the early days of the monarchy and a number of double stories. One account, for example (1 Samuel 9: 1 to 10: 16) shows Samuel as the seer of Ramah who anoints Saul to be prince over God's people Israel in the days of their struggle against the Philistines. A very different account (1 Samuel 7: 2-17; 8; 10: 17-21; 12) states that the demand for a king comes from the people and does not at all please Samuel, who declares it to be alien to the will of God. It is probable that here and elsewhere in the O.T. we find two later viewpoints, one for and one against the whole idea of monarchy.

The two books of Samuel as we have them may be roughly

divided thus:

(a) 1 Samuel 1: 1 to 7: 2: Stories of the birth and boyhood of Samuel the man of God.

(b) 1 Samuel 7: 3 to 15: 35: Stories of Samuel and Saul and the war with the Philistines.

(c) 1 Samuel 16: 1 to 2 Samuel 1: Stories of David and Saul.

(d) 2 Samuel 2-24: The life and times of David the king.

It must be added that the tales of these early rulers of Israel were recorded and revised by Jerusalem writers of the court circle who wished to show David in a favourable light as the hero-king. They tend to cast a shadow on Saul to make David shine all the more brightly.

Sanhedrin *See* COUNCIL

Sarah or **Sarai** The wife of Abraham and mother of Isaac. Sarah journeyed with Abraham from Ur to Haran and then to unknown Canaan. She grew old and was still childless. A messenger of God told Abraham that Sarah would bear a son who would be heir of the promise and father of a great nation. Sarah overheard and laughed bitterly. But it came true, and her son was called Isaac which is a Hebrew pun on 'laughter'. 'God has made laughter for me', said Sarah. [*Refs.* Genesis 11: 29; 16: 1; 17: 15-19; 18: 9-15; 21: 1-7. Romans 9: 9.]

Satan The name of the chief of the evil spirits, sometimes called the Devil. It originally meant no more than 'enemy' or 'adversary'. The idea of a personalized devil may have come into Jewish thought from Persian influences. In the Gospels Satan is depicted as the one who 'tempts' Jesus in the wilderness. In Christian writings Satan is used as a proper name for the fallen angel who has become the chief enemy of God. In the Book of the Revelation the final victory comes after the binding and imprisonment of 'the dragon, that ancient serpent, who is the Devil and Satan'. [*Refs.* Job 1: 6, 8. Zechariah 3: 1, 2. Matthew 4: 10; 12: 26; 16: 23. Mark 1: 13, 4: 15; 8: 33. Luke 22: 3. John 13: 27. Revelation 2: 9, 13; 20: 2, 7.] *See also*: BEELZEBUB; DEVIL

Saul The name of the first king of Israel. Saul was the son of Kish, a man of wealth, of the tribe of Benjamin. Various stories of Saul from different sources can be found in 1 Samuel. He was a handsome young man, taller than any of the people of Israel, who was anointed by Samuel in the name of God to be prince over his people Israel. Another tradition suggests that Saul was chosen to be king by lot. His first test came when he rallied the men of Israel against the Ammonites. The more famous stories of Saul, however, tell of the war he and his son Jonathan waged against the powerful Philistines: 'There was hard fighting against the Philistines all the days of Saul.' Young David is introduced into the narrative as shepherd boy, musician in the service of the king, victor over Goliath, friend of Jonathan, and Saul's son-in-law. Thereafter the writers portray Saul as a moody, vengeful man whose fortunes wane as those of David rise. At last Saul and his sons and the men of Israel fought a battle with the Philistines at Mt. Gilboa. They were disastrously defeated, the sons of Saul were slain, and the king himself fell upon his sword. One of the most famous poems in Hebrew literature is the lament which David made over Saul and Jonathan:

'Saul and Jonathan, beloved and lovely!
In life and in death they were not divided
They were swifter than eagles,
They were stronger than lions.'

[*Refs.* 1 Samuel 9-31. 2 Samuel 1. 1 Chronicles 10.] *See also*: PAUL

Scribes Jewish scribes were originally writers attached to the Temple and court, who kept official and sacred records, copied documents and acted as secretaries in affairs of state in days long before the age of printing, when only a few could write and read. After the Exile, scribes such as Ezra played an important part in copying, preserving and teaching the sacred scriptures to the Jews who returned to Jerusalem. In n.t. times the scribes were sometimes Pharisees and thus laymen, sometimes priestly and thus attached to the Temple. We read of their encounters with Jesus and their criticism of him.

There is a portrait of the ideal scribe in the Apocryphal Book of Ecclesiasticus: 'He will seek out the wisdom of all the ancients, and will be occupied in prophecies. He will keep the discourse of the men of renown, and will enter in amidst the subtleties of parables. He will seek out the hidden meaning of proverbs, and be conversant in the dark sayings of parables. He will serve among great men, and appear before him that ruleth ... If the great Lord will, he shall be filled with the spirit of understanding: he shall pour forth the words of his wisdom, and in prayer give thanks unto the Lord.' [*Refs.* 2 Kings 12: 10; 22: 8-10. Ezra 7: 6. Nehemiah 8: 1, 4. Matthew 2: 4; 5: 20; 16: 21. Mark 1: 22; 2: 6; 12: 38; 14: 43; 15: 1. Luke 22: 66; 23: 10.]

Selah *See* PSALMS

Seleucia The seaport of the city of Antioch in Syria, about five miles from the mouth of the river Orontes. From there Barnabas and Paul, with John Mark to assist them, sailed to Cyprus on their first missionary journey. [*Ref.* Acts 13: 4.]

Sennacherib Son of Sargon II, king of Assyria, 705-681 B.C. Ancient Assyrian records from his own time boast of Sennacherib as 'the great king, the mighty king, the king of the universe, the king of the four quarters of the earth, the favourite of the great gods, defender of the right, lover of justice ...'. He appears in the Bible account of the Assyrian attack on Judah and siege of Jerusalem in the time of King Hezekiah: 'Sennacherib king of Assyria came up against all the fortified cities of Judah and took them.' Hezekiah paid tribute of silver and gold, stripping the very doors of the Temple to do so. Sennacherib's own account of the siege of Jerusalem states: 'He himself (Hezekiah) I shut up like a caged bird within Jerusalem his royal city.' The Bible record tells how 'the angel of the Lord went forth, and slew a hundred and eighty-five thousand in the camp of the Assyrians'—i.e. plague broke out among the enemy. The Assyrians withdrew and Sennacherib was assassinated by his sons in Nineveh. Byron has his own version in the famous poem which begins: 'The

Assyrian came down like a wolf on the fold.' [*Refs.* 2 Kings 18: 13 to 19: 37. Isaiah 36-7.]

Septuagint The Greek version of the O.T. The Greek word *septuaginta* means 'seventy' and refers to the tradition that the work of translation from the original Hebrew was carried out by seventy (or seventy-two) learned Jews in Alexandria in the third century B.C. It is often denoted by the symbol LXX. The Septuagint was the version of Hebrew Scriptures known and used by Greek-speaking Jews and Gentiles in the Mediterranean world of the N.T. times. It is thus the translation usually quoted in such writings as the Gospels, the Acts of the Apostles, and the Letters of Paul.

Seraphim *Seraphim* is the Hebrew plural of the word *seraph*. They were mythical, half-human, half-animal creatures with six wings, hands and feet which Isaiah saw and heard about the throne of God in his vision in the Temple in Jerusalem. The vision was possibly suggested by carved decorations in Solomon's Temple. The name *seraphim* seems to mean 'the burning ones'. The seraphim had a much older ancestry than Hebrew symbolism, being found in various forms in Egyptian and early Mesopotamian art. [*Ref.* Isaiah 6: 2, 6.]

Sermon on the Mount The Sermon on the Mount forms part of the teaching of Jesus in the Gospels of Matthew and Luke. It is found in Matthew 5-7 and in briefer form in Luke 6: 20-49. The title Sermon on the Mount comes from the setting mentioned in Matthew 5: 1-2: 'Seeing the crowds, Jesus went up on the mountain, and when he sat down his disciples came to him. And he opened his mouth and taught them, saying...'. As Moses gave the old law on Mt. Sinai to God's chosen people, so Jesus is shown to be giving the new law of the kingdom of God on a mountain to his chosen disciples who are the nucleus of the new Israel of God. The words 'he sat down' are a reminder that this is serious teaching, not mere conversation. Jewish rabbis sat in the synagogue and in school to instruct their disciples, and the pupils gathered round them.

An outline of the account in Matthew's Gospel is:

(a) Matthew 5: 3-12: The sermon opens with the beatitudes which declare a blessing on those who are true citizens of the kingdom of heaven, such as the poor in spirit, the meek, the merciful, the pure in heart, the peacemakers.

(b) Matthew 5: 13-16. There follow two parables about the special quality of the members of the kingdom—they are to be the salt of the earth and the light of the world.

(c) Matthew 5: 17-47: The old law is not set aside, rather it is fulfilled in Christ. Six times over there is a reminder of the old law followed by positive statements of the new way of life of the kingdom of heaven. These are introduced by the phrases: 'You have heard that it was said ... But I say to you.' The six themes dealt with are: murder, adultery, divorce, truthfulness, revenge, loving your neighbour.

(d) Matthew 5: 48: This part of the sermon is summed up by the ideal requirement for membership of God's kingdom: 'You, therefore, must be perfect, as your heavenly Father is perfect.'

(e) Matthew 6: 1-18: Deals with some of the forms of religion, almsgiving, prayer, fasting. It is a warning against outward show and hypocrisy. It includes the Lord's Prayer as a model of how his disciples are to pray.

(f) Matthew 6: 19-34: A warning about wordly possessions and needless anxiety about everyday things. This collection of teaching leads up to the sentence: 'Seek first his kingdom and his righteousness, and all these things shall be yours as well.'

(g) Matthew 7: 1-12: Ethical teaching about judging and about giving. This section ends with the Golden Rule which sums up in one sentence all the rules of the law and the prophets.

(h) Matthew 7: 13-27: There follow four sets of parable pictures about two ways—the wide and easy contrasted with the narrow and hard; two kinds of prophets, the false and the true—they will be known by their fruits; two disciples—those who merely talk without meaning, and those who do the will of God; two houses—one built on sand and the other on foundations of rock.

(i) Matthew 7: 28-9: The Sermon on the Mount according to Matthew ends with the impression made by Jesus: 'the crowds were astonished at his teaching'. Here was one who did not quote written laws but spoke and lived with the authority of one whose words and deeds were one. That authority was to be heeded.

Luke's version of this teaching material is more properly called 'the sermon on the plain' for his setting for the words of Jesus is 'a level place' (Luke 6: 17). It follows immediately on the choosing of the twelve disciples and to them, as in Matthew, the Master's teaching is given. Luke draws on the same common source as Matthew, but he sets down the teaching of Jesus in a different way. Where Matthew brings it together in an orderly system, as if for a catechetical purpose, Luke scatters it through the latter part of his Gospel, attached to other material.

(a) Luke 6: 20-6: Luke's version of the beatitudes, four 'blesseds' with four contrasting 'woes'.

(b) Luke 6: 27-36: The character and conduct of those who live in the kingdom: love your enemies, do good, bless, pray, lend, give and forgive. The Golden Rule sums it all up, and the motive is the nature of God himself: 'He is kind to the ungrateful and the selfish. Be merciful even as your Father is merciful.'

(c) Luke 6: 37-49: Luke's parallel to the teaching found in Matthew 7: 1f, concluding with the same parable of the two houses.

The whole Sermon on the Mount may be regarded as the teaching of Jesus treasured by the early Church on the theme: 'living in the kingdom'. *See also*: BEATITUDES; LORD'S PRAYER

Sharon A plain on the Mediterranean coast of Palestine, from Joppa to Mt. Carmel, famous for its fertility and its flowers. [*Refs*. Song of Solomon 2: 1. Isaiah 33: 9; 35: 2; 65: 10.]

Sheba A country on the south-west coast of Arabia, famous in O.T. times for its trade in frankincense, gold and precious stones to east and west. The legendary Queen of Sheba came with a great camel-caravan to visit Solomon and no doubt to enter into trade agreements with him. She brought the king 'spices and very much gold and precious stones'. The names Seba and Sabean refer to the same place, and are always associated with exotic wealth. Modern archaeologists have uncovered rich ancient cities in this part of Yemen. [*Refs.* 1 Kings 10: 1-10. Psalm 72: 15. Isaiah 60: 6. Jeremiah 6: 20. Ezekiel 27: 22.]

Shechem An important town in the hill country of Canaan mentioned in the stories of Abraham, Jacob, and Joseph. It was there, according to tradition, that the bones of Joseph were buried. Joshua gathered the tribes of Israel to Shechem and united them in a covenant of obedience to the Lord who had brought them out of Egypt. Thus the scattered tribes were bound together in one common loyalty. Rehoboam, son of Solomon, went to Shechem to be made king on the death of his father, and it was there that Jeroboam the rebel confronted him on behalf of the northern tribes. When Jeroboam set himself up as king, he fortified Shechem as his capital. The place was remembered in Jewish history as one of the most significant centres of their early history, as a sanctuary and place of pilgrimage. The Samaritans of post-exilic days built their temple at Mt. Gerizim near ancient Shechem. [*Refs.* Genesis 12: 6; 33: 18-20; 37: 12-14. Joshua 2 : 7; 24: 1*f*; 1 Kings 12: 1, 25.]

Shewbread The word used in the Authorized Version for the sacred loaves of hot, fresh, unleavened bread which were laid on a table in the shrines of Israel and later in the Temple 'before the face of God'. They were made of the finest flour, holy, only to be eaten by the priests, and were offered fresh sabbath by sabbath. Probably the custom arose in earliest times from the idea of setting food before a hungry god. Later, the loaves were a reminder to Israel that it is God who gives our daily bread. Modern versions of the Bible usually translate the word as 'bread of the Presence'. [*Refs*. Exodus 25: 30. Leviticus 24: 5-9. 1 Samuel 21: 1-6. 1 Kings 7: 48. Matthew 12: 3-4.]

Shibboleth The Hebrew word used by Jephthah at the fords of Jordan to test the fleeing Ephraimites who had been in battle with his own men of Gilead. The Ephraimites could not pronounce *sh* and said *Sibboleth* instead of Shibboleth. They were thus detected and slain. The word has passed into the English language as meaning a catchword or rallying cry for a group. [*Ref*. Judges 12: 4-6.]

Shiloh An important religious centre in the early days of the Israelite conquest and occupation of Canaan. The Ark of the Covenant was placed in the shrine at Shiloh and there the tribes gathered at times of religious festival. Samuel 'served before the Lord' at Shiloh when he was a boy. Shiloh was captured and destroyed by the Philistines, and the Ark of the Covenant was carried off by them. [*Refs*. Joshua 18: 1. 1 Samuel 1: 3; 3: 21; 4: 3-4, 11. Jeremiah 7: 12, 14.]

Shinar A name given in the early chapters of Genesis to the land better known as Babylonia, the cradle of Hebrew civilization. [*Refs*. Genesis 10: 10; 11: 2.] *See also:* BABYLON

Shishak *See* REHOBOAM

Sidon An ancient seaport on the northern coast of Palestine and chief city, along with Tyre, of the kingdom of Phoenicia. The Sidonians were sea traders from earliest times, and merchants of Sidon were known wherever ships could sail. Sidonian woodworkers were famous in the time of Solomon and they helped to build his Temple and palace. This skilled craft was still going on when the second Temple was built. Religious and moral disaster befell Israel when Ahab the king married Jezebel, daughter of the king of Sidon. She brought heathen Baal worship and priests of Baal to the land of Israel.

After a stormy history Sidon rose to prominence again in Roman times. It is mentioned in the Gospels and Paul visited friends there on his way to Rome as a prisoner. [*Refs*. 1 Kings 5: 6; 16: 31-3. Ezra 3: 7. Isaiah 23: 2. Ezekiel 27: 8. Matthew 11: 21. Mark 7: 24, 31. Acts 27: 3.]

Silas Silas (or Silvanus) was a leader of the Church in Jerusalem who was sent to Antioch with Paul and Barnabas to announce the findings of the council of apostles and elders regarding relationships between Jewish and Gentile Christian believers. Silas is named as a prophet. Paul chose him to accompany him on his second missionary journey through Syria and Cilicia. He shared imprisonment with Paul at Philippi and is mentioned as being with him in Corinth. His name also appears at the opening of the Letters to the Thessalonians and at the end of the first Letter of Peter, where he is described as 'a faithful brother' who as secretary wrote down this particular Letter. [*Refs.* Acts 15: 22 to 18: 5. 2 Corinthians 1: 19. 1 Thessalonians 1: 1. 2 Thessalonians 1: 1. 1 Peter 5: 12.]

Siloam Also called Siloah and sometimes 'the king's pool'. It was the conduit which carried water from the spring Gihon in the Kidron valley below Jerusalem to a pool inside the city. King Hezekiah is credited with this remarkable engineering feat which was achieved by tunnelling in zig-zag fashion from opposite ends through solid rock. The tunnel is more than 1,700 feet long, about two feet wide and five feet high. This water supply was of vital importance to Jerusalem in time of siege. The name Siloam applies to the tunnel and to the pool. In the Gospel of John we find that Jesus sent a man blind from birth to wash in the pool of Siloam as part of the act of faith which brought him sight.

Visitors to Jerusalem today can still wade along the Siloam tunnel and see the marks made by the tools of workmen in the eighth century B.C. An inscription, found by a boy in A.D. 1880 says: 'While the stonecutters were swinging their axes, each towards his fellow and while there were yet three cubits to be pierced through there was heard the voice of a man calling to his fellow, for there was a crack on the right. And on the day of the piercing through, the stonecutters struck through each to meet his fellow, axe against axe.' This inscription dates from the time of Hezekiah. [*Refs.* 2 Kings 20: 20. 11 Chronicles 32: 30. Nehemiah 2: 14; 3: 15. John 9: 7, 11.]

Simeon (1) The second son of Jacob and Leah and therefore the ancestor of one of the tribes of Israel. [*Refs.* Genesis 29: 33; 42: 24.] (2) An old man who was in the Temple at Jerusalem who was 'looking for the consolation of Israel'. When Mary and Joseph brought their son to the Temple according to the Law, Simeon took the child Jesus in his arms and gave thanks to God. The prayer of Simeon is known as the *Nunc Dimittis* from the opening words: 'Lord, now lettest thou thy servant depart in peace.' [*Refs.* Isaiah 49: 6. Luke 2: 22-35.] (3) A form of the name Simon, used of Simon Peter. [*Refs.* Acts 15: 14. 2 Peter 1: 1.] (4) A member of the Church at Antioch who was a prophet and teacher 'Symeon who was called Niger' means presumably that he was a black man. [*Ref.* Acts 13: 1.]

Simon (1) Simon Peter. *See* PETER. (2) Another of the twelve chosen disciples of Jesus, called 'Simon the Cananaean' in the Gospels of Matthew and Mark and 'Simon who was called the Zealot' in the Gospel of Luke and in the Acts. [*Refs.* Matthew 10: 4. Mark 3: 18. Luke 6: 15. Acts 1: 13.] (3) A brother of Jesus. [*Ref.* Matthew 13: 55. Mark 6: 3.] (4) A leper in Bethany in whose house a woman anointed Jesus' head with precious ointment. [*Ref.* Matthew 26: 6. Mark 14: 3.] (5) A man of Cyrene who was compelled to carry Jesus' cross on the way to Calvary. [*Refs.* Matthew 27: 32. Mark 15: 21. Luke 23: 26.] (6) A Pharisee who invited Jesus to eat with him and in whose house a woman of the city anointed Jesus' feet with ointment. This is, no doubt, Luke's version of (4), above. [*Ref.* Luke 7: 36-47.] (7) The father of Judas Iscariot, named only in the Gospel of John. [*Refs.* John 6: 71; 13: 2, 26.] (8) A magician in Samaria who was converted by Philip the evangelist and was baptized. He then tried to buy the gift of the Holy Spirit from the apostles Peter and John. The term simony comes from this story. [*Ref.* Acts 8: 9-24.] (9) A tanner in Joppa whose house was by the seaside and with whom Peter stayed for many days. [*Refs.* Acts 9: 43; 10: 6, 17, 32.]

Sinai Another name for Mt. Horeb, the sacred mountain where Moses saw the burning bush and heard God speak to him. It was also the place of awesome thunder and lightnings, smoke and flame, where the Law was given. There is no agreement about the exact site of Sinai, but it was probably in the south of the Arabian peninsula. [*Refs*. Exodus 3: 1-6; 19; 34: 1-10. Leviticus 25: 1.] *See also*: COVENANT

Sion *See* ZION

Sisera A Canaanite commander whose charioteer army oppressed the Israelites in the days of the Judges. Deborah the prophetess gave Barak orders to entice Sisera to fight in the valley of the river Kishon. Torrential rain fell, the river was in full flood and overflowing, and the chariots of Sisera were bogged down. His men fled on foot and were cut down by the Israelites. Sisera escaped on foot and sought refuge in the tent of Jael. She gave him hospitality and then killed him with a tent peg through his head as he lay asleep. The battle against Sisera is celebrated in one of the oldest poems in the O.T. [*Refs*. Judges 4-5.]

Sodom A city of the Jordan valley mentioned with Gomorrah on the shore of the Dead Sea. A catastrophe which destroyed these cities is mentioned in the story of Abraham and his nephew Lot. The cities now lie under the salty waters of the Dead Sea. Sodom and Gomorrah became legendary in Jewish tradition for the wickedness of their inhabitants [*Refs*. Genesis 13: 10; 19: 24-5. Deuteronomy 29: 23. Matthew 10: 15.]

Solomon The youngest son of David and Bathsheba and one of the most famous kings of Israel. Solomon is remembered in Jewish tradition for many things—his wisdom, his splendour, his marriages, his building of the Temple. He came to the throne by intrigue, aided by his mother, Nathan the prophet and Zadok the priest, and his first act was to bring about the death of his elder half-brother and rival, Adonijah. Solomon strengthened his position by a number of political marriages, his queen, for example, being a daughter of the Pharaoh of Egypt. His magnificence is expressed in the phrase: 'Solomon ruled over all the kingdoms from the Euphrates to the land of the Philistines and to the border of Egypt; they brought tribute and served Solomon all the days of his life.' It involved, however, heavy taxation of his people, in food and provisions for his vast household, their servants and horses. The king made a treaty with Hiram of Tyre to build the Temple. The Phoenician king was to supply timber and skilled craftsmen. Solomon in return was to pay with wheat and oil and to supply the forced labour. The result was a splendid and costly Temple and an even more opulent royal palace. But the political outcome was restlessness among the slave labour and open revolt on the death of Solomon, with the eventual break-up of the kingdom.

Many legendary tales are woven into the narrative of this magnificent monarch. His wisdom, which in truth is better described as shrewdness, is seen in the tale of the two harlots, as well as in references to his many proverbs, songs and stories. 'He spoke also of beasts, and of birds, and of reptiles, and of fish. And men came from all peoples to hear the wisdom of Solomon, and from all the kings of the earth, who had heard of his wisdom.' His fame brought the queen of Sheba to his court, and she marvelled at all she saw and heard. Solomon's devotion is set forth in his prayer at the dedication of the Temple, but we must recognize here also the work of pious revisers and editors of a much later date.

There is no doubt that the kingdom in Solomon's time was strong, wealthy and extensive. His trade relationships with Asia Minor, Egypt, Arabia and East Africa and the copper-mines at Ezion-geber on the Gulf of Aqaba brought a vast income as well as stores of ivory, spices, precious stones, silver and gold. Foreign goods, however, brought an interest in foreign gods, for which the Bible writers condemn him. It is also true that a great deal of Solomon's magnificence depended on slave labour as well as an intolerable burden of taxation on the peasant farmer. The top-heavy united kingdom could not, and did not, outlast him. Although Solomon remains forever in Jewish memory as the splendid Eastern potentate, the N.T. has almost nothing to say of him except Jesus' passing comment on his outward show: 'Consider the lilies of the field. . . I tell you, even Solomon in all his glory was not arrayed like one of these.' [*Refs.* 1 Kings 1-11. 2 Chronicles 1-9. Matthew 6: 28-9.] *See also*: JEROBOAM

Solomon's Porch A long colonnade which ran along the east side of the outer court of Herod's Temple in Jerusalem. It is mentioned in John's Gospel as a place where Jesus taught, and it appears to have been the regular meeting-place of the early Christians in Jerusalem. [*Refs.* John 10: 23. Acts 3: 11; 5: 12.]

Song of Solomon This book forms part of the Writings of the Hebrew Scriptures, where it is known as The Song of Songs. It is a collection of poems and bridal songs in praise of sexual love between man and woman. Solomon's name appears here and there, no doubt because of the ancient tradition that he was a composer of songs, and perhaps his fame ensured that this work found a place among the religious books of the O.T. These songs are in fact pagan and sensuous, a string of little poems describing with a good deal of erotic detail how lovers delight in one another. They have nothing directly to do with Solomon and belong to a date after the Exile.

Since the book seems out of keeping with the rest of godly Scripture, there has been a tradition of treating the words and ideas metaphorically. The Jews teach them as a picture of love between God and his chosen people Israel. The Christian Church came to regard the whole book as an allegory of the love of Christ for his Church, and so the words could be used in prayer and preaching in a spiritual rather than a literal sense. Regarded simply as poetry, there are many phrases of pure delight, as in the description of springtime, in 2: 1-13.

Spain Mentioned only in connection with Paul's hopes to visit Spain. It is not known whether he did so. [*Refs.* Romans 15: 24, 28.]

Stephen The name means 'crown'. Stephen was the first among the 'seven men of good repute' chosen by the early Church to see to it that Greek-speaking widows were not neglected in the daily distribution of food and necessities. Stephen became known as a man 'full of grace and power and a wise speaker, inspired by the Spirit of God. The Hellenist Jews, however, brought false witnesses against him, accusing him of blasphemy. Stephen had to stand trial before the Council of the Jews. When he in turn accused them of betraying and murdering their Messiah, they cast him out of Jerusalem and stoned him. Saul, as a young man, was a witness of his death and was profoundly affected by it. Stephen was the first believer to be put to death for his faith and his dying words closely parallel those of Jesus on the cross. The outcome was persecution of the Church in Jerusalem and the scattering of believers. It is also true to say that it was the beginning of the break with traditional Judaism and the birth of a separate Christian community. The Church has ever since remembered St. Stephen as the first martyr. [*Refs.* Acts 6: 1 to 8: 4; 11: 19.]

Synagogue The word literally means 'meeting' or 'assembly'. It is applied to the regular coming together of the Jews for religious instruction and prayer. The origins of the synagogue are lost in obscurity, but it probably began in the time of Exile, when the Jews were far from Jerusalem and their sacred Temple, the only place where sacrificial worship could take place. We read in the Book of Ezekiel of groups of Jews meeting at the house of the prophet 'to enquire of the Lord'. Apart from these allusions there is no direct mention of the synagogue in the O.T.

In N.T. times there were synagogues wherever Jews were to be found, not only in Palestine, but throughout the Mediterranean world. Sometimes the name is used of the building where they met, sometimes of the meeting itself which might be in the open air, for example, by the side of a river. There were several synagogues in the larger towns, many in the sacred city of Jerusalem. Ten or more male Jews form a synagogue, which is controlled by a group of elders responsible for the proper order of worship. Women take no part in the service, though they may attend and watch from a part of the building reserved for their use. The main purpose of the synagogue is the study of the Scriptures and the diligent teaching of the people. The furnishings must include an Ark or chest where the scrolls of Scripture are kept and the reading-desk or pulpit from which they are read.

In the early days of the spread of the Christian gospel, Paul and other missionaries went first to the Jewish synagogues with their message. Only when the Jews rejected and persecuted them did they deliberately turn to the Gentiles. Nevertheless, the outline of prayer, reading and sermon, as well as some of the furniture of Christian churches owe a great deal to the Jewish synagogue. Since the final downfall of the Temple in A.D. 70 the synagogue has remained all through the centuries in many lands, in times of peace and of persecution, the centre of Jewish teaching, faith, hope, and communal life. [*Refs.* Ezekiel 8: 1; 20; 1, 31. Matthew 4: 23; 9: 35; 13: 54; 23: 6. Mark 1: 21, 39; 3: 1; 6: 2. Luke 4: 15; 8: 41; 13: 10. Acts 6: 9; 9: 2, 20; 13: 5, 14, 43; 14: 1; 15: 21; 17: 1, 10, 17; 18: 4, 19, 26; 19: 8; 22: 19; 24: 12.]

Syria Ancient Syria in O.T. times consisted of the land to the north-west of Palestine, and the tribes therein, one of their chief city-states being Damascus. Syria was sometimes known as Aram, and its inhabitants therefore as Aramaeans. The northern kingdom of Israel had ill-defined boundaries with Syria and suffered continual raids and attacks from Damascus. In the time of Ahab, for example, the king of Syria laid siege to Samaria and demanded tribute, but in the war that followed the Israelites drove the Syrians from their land. Later, Ahab was himself killed in battle against the Syrians. Syria eventually fell to the Assyrians, shortly before the downfall of Israel. Thereafter, like the rest of Palestine, Syria came under the control in due course of Babylon and Persia and Alexander the Great and his successors.

In N.T. times the Romans named Syria a province of the Empire and it took in terrritory from Asia Minor to Egypt, including Palestine. Saul, late called Paul, was converted on the ancient road to Damascus, and Antioch of Syria became one of the first great centres of the Christian Church. [*Refs.* Deuteronomy 26: 5. 2 Samuel 8: 6. 1 Kings 20. 2 Kings 5: 1 Amos: 5. Matthew 4: 24. Luke 2: 2. Acts 9: 3; 13: 1; 15: 41.]

T

Tabernacle The name literally means 'a temporary, movable dwelling', such as a hut or tent. In Jewish history the Tabernacle was the tent which contained the Ark of the Covenant and which was carried from place to place as the Hebrews wandered through the wilderness on their way to the promised land of Canaan. It is sometimes known in the O.T. as 'the tent of meeting' or 'the tent of testimony'. The elaborate details of the making of the Tabernacle are set out in *Exodus* 20-7 and 35-40. Curtains of fine linen in blue, purple and scarlet, clasped with bronze are mentioned, as well as tanned rams' skins and goat skins and a frame of acacia wood and woven veils to screen the sacred Ark. Further details are concerned with the altar, its furnishings and utensils, the table, lampstand and lamp. Lavish use of gold is mentioned and silver for adornment. A summary of the Tabernacle and its contents is to be found at Exodus 39: 32-43.

As a sign of divine approval, 'the cloud covered the tent of meeting, and the glory of the Lord filled the Tabernacle'. Throughout all their journeys, whenever the cloud was taken up from over the Tabernacle, the children of Israel would go on their way; but if it was not taken up, they stayed where they were. The Tabernacle, in short, was a symbol of God's presence in the midst of their camp.

No doubt this account of the Tabernacle is greatly embellished by pious later editors. The richly adorned tent as here described was far too elaborate for the time and the setting of the wilderness wanderings. Nor is there much mention of the Tabernacle in the story of the settlement in Canaan. It is difficult to believe that the account of the Tabernacle is historical. Rather it is an idealized account from the much later days of the Exile and priestly teaching about the importance of a single central shrine. Nevertheless, the central thought of God in the midst of the camp, going ever onwards with his people, is a powerful religious idea. Thus even in the N.T. we find the Jewish writer of the Gospel of John declaring: 'the Word became flesh and dwelt ("tented") among us, full of grace and truth; we have beheld his glory, glory as of the only Son from the Father.' [*Refs.* Exodus 26-7; 35-8; 39: 32-43; 40. Numbers 9: 15-23. Psalm 15: 1. John 1: 14. Hebrews 9: 1-5. Revelation 21: 3.]

Tabernacles, Feast of *See* BOOTHS

Tabitha *See* DORCAS

Tarshish, Tharshish The place is difficult to identify. It may have been a ship-building or sea-trading port somewhere in the ancient Mediterranean. Tartessus in southern Spain has been suggested. The Biblical name, however, is usually used to describe a heavy, cargo-ship merchant fleet known as 'ships of Tarshish'. Thus King Solomon had at sea 'a fleet of ships of Tarshish' which brought him 'gold, silver, ivory, apes and peacocks'. [*Refs.* 1 Kings 10: 22; 22: 48. Psalm 48: 7. Isaiah 2: 16; 23: 1, 14; 60: 9. Jeremiah 10: 9. Ezekiel 27: 25. Jonah 1: 3; 4: 2.]

Tarsus A city of Asia Minor on the banks of the river Cydnus and capital of the Roman province of Cilicia in N.T. times. Tarsus was the birthplace of Saul or Paul who called it 'no mean city'. The citizens of Tarsus enjoyed the privileges of full Roman citizenship. [*Refs.* Acts 21: 39; 22: 3.]

Tekoa The home town of the prophet Amos who was a shepherd there. The whole area is a stony wilderness in the hills which run down to the Dead Sea. Tekoa is about five miles from Bethlehem. [*Refs.* 2 Samuel 14: 2. 2 Chronicles 2: 6. Amos 1: 1. Jeremiah 6: 1.]

Temple The Temple in Jerusalem was the central shrine of Jewish worship for a thousand years. It was built in three times. The first, and most famous, is usually known as Solomon's Temple. King David had brought the Ark of the Covenant to his capital city and enshrined it in a tent—the traditional symbol of the wilderness wanderings when God went with his people. David had it in mind to build a permanent 'house of the Lord' but it was his son Solomon who brought it about. His ally in the work was King Hiram of Tyre, and indeed the first Temple was entirely of Phoenician design and craftsmanship, although it was the subjects of Solomon who supplied forced labour by the thousand to quarry the stones and to drag the timber for the building. The details of the work are clearly set down in 1 Kings 5-7. The Temple was begun about 961 B.C. and was seven years building. It was very much smaller than most imaginative pictures and poetic descriptions would suggest, being no more than ninety feet long, thirty feet wide and forty-five feet high. The flat-roofed building was of white limestone lined inside with cedar of Lebanon. At the entrance were two free-standing pillars, carved and ornamented, named Jachin and Boaz. Inside, steps led up to a large inner room known as the holy place, furnished with an altar, lamp-stands, and a table for the shewbread. The inmost room, which was in complete darkness, was the holy of holies, where the Ark of the Covenant was kept, and an altar. There were also two cherubim of olivewood overlaid with gold and ornate carvings of palm trees and flowers on every wall. Everything in this room was overlaid with gold. The doors of the Temple were of olivewood and cypress, carved and gilded, and the linen curtains were blue, purple and crimson. In the open court near the entrance to the Temple was a bronze altar for the daily sacrifice of animals, and a 'molten sea', which was a vast basin of bronze supported on twelve metal oxen, three facing north, three facing west, three facing south, and three facing east. Many other furnishings of Solomon's Temple are described with proud and devoted detail—lavers, pots, shovels, basins, lamp-stands, lamps tongs, cups, snuffers, dishes, firepans, fashioned of gold, silver and bronze.

Solomon's Temple was, in fact, built to be the king's chapel, as part of a vast complex of buildings which included his large and splendid palace. It was the presence of the Ark of the Covenant which made the Temple a national sanctuary. The Temple was not regarded as a place to be thronged by pious worshippers from near and far. It was 'the house of the Lord', a permanent dwelling-place for the God of their fathers who had brought them to this promised land. The prayer of Solomon at the dedication of the Temple declares: 'I have built thee an exalted house, a place for thee to dwell in for ever.' At the same time, the Bible writers acknowledge that God cannot be confined to any earthly dwelling: 'Behold heaven and the highest heaven cannot contain thee, how much less this house which I have built!' All of these are the pious words of a later age, but they record the belief that the Temple in the holy city of Jerusalem is the place where God's name is, where he listens to the prayers of his people, and where his altar stands to which they must bring their offerings for forgiveness and blessing.

Solomon's Temple was destroyed by the army of Nebuchadrezzar in 587 B.C. and those treasures which remained were plundered and carried to Babylon, pillars, bronze sea, vessels and all. The shrine remained a memory of Israel's golden age, to be described in love and reverence by later chroniclers. [*Refs.* 2 Samuel 6: 17; 7: 2*f*. 1 Kings 5-8. 2 Kings 16: 17; 24 10-16; 25: 13-17. 2 Chronicles 2-7. Isaiah 6: 1*f*. Jeremiah 52: 17-23.]

The second Temple, completed by returned exiles about 515 B.C., is known as Zerubbabel's Temple. It was set on the same site as the first, of loved memory, but was a greatly inferior building. The Book of Ezra tells of the decree of Cyrus of Persia granting the Jews permission to return from Babylon to rebuild their Temple in Jerusalem. Cyrus also restored to them some of the Temple furnishings which has been looted by Nebuchadrezzar, particularly the sacred implements of sacrifice. The second Temple, however, was slow in building. Drought, bad harvests, harassment by enemies and monetary inflation held up the work. The Books of Haggai and Zechariah tell of the prophets urging Zerubbabel the governor of Judah and Joshua the high priest to stir the people to their task. No detailed descriptions are available of the structure of the second Temple. There was no Ark in it, for the sacred box seems to have disappeared during or before the destruction of Solomon's Temple. The Book of Ezra records both weeping and rejoicing at the laying of the foundations of this new 'house of the Lord'—weeping, because many of the priests and old men among them remembered the glory of the first Temple, joy, because once again Jerusalem had a shrine where God the Lord was to be sought and worshipped. Once again God was in the midst of his people, and all the ritual of priestly service, animal sacrifice, music and prayer was set up to render the people's devotion. Many of the psalms belong to this time.

The second Temple was desecrated in the second century B.C. when Antiochus Epiphanes despoiled it of its gold and set up in its court an 'abomination of desolation', that is, an altar to the Greek god Zeus, where the Jewish altar of burnt offering stood. There he sacrificed swine, thus defiling the whole place in the eyes of the Jews. Judas Maccabaeus led his people in revolt, and in the year 165 B.C. the Temple was cleansed and restored to normal worship. The Jewish festival of Hanukkah, or Feast of Lights, celebrates that rededication, and is observed to this day. (*Refs.* Ezra 1; 3: 8-13; 5: 1-2; 6: 3-5.]

The third Temple, which is known as Herod's Temple, was a complete reconstruction of the second building. Josephus, the Jewish historian, describes it thus: 'And now Herod, in the eighteenth year of his reign, undertook a very great work, that is, to build himself the temple of God, and make it larger in compass, and to raise it to a most magnificent altitude, as

esteeming it to be the most glorious of all his actions...'
Herod's Temple was begun in 20 B.C. It included courts (the
court of the Gentiles, the court of the Women, the court of
Israel, the court of the Priests), porches, gates and walls, as
well as the traditional shrine with its altar, holy place, and
screened-off holy of holies. So elaborate was the Temple area
that the work was not completed until after the time of Jesus,
long after the death of Herod the Great. The shrine itself was
Greek in design. It could be seen from afar by pilgrims to
Jerusalem shining in white marble with gold adornment. This
was the Temple to which, Luke tells us, Jesus was brought as
a child, where he was found among the teachers when he was
twelve, where he drove out the traders and money-changers,
where he taught the people, and where at last he was brought
to trial by the Council of the Jews and condemned to death.
His disciples spoke once in awe of the splendour of the building: 'how it was adorned with noble stones and offerings'.
This Temple was destroyed by the Romans in A.D. 70, and no
Jewish shrine rose there again. The priesthood came to an
end with the whole elaborate sacrificial system. The symbol
of a people's soul had perished for ever. On the traditional
Temple site there stands today the Moslem mosque known
as 'the Dome of the Rock'.

The worship of the Temple centred on the daily morning
and evening sacrifice, and the special festivals which brought
pilgrims in their thousands to Jerusalem. The Book of Psalms,
which has been called 'the hymn-book of the second Temple,
tells time and again of Jewish joy in the house of God:

'His holy mountain, beautiful in elevation, is the joy of all
the earth.'
'How lovely is thy dwelling-place, O Lord of hosts!'
'I was glad when they said to me, "Let us go to the house of
the Lord!" '
'Our feet have been standing within your gates, O Jerusalem!'

[*Refs.* Psalm 2: 4; 48: 2; 65: 4; 84; 122. Luke 2: 22, 41*f*. 19:

45*f.* 21: 5; 22: 54*f.* Revelation 21: 22.] *See also*: SOLOMON; ZERUBBABEL; HEROD; PRIEST; HIGH PRIEST

Ten Commandments *See* COMMANDMENTS

Terah The name of the father of Abraham, mentioned in connection with Ur and Haran in Mesopotamia. [*Ref.* Genesis 11: 26-32.]

Teraphim Primitive idols, household gods in human form, no doubt used as magic charms to bring good luck. They may even have served, before the days of legal documents, as title-deeds to family property. [*Refs.* Genesis 31: 19, 34-5. Judges 17: 5; 18; 14-20. 1 Samuel 19: 13-16. 2 Kings 23: 24. Ezekiel 21: 21.]

Tetrarch A ruler of a fourth part of a province in Roman times Herod Antipas, his brother Philip, and Lysanias are mentioned as tetrarchs in the Gospels. [*Refs.* Matthew 14: 1. Luke 3: 1; 9: 7. Acts 13: 1.]

Thaddeus One of the twelve disciples of Jesus mentioned in the Gospels of Matthew and Mark. Some ancient versions read Lebbaeus, or Lebbaeus called Thaddaeus. He is not named elsewhere and nothing else is known of him. [*Refs.* Matthew 10: 3. Mark 3: 18.]

Theophilus The 'most excellent' official to whom the Gospel of Luke and the Acts of the Apostles are addressed by their author. No one knows who Theophilus was, but he may have been a Roman official sympathetic to the Christian faith, or one who himself became a Christian. [*Refs.* Luke 1: 3. Acts 1: 1.]

Thessalonica A wealthy and important city of Macedonia visited by Paul on his second missionary journey. The Jews there set the city in an uproar against Paul and Silas. Nevertheless, a strong Church was founded in Thessalonica, with Jewish converts, devout Greeks, and some leading women of the place among its members. To the Christians there Paul wrote the Letters to the Thessalonians. [*Ref.* Acts 17: 1*f.* Philippians 4: 16. 1 Thessalonians 1: 1. 2 Thessalonians 1: 1.]

Thessalonians, The First and Second Letters of Paul to the Both of these letters open with the same greetings—'Paul,

Silvanus, and Timothy, To the church of the Thessalonians'—and with almost the same customary words of blessing. They are addressed to the Christians in the busy trading and seaport town of Thessalonica, the chief city of Macedonia. Paul founded the Church at Thessalonica on his second missionary journey (Acts 17: 1-9). There is some evidence that he stayed there longer than the Acts reference would indicate. Philippians 4: 16 mentions that he was there long enough to receive gifts sent by the Christians of Philippi more than once, and he seems to have taken up his trade of tent-making for a time (1 Thessalonians 2: 9. 2 Thessalonians 3: 8). As Paul went on to Athens and then Corinth after this, it is probable that he wrote at least the first Letter to the Thessalonians from the latter city. The date would be about A.D. 50-1, thus placing this Letter second only to the Letter to the Galatians among Paul's writings.

Paul's visit to Thessalonica had caused an uproar when he preached in the synagogue of the Jews about the suffering of Christ and the Resurrection. The Christians there are anxious to see him again, but since he cannot come he writes to them instead. The first half of this first Letter to the Thessalonians urges them to stand firm in the face of like sufferings which have come upon them because of their faith. The rest of the Letter takes up a matter which particularly troubles the Christians of Thessalonica, namely, what happens to believers who have died before the second coming of the Lord? Paul writes to assure them that 'living and dead alike will always be with the Lord'.

A brief outline of the contents of the first Letter is:

(a) 1 Thessalonians 1: 1: Greetings and brief blessing.
(b) 1 Thessalonians 1: 2-10: Warm thanksgiving for the faithfulness of the Christians of Thessalonica.
(c) 1 Thessalonians 2: 1-12: A personal note about Paul's own way of life when he was among them—'like a nurse taking care of her children'.
(d) 1 Thessalonians 2: 13-16: He again gives thanks for their courage under persecution.

(e) 1 Thessalonians 2: 17 to 3: 13: Paul wanted to visit them again, but was hindered. Instead, he sent Timothy, who brought back news of their constant faith and love. He prays that this may continue.

(f) 1 Thessalonians 4: 1-10: Paul adds a familiar note here about the importance of moral behaviour in the sight of the pagan world: 'We exhort you...to live quietly, to mind your own affairs, and to work with your hands...so that you may command the respect of outsiders, and be dependent on nobody.'

(g) 1 Thessalonians 4: 13-18: Timothy has brought back news of their special problem concerning some Christians who have died. Paul assures his readers that he is quoting the Lord when he says: 'We who are alive, who are left until the coming of the Lord, shall not precede those who have fallen asleep.' Obviously Paul expected the second coming of Christ very soon, and he portrays it as a dramatic event.

(h) 1 Thessalonians 5: 1-11: He warns them to be watchful and ready, 'for you yourselves know well that the day of the Lord will come like a thief in the night'.

(i) 1 Thessalonians 5: 12-28: More ethical instruction for daily behaviour. Finally, a prayer, a Christian greeting, and the blessing.

The whole of this letter convinces us of Paul's warm missionary concern for these children in the faith to whom he is both an example and a father in God.

The second Letter to the Thessalonians is at first sight very similar to the first. Its opening greeting leads into thanksgiving for their steadfast faith and love. But after that, a good deal of the material seems like a bloodless repetition of 1 Thessalonians, and there is reason to doubt whether this is a genuine letter of Paul. Once again the second coming of Christ is dealt with at length, but the writer's view of the Last Judgment seems to have changed. It is, in fact, impossible to prove whether Paul is the author or not.

An outline of the contents is:

(a) 2 Thessalonians 1: 1-2: Greetings and a blessing.

(b) 2 Thessalonians 1: 3-12: Thanksgiving for the steadfast-ness and faith of the Thessalonians in the face of persecu-tion and affliction. A reminder that Christ is coming again in fire and vengeance.

(c) 2 Thessalonians 2: 1-12: Paul tells his readers that the coming of the Lord Jesus Christ will not be at once. First, the Anti-Christ is to appear and do his worst. This seems to contradict the immediacy of similiar writing in the first Letter.

(d) 2 Thessalonians 2: 13-17: A repetition of 1: 3-12.

(e) 2 Thessalonians 3: 1-5: A prayer for the writer and for them all.

(f) 2 Thessalonians 3: 6-16: A warning, as in 1 Thessalonians 4: 1-10, that they are not to be idle.

(g) 2 Thessalonians 4: 17-18: A final signature, it is claimed, in Paul's own writing, and the usual blessing.

Thomas One of the twelve chosen disciples of Jesus. In John's Gospel he is also called the Twin, the English form of the Greek word *didymos*. Only in this Gospel do we hear anything about Thomas, for example, when he refused to believe the other disciples who said 'We have seen the Lord.' His later encoun-ter with the risen Christ, however, evoked from Thomas the confession of faith: 'My Lord and my God!' [*Refs.* Matthew 10: 3. Mark 3: 18. Luke 6: 15. John 2: 16; 14: 5; 20: 24*f*; 21: 2. Acts 1: 13.]

Thummim *See* URIM

Tiberias, Sea of Another name for the Sea of Galilee. It is called after the Roman emperor Tiberius, but would not be known by this name in the time of Jesus. [*Refs.* John 6: 1; 21: 1.] *See also*: GALILEE, SEA OF

Tiberius The Roman emperor called Caesar in the Gospels (ex-cept in Luke 2: 1). Tiberius ruled A.D. 14-37, and was emperor at the time of the ministry and Crucifixion of Jesus. [*Refs.* Mat-thew 22: 17. Mark 12: 14-17. Luke 3 1. John 19 12, 15.]

Timon One of the seven men of good repute chosen to help in the daily distribution of food in the early Church. Stephen is the first named and most famous of the seven. Nothing more is known of Timon. [*Ref.* Acts 6: 5.]

Timothy The name means 'honourer of God'. Paul found him in the town of Lystra in Asia Minor on his second missionary journey, where he was already 'a disciple ... the son of a Jewish woman who was a believer; but his father was a Greek'. Elsewhere we learn that his mother's name was Eunice and his grandmother, Lois. Paul circumcised Timothy so that he might enter the company of Jewish-Christians without offence, and thereafter he became known as the companion and helper of the apostle. Paul refers to him many times affectionately as his 'fellow-worker' and 'beloved and faithful child in the Lord', who has served with him 'as a son with a father'. Some of the references in the Letters to Timothy, however, scarcely fit the man portrayed in the Acts and in Paul's other letters. [*Refs.* Acts 16: 1-3. Romans 16: 21. 1 Corinthians 4: 17; 16: 10. 2 Corinthians 1: 1. Philippians 2: 19-23. 1 Thessalonians 3: 2, 6. 1 Timothy 1: 2. 2 Timothy 1: 2.]

Timothy, The First and Second Letters of Paul to The Letters to Timothy and to Titus are known as the Pastoral Letters. They contain advice about the day-to-day oversight of the Church, the household of God. Timothy was the friend and companion of Paul, his messenger to several of the Churches he founded, and, by tradition, his successor. According to Acts 16: 1-3 Paul met him in the town of Lystra on his second missionary journey. Information about Timothy is to be found here and there in a number of Paul's letters and other N.T. writings.

Whether these letters were written by Paul to the real Timothy is another matter. It is usually agreed by scholars today that the style, ideas and language are unlike the genuine letters of Paul to the Churches. Probably they belong to a later age. Certainly we cannot fit the Pastorals to any particular events or time in Paul's life as outlined in the Acts of the

Apostles. These letters seem to apply to a time when the Church at large is having to come to terms with daily living in a pagan world. Christians find it difficult to hold fast to the faith in an age of many gods and many lords. They need instruction in how to live the Christian life in the market-place of common man.

Probably the Pastoral Letters belong to the very end of the first century. They are largely concerned with the organiza-tion of the Church, with proper teaching and good behav-iour. We read of a Church which has some kind of rule and structure, with bishops, elders, deacons, wives and widows. Doctrine has become a system of belief. Faith is no longer declared as simple trust in the Lord Jesus Christ or in saying 'Jesus is Lord'. It is now the pattern of 'sound words' (2 Timo-thy 1: 13), teaching which can be formulated in a written statement to be agreed to. The 'Timothy' of these letters may be an idealized leader of the Church rather than the flesh and blood friend of the apostle whom we hear about else-where in the N.T.

It is possible, however, that personal references here and there reveal genuine fragments of writing preserved from the hand of Paul, autobiographical snapshots, as it were. For ex-ample, 2 Timothy 1: 16-18, where there is a reference to Paul's imprisonment in Rome; 2 Timothy 3: 10-11 which refers to the apostle's sufferings at Antioch, Iconium and Lystra, 2 Timothy 4: 1-22, which reads like Paul's last message from prison and is full of references to his closest friends and his personal affairs. It may be that we have indeed here part of a farewell letter of Paul.

A brief outline of the contents of the two Letters is:

(a) 1 Timothy 1: 1-2: Greeting from Paul to Timothy, and the blessing.

(b) 1 Timothy 1: 3-20: Timothy is to remain at Ephesus to deal with false teachers who are spreading 'myths and end-less genealogies'. He is to 'wage the good warfare, hold-ing faith and a good conscience'.

(c) 1 Timothy 2-3: Is taken up with instructions for the orderly worship of the Church, in prayer, the correct behaviour of women, the work and life of a bishop and of deacons.

(d) 1 Timothy 4: 1-11: A warning about heretics who will disturb the true faith. Again the counsel: 'have nothing to do with godless and silly myths.'

(e) 1 Timothy 4: 12 to 6: 19: Personal advice to Timothy, and instruction about his work in the Church—the reading of scripture, preaching, teaching, the pastoral care of Church members, especially widows, the work of the elders. The upright life of a man of God, and the ethics of the Christian community.

(f) 1 Timothy 6: 20-1: Final personal warning to Timothy against false wisdom, and the blessing.

It is interesting to note fragments of prayers and hymns here and there as used in the early Church, e.g. at 1: 17, 3: 16, 6: 15. It is likely that the Christians of these days sang their belief together as a hymn rather than saying it together as a prayer. These are the first steps towards the more formal creeds which became necessary in the second century of the Church's life.

(g) 2 Timothy 1: 1-2: Greetings from Paul to Timothy and the blessing, very similar to the opening of the first Letter.

(h) 2 Timothy 1: 3-18 A personal tribute to Timothy, a reference to his own imprisonment, and advice to 'follow the pattern of the sound words which you have heard from me'. Some more personal references, including a tribute to Onesiphorus.

(i) 2 Timothy 2: 1-26: Timothy is to be resolute in faith and deed, like a soldier on active service, an athlete, a hard-working farmer, a workman rightly handling the word of truth. He is to avoid controversies and quarrels.

(j) 2 Timothy 3: 1 to 4: 5: The menace of false teachers and their ways is contrasted with Timothy's task to 'preach the word...convince, rebuke and exhort'.

(k) 2 Timothy 4: 6-18: Paul's farewell, possibly containing fragments of a genuine letter.

(l) 2 Timothy 4: 19-22: Final greetings to Timothy and to friends in Ephesus, and the blessing.

As we have seen, it is almost impossible to decide how much of Paul there is about these two Letters. Their value is in the picture they give of the Christian towards the end of the first century, beset by false teaching and trying to maintain faith and order and Christian standards in a pagan world.

Titus A Greek companion and fellow-worker of Paul, affectionately called by him 'my brother Titus'. Although not mentioned in the Acts of the Apostles, he was apparently well known in the early Church as a trusted messenger of Paul. An early tradition suggests that Titus may have been a brother of Luke. [*Refs.* 2 Corinthians 2: 13; 7: 6, 13, 14; 8: 6, 16, 23. Galatians 2: 1, 3.]

Titus, The Letter of Paul to The Letter to Titus should be read along with the Letters known as 1 and 2 Timothy. Together they form the Pastoral Letters which are largely concerned with the rule and order of the Christian Church towards the end of the first century A.D. It is usually agreed today that they are not by Paul but contain some reminiscences of the apostle.

Titus, the man, is not mentioned in the Acts of the Apostles, but does appear in 2 Corinthians 8: 23 as Paul's 'partner and fellow worker'. It was apparently Titus who took the collection of money for the relief of the Church in Jerusalem.

The Letter to Titus presupposes that Paul and Titus had been working together in Crete, though there is no evidence for this in the Acts. According to 1: 5*f*, Paul is writing to instruct Titus concerning the proper organization of the Church in a number of towns on the island. If we accept the theory that the Pastorals belong to a later date than Paul we may doubt specific historical reference to people and places, e.g. the mention of Nicopolis at 3: 12. This brief Letter is of value, however, in showing the shape of the Church at the end of the first century.

A brief outline of the contents is:

(a) Titus 1: 1-4: A longer than usual opening greeting from Paul to Titus, and a blessing.

(b) Titus 1: 5-9: Instructions regarding the character and conduct of elders and a bishop.

(c) Titus 1: 10-16: A strong attack on 'the circumcision party' who have been upsetting people by spreading heresies and Jewish myths.

(d) Titus 2: 1-3, 8: Teaching concerning Christian standards and conduct.

(e) Titus 3: 9-11: Another warning against stupid controversies and heresy.

(f) Titus 3: 12-15: A personal ending, and the blessing.

Tobiah An Ammonite, partly Jewish leader who, in company with Sanballat, did everything he could to prevent Nehemiah from rebuilding the walls of Jerusalem. Tobiah taunted the builders, derided their work, plotted an attack, and wrote letters to his influential relatives to stir them up against Nehemiah. But all in vain. [*Refs.* Nehemiah 2: 10, 19; 4: 3, 7; 6: 17-19; 13: 4-9.]

Trachonitis An area of Palestine, north of Galilee, which was ruled by Philip the tetrarch in N.T. times. [*Ref.* Luke 3: 1.]

Transfiguration The word literally means 'to change the appearance or form'. The Transfiguration of Jesus refers to an experience recounted by the writers of the Synoptic Gospels just after his disciples' acknowledgment at Caesarea Philippi that he is the Christ, and before the final journey to Jerusalem. The account in Mark's Gospel tells how Jesus took with him Peter and James and John to a high mountain and was transfigured before them. His garments became intensely white. There appeared to them Elijah with Moses, talking to Jesus. The mystic experience concluded with a cloud overshadowing them, and a voice came out of the cloud: 'This is my beloved Son; listen to him.' The accounts in Matthew and Luke are substantially the same.

The description of the event is full of symbolism. No doubt

it is linked in the Gospel-writer's mind with the turning-point at Caesarea Philippi and the prediction of the passion. Jesus' disciples have discovered that he is the Christ (Messiah). He has told them that he must suffer. The two ideas 'Messiah' and 'suffering', were contradictory. On the Mount of Transfiguration the three most intimate disciples, Peter, James and John, have an experience of the divine in which God confirms before their eyes and in their hearing that Jesus is indeed his Chosen One. Jesus takes precedence over Moses and Elijah—the sacred Law and the prophet. He is indeed to be listened to and obeyed. The story of the Transfiguration has no doubt been adapted by later telling and transmission, but its teaching is clear: 'This is my beloved Son; listen to him.' The whole event is described from the point of view of the disciples, perhaps especially of Peter. The truth which has puzzled them at Caesarea Philippi has been made clearer if they have eyes to see, ears to hear, minds to understand. The Master who led them up the mountain now appears in his true glory as the very Son of God. [*Refs.* Mark 9: 2-8. Matthew 17: 1-8. Luke 9: 28-36.]

Trial of Jesus The trial of Jesus is recorded in all four Gospels, though their accounts do not exactly agree, nor is it possible now to know what the historical facts were. All the Gospels state that Jesus was arrested in a garden on the slopes of the Mount of Olives. Thereafter the Gospels set down various stages in the trial:

(a) All the writers emphasize that the arrest, trial and condemnation of Jesus was the work of the Jewish religious authorities. John alone mentions that the soldiers led Jesus, bound, to Annas, the father-in-law of Caiaphas, and former high priest. This Gospel also mentions a disciple who was known to the high priest and who was therefore admitted to the court, and who contrived the admission of Simon Peter as well. Nothing more is said or known about Jesus' appearance before Annas.

(b) The Synoptic Gospels begin with the trial before Caiaphas the high priest. Matthew follows Mark in his general account. So also does Luke, but he adds information which he has acquired from some other source. Mark mentions the Sanhedrin or Council of the Jews where 'all the chief priests and the elders and the scribes were assembled'. They could not find adequate testimony against Jesus to put him to death. There were false witnesses, but their testimony did not agree. Finally the high priest stood up and asked Jesus himself for an answer; but he was silent until the high priest asked if he were the Christ. After that the high priest called for the verdict of death for blasphemy. Jesus then endured spitting and blows.

(c) The next scene is at dawn, when 'the chief priests with the elders and scribes and the whole council held a consultation; and they bound Jesus and delivered him to Pilate'. It is difficult to discern whether there is a further stage in the Jewish trial at daybreak or not. Luke's Gospel seems to say so. It is possible, however, that Mark and Luke give different versions of the same trial and that it indeed took place early in the morning rather than in the middle of the night. It is highly probable also that the open acknowledgment of Jesus as 'Christ, the Son of God' is a later Christian addition to the story.

(d) The trial before Pilate, the Roman governor, involves the civil power, and the charge against Jesus is now that he claims to be King of the Jews. The chief priests accused Jesus of 'many things'. One must assume that they were imputations of sedition or treason, otherwise a Roman governor would have paid little heed. Luke gives the details: 'We found this man perverting our nation, and forbidding us to give tribute to Caesar, and saying that he himself is Christ, a king.' Also that he 'stirs up the people'. Jesus stood silent before Pilate, in spite of questioning. The Gospel writers portray Pilate as unwilling to condemn Jesus: 'I find no crime in this man'.

(e) It is Luke also who tells how Pilate sent Jesus to Herod of Galilee who was in Jerusalem at that time. Again Jesus stood silent and made no answer, while the chief priests and the scribes stood by, vehemently accusing him. Herod treated Jesus with contempt, had him arrayed in gorgeous apparel, and sent him back to Pilate.

(f) Finally, Jesus stood before Pilate again. According to the Gospels the governor sought repeatedly to release Jesus. He offered to set him free because it was a time of festival, but the crowd chose Barabbas instead. He asked: 'What evil has he done?' and they shouted all the more: 'Let him be crucified." So Pilate gave sentence that their demand should be granted. John's Gospel adds the details that he had Jesus scourged and that the soldiers arrayed him in a purple robe and put a crown of thorns on his head. Pilate again declared that he found no crime in him. When the Jews cried out: 'If you release this man, you are not Caesar's friend', the governor took fright. After a final appeal to the Jews, he handed Jesus over to be crucified.

Many of the details in the various stages of the trial (or trials) of Jesus are lifelike and credible. It is, however, impossible to piece together a step-by-step account of what happened to Jesus during the last night before the Crucifixion. The purpose of the Gospel-writers over-rides their desire to present a coherent historical statement. That purpose includes their desire to put the blame for the death of Jesus on the Jewish leaders and to show the Roman authority in as favourable a light as possible, and to reveal Jesus standing silent before his accusers as in very truth the obedient, suffering, servant-Messiah of God: 'He was oppressed, and he was afflicted, yet he opened not his mouth.' [*Refs*. Matthew 26: 57 to 27: 31. Mark 14: 53 to 15: 20. Luke 22: 54 to 23: 25. John 18: 12 to 19: 16.]

Troas A seaport city of Asia Minor, on the Aegean, and a Roman colony in N.T. times. It was near the ancient Troy of Homer's *Iliad*. Paul had a vision in the night at Troas in which a man begged him to come over into Macedonia. He took it as a sign from God, and thus embarked on the first missionary visit to Europe. It was at Troas that a young man named Eutychus went to sleep while Paul talked and fell from a third-story window to the ground. Paul went down and restored him to life. [*Refs.* Acts 16: 8, 11; 20: 5-12. 2 Corinthians 2: 12. 2 Timothy 4: 13.]

Tyre An ancient seaport and trading city of the Phoenicians set on an island off the coast of Palestine. The golden age of Tyre coincided with the reigns of David and Solomon, both of whom made trade alliances with Hiram, king of Tyre. Solomon, for instance, built his trading fleet at Ezion-geber in treaty with Hiram who supplied skilled Phoenician seamen. Another Hiram of Tyre, a skilled craftsman, was the chief architect of the Temple.

King Ahab of Israel married Jezebel, daughter of the king of Tyre, who brought her heathen ways and worship to trouble Israel in the ninth century B.C. Tyre was the greatest symbol of wealth in the Mediterranean world of O.T. times: 'Tyre has built herself a rampart and heaped silver like dust, and gold like the dirt of the streets.' Apart from her vast commercial enterprises she was famous for Tyrian purple, the royal colour of the ancient world. The purple dye was obtained from the murex shellfish of the Phoenician coast and was exported all over the known world. The Hebrew prophets cried out against the wealth and wickedness of Tyre. One of the most splendid poems in O.T. literature is the lament of Ezekiel over the doom of 'the good ship Tyre', in Ezekiel 26-8. All the splendours of an Eastern market are here, and the trade of the Orient.

Tyre survived the attack of many powerful enemies, but fell at last to the army of Alexander the Great, who built a causeway from the mainland to the island to bring about its conquest. In the N.T., Tyre is mentioned along with Sidon as a place visited by Jesus and later by Paul. [*Refs.* 2 Samuel 5: 2. 1 Kings 5: 1; 7: 13; 9: 2. Isaiah 23: 1*f.* Ezekiel 26-8. Amos 1: 9-10. Zechariah 9: 3. Matthew 15: 21*f.* Mark 7: 24*f.* Acts 21: 3, 7.]

U

Unleavened Bread, The Feast of *See* PASSOVER

Ur The city usually known as Ur of the Chaldees is first named as the place from which Abraham and his father Terah and their household set out for Haran. Ur was a very old centre of early civilization in Mesopotamia near the mouth of the Euphrates, and capital city of the Sumerians. Archaeology has revealed that Ur was a magnificent and highly-developed city in the time of Abraham, with spacious houses, schools, and a temple to the moon god. Treasures and jewels from the ruins of Ur are to be seen today in the museums of the world. [*Refs.* Genesis 11: 28-31; 15: 7. Nehemiah 9: 7.]

Uriah There are a number of men known as Uriah in the O.T. Uriah the Hittite, the best known of them, was a soldier in David's army and had a wife called Bathsheba. David commited adultery with her and then arranged that Uriah was set in the forefront of the battle line so that he was struck down and killed. Nathan the prophet rebuked David for this sin. [*Ref.* 2 Samuel 11: 1 to 12: 15.]

Urim and Thummim Objects which were put in the breastpiece worn by the high priest and which were used in casting lots to determine the will of God. They were probably small stones which were used like dice to give a 'Yes' or 'No' answer. [*Refs.* Exodus 28: 30. Leviticus 8: 8. 1 Samuel 14: 41-2; 28: 6. Nehemiah 7: 65.]

Uzzah The name of one of the drivers of a new cart on which the Ark of God was placed when it was brought from the house of

Abinadab by King David. The oxen stumbled, Uzzah put out his hand to steady the Ark, and for this sacrilegious act was struck dead. It is a tale of the fetish fear which clung to the sacred Ark. [*Refs.* 2 Samuel 6: 3, 6, 7. 1 Chronicles 13: 6-11.]

Uzziah Also known as Azariah. The son of Amaziah, king of Judah, Uzziah reigned in Jerusalem 783-742 B.C. through the most prosperous period the kingdom of Judah ever knew. Although the second book of Kings mentions him only briefly, Uzziah was a very able and powerful ruler. He recaptured Solomon's ancient port of Elath on the Gulf of Aqaba, conquered Philistine territory on the coast of Palestine, and extended his power to the border of Egypt. In Jerusalem he strongly fortified the city wall with garrison towers, established an efficient, well-equipped army, and provided it with weapons of war. He was also famous as an agriculturalist, 'for he loved the soil'. Eventually, however, Uzziah contracted leprosy, which the writer of his story in Chronicles sets down as a punishment from God. He withdrew from all public view and his son Jotham ruled as regent before he eventually became king on the death of his father. It was 'in the year that king Uzziah died' that the young man Isaiah heard his call to be a prophet of God. His experience is movingly described in Isaiah 6. [*Refs.* 2 Kings 15: 1-7. 2 Chronicles 26. Isaiah 6. Amos 1: 1.]

W

Weeks, Feast of *See* PENTECOST

Z

Zacchaeus The name means 'pure'. Zacchaeus was chief tax-collector in Jericho and he was rich. When Jesus came there, Zacchaeus being small of stature climbed a tree to see him. Jesus saw him and invited himself to the house of the tax-collector, thus making himself unclean in the sight of the orthodox Jews. His words and his act brought about the wholesome repentance of Zacchaeus. [*Ref.* Luke 19: 1-9.]

Zacharias *See* ZECHARIAH

Zadok The name of a number of men in the O.T., particularly the priest who lived in the time of David and Solomon and gave his loyalty and considerable political support to the royal house. Zadok guarded the Ark of God in Jerusalem when David was a refugee from his capital during the revolt of Absalom. Through his son Ahimaaz he was able to warn the king of Absalom's plan of campaign, and thus bring about his defeat. In David's old age Zadok kept his loyalty to the king and helped to bring about the succession of Solomon, whom he anointed as king. Later high priests of Judaism claimed descent from Zadok. [*Refs.* 2 Samuel 8: 17; 15: 24-9, 35-6; 18: 15*f*. 1 Kings 1: 8, 32*f*.]

Zealots The name does not appear in the Authorized Version of the Bible, but is applied in the R.S.V. to Simon the disciple of Jesus mentioned in Luke 6: 15. The Zealots were a fanatical nationalist party in Palestine, in the time of Jesus, who wanted to win independence from the Romans by armed rebellion. No doubt they were interested in Jesus as a possible war-like, Messianic leader. [*Refs.* Luke 6: 15. Acts 1: 13.]

Zebedee The father of James and John, the disciples of Jesus, Zebedee was a fishermen of Galilee who had a boat and hired servants. We hear no more of him, but his wife was apparently one of the women of Galilee who went with Jesus to Jerusalem and who witnessed the Crucifixion. [*Refs.* Matthew 27: 56. Mark 1: 19-20.]

Zechariah or **Zacharias** Zechariah (or Zacharias) was the father of John the Baptist. Zechariah was a priest of the Temple to whom the angel Gabriel appeared to announce that his elderly wife would bear a son whose name was to be John. The news made Zechariah speechless, but when the child was born his tongue was loosed and he praised God in the poem which we call the Benedictus. [*Refs.* Luke 1: 5-23, 57-79.]

Zechariah, The Book of The book of Zechariah is to be found among the 'Latter Prophets' of the Hebrew Scriptures and is one of the twelve minor prophets of our o.t. The prophet was contemporary with Haggai and shared his concern for the rebuilding of the Temple in Jerusalem. They are mentioned together in Ezra 5: 1. Nothing more is known of Zechariah except that he was probably a returned exile. His fellow-Jews in Jerusalem were no more than a colony living under the favour of the Persian emperor. The Book of Zechariah falls into two parts:

(a) Zechariah 1-8: A series of eight dream-visions written in the first person, the aim of which is to inspire his people with a purpose and a hope in the ideal Jerusalem that is to be. The dreams are full of strange symbolism reminiscent of the visions of Ezekiel and even more difficult to interpret. There is a man on a red horse followed by red, sorrel and white horses, next four horns and four smiths; then, a man with a measuring line in his hand, Joshua the high priest; a lamp-stand of gold; a flying scroll; a woman in an ephah (measure); four chariots drawn by red, black, white and dappled horses. Throughout these mysterious dreams runs the proclamation of the restoration of the Temple in the midst of the holy city, God's blessing on his people, and the supremacy of Zerubbabel as the anointed king of God's favour and Joshua as the high priest. These chapters end with a picture of the ideal Jerusalem where God will dwell in the midst, old men and women will sit peacefully in the open air, and 'the streets of the city shall be full of boys and girls playing in its streets' (8: 4-5).

(b) Zechariah 9-14: This part cannot be accurately dated and is concerned with different themes. Here are a number of prophetic oracles, mainly in poetic form, and mostly of very obscure meaning. Our main interest in these passages lies in the use made of portions of them by N.T. writers. For example: Zechariah 9: 9-10 is quoted in Matthew 21: 5 and in John 12: 15 where Jesus comes to Jerusalem riding on an ass. Zechariah 2: 12-13 mentions 'thirty pieces of silver' and the phrase is taken up in Matthew 26: 15; 27: 9 (where it is wrongly attributed to Jeremiah).

Zedekiah The last king of Judah, youngest son of Josiah, brother of Jehoiakim, uncle of Jehoiachin. When Nebuchadrezzar sacked Jerusalem in 597 B.C. and took the royal house and notables of the people to exile in Babylon, he made Zedekiah his vassal king, having changed his name from Mattaniah to Zedekiah. He was twenty-one years old when he became king, and he reigned eleven years in Jerusalem. We see him through the eyes of Jeremiah who was imprisoned in Jerusalem throughout a good deal of his reign, and whose advice Zedekiah both sought and scorned. The pathetic puppet Zedekiah, however, proved a rebel in the end, and Nebuchadrezzar's army once again laid seige to Jerusalem. The city held out for three years, but famine and disease destroyed its people. Finally in 587 B.C. the walls were breached and the Babylonian soldiers swept in. Zedekiah fled, but he was caught at Jericho. His eyes were put out, he was bound in fetters and led away to captivity in Babylon. The end had come to the royal

house of David in Jerusalem and to the kingdom of Judah.
[*Refs.* 2 Kings 24: 17 to 25: 7. Jeremiah 21: 1-7; 27: 12-22; 37:
1 to 39: 7; 52: 1-1.]

Zephaniah The name of several men in the O.T., including the
seventh century prophet whose book bears his name. According to the opening words of that work, he was the descendant
of King Hezekiah of Judah and lived and prophesied in Jerusalem in the days of Josiah. We know nothing else of him.
[*Ref.* Zephaniah 1: 1.]

Zephaniah, The Book of The Book of Zephaniah is one of the
'Latter prophets' of the Hebrew Scriptures and one of the
twelve minor prophets of our O.T. According to 1: 1 the prophet
was a descendant of King Hezekiah of Judah. He was probably a contemporary of Jeremiah, and prophesied in Jerusalem just before the time of King Josiah's great religious reform of 621 B.C. Zephaniah's message concerns the immi-
nent 'day of the Lord'. A collection of short oracles warns
again and again of the dread day of God's punishment about
to fall on the wicked priests, officials and citizens of Jerusalem. Zephaniah's condemnation of social iniquity and false
worship echoes the earlier message of Amos. Wailing, distress, anguish, ruin, devastation, thick darkness, fire, the wrath
of the Lord—these are the key words piled one on another.
Nor will the surrounding nations escape. The language of the
whole book is urgent, violent, passionate. Only at the end is
there a note of hope for 'a people humble and lowly'.

One of the most famous of medieval Latin hymns, still sung
in many translations, is based on the words of Zephaniah. It
is the *Dies Irae*, 'That day of wrath, that dreadful day.'

Zerubbabel Zerubbabel was the grandson of Jehoiachin
(Jeconiah) the second last reigning king of Judah before the
Exile of the Jews in Babylon. Zerubbabel went back to Jerusalem with the first group of Jews liberated by the decree of
Cyrus, king of Persia. He took part in the setting up of the
altar of burnt-offering in Jerusalem and the eventual rebuilding of the Temple. Zerubbabel's name is important in Jewish

history because he was a descendant of David, but the throne was not restored in him. In fact, he, and the Davidic line, disappear from the Bible record, except that the second Temple is usually known as 'Zerubbabel's Temple'. [*Refs.* Ezra 2: 2; 3: 2*f*; 5: 2. Haggai 1: 1, 12*f*. Zechariah 4: 6*f*.]

Zion Name of the original hilltop fortress captured by David from the Jebusites, which became the oldest part of the city of Jerusalem. Zion came to be known as the city of David, and eventually the name was applied to the whole of the enlarged sacred city. Time and again in the Psalms and poetry of the O.T. Zion is mentioned symbolically as 'the holy hill', the dwelling-place of God, 'the City of the Lord', and in N.T. writings it appears as the idealized 'city of the living God, the heavenly Jerusalem'. [*Refs.* 2 Samuel 5: 7. 1 Kings 8: 1. Psalm 2: 6; 9: 2; 50: 2; 132: 13*f*. Isaiah 8: 18; 28: 16; 60: 14. Hebrews 12: 22. 1 Peter 2: 6. Revelation 14: 1.]